DISCARDED

D1024747

Blacks in Power

Blacks in Power

A Comparative Study of Black and White Elected Officials

Leonard A. Cole

Princeton University Press
Princeton, New Jersey

COLLEGE OF THE SEQUOIAS
LIBRARY

Copyright © 1976 by Princeton University Press
Published by Princeton University Press, Princeton and
Guildford, Surrey
All Rights Reserved

Chapter IV originally appeared as an article, "Electing Blacks to
Municipal Office: Structural and Social Determinants," in *Urban
Affairs Quarterly*, 10, no. 4 (September 1974), 17-39, and is
reprinted here by permission of the publisher, Sage Publications, Inc.

Library of Congress Cataloging in Publication Data will
be found on the last printed page of this book

Publication of this book has been aided by a grant from The
Andrew W. Mellon Foundation

This book has been composed in Linotype Baskerville

Printed in the United States of America
by Princeton University Press, Princeton, New Jersey

Second printing, 1977

COLLEGE OF THE SEQUOIAS

LIBRARY

For Wendy,
  Philip,
    and Bill

Contents

List of Tables

List of Figures

Preface

Early in 1971 I sat in an audience addressed by Mayor William S. Hart, Sr., of East Orange, New Jersey. He proclaimed his city a racial success, populated evenly by blacks and whites, with interracial harmony and no ghettos. I wondered about the relationship between the "success" of East Orange and its elected leaders, particularly its black officials. Were the political leaders a reflection of the city's social composition? Did they substantially influence community relations and issues? Later I met another East Orange elected official, who hoped I would expose the city's social disintegration, reflected in whites leaving the public school system, increased crime rates, and fear. The difference between this official's East Orange and the mayor's was shocking. Racial harmony or disharmony seemed largely a state of mind.

As I expanded my inquiry to other New Jersey municipalities, I remained curious about the roles of elected officials. But attempts to understand them, to separate perception from reality, fastened on the original questions. The interdependence of perception, behavior, and external constraints became more insistent as the study progressed.

No one, not elected officials, nor authors, can avoid bringing individual perceptions to the definition of reality. Events chosen for discussion, questions asked, quotations cited, the subject of a book reveal an author's priorities, what he *believes* to be important. I have not sought to disguise my prejudices, but I have attempted to report fairly the views and actions of elected officials. These men and women are the book; and to them I owe my deepest gratitude. Every one of the 127 officials interviewed was gracious and responsive. Additionally, friends, students, residents of communities in this study shared ideas, collated data, or helped with telephone interviews in the citizens survey. They are too numerous to name, but I am indebted to them all.

I owe special thanks, however, to Nida E. Thomas, director of the Office of Equal Educational Opportunity in the state Department of Education, for information about school integration in New Jersey; and to Charles C. Jury and his staff at the William Paterson College Computer Center, for continual cooperation. Professors Michael N. Danielson, Inez Smith Reid, William Small, and George S. Sternlieb read the manuscript and offered valuable comments. I am grateful also to Sanford G. Thatcher, social science editor at Princeton University Press, for his early interest in the project; and to Joanna Hitchcock, for her judicious editing of the text. Faith Moneypenny and Margie O'Kane typed on a hurried schedule, often at personal inconvenience. My wife Ruth helped at every stage, from preparing questionnaires to proofreading. She has been sounding board and critic, and her suggestions have benefited the study immeasurably.

Finally, I dedicate this book to my children, Wendy, Philip, and Bill. I hope they share the exhilaration prompted by its completion, as they did the impositions caused by its preparation. The future of black–white relations is uncertain, though many studies are pessimistic. But if, as suggested here, the growing number of black elected officials represents an encouraging trend, the tide of racial discrimination may continue to recede during my children's generation. To this hope I devote these pages.

Blacks in Power

Blacks, Elected Officials, and New Jersey as a Political Forum

Many American municipalities will be shaped largely by black elected officials. This book is about these officials, the mayors and local legislators who are gaining office in increasing numbers. While our focus centers on local officials in New Jersey, the significance of this study should reach far beyond. For New Jersey, the most densely populated state, typifies urban and suburban America.

Politicians, of course, are not the only components of a political system. Interest groups, voting behavior, political parties, and historical and sectional patterns also contribute to the mosaic of black politics, described by Hanes Walton as efforts of blacks "in the American political system to implement their preferences as public policy."[1] Moreover, blacks are attaining political leadership at a time when many cities are in shambles. To expect them alone to solve problems of housing, unemployment, and shrinking tax bases is unrealistic. But however the problems of the cities are to be solved, blacks will play a central role. And while elected officials may be only a part of a political system, in a representative democracy they are its heart.

Not all cities will have black officials, let alone be dominated by them. Blacks comprise, after all, only 11 percent of a national population of 209 million. Yet three trends are

[1] Hanes Walton, Jr., *Black Politics* (Philadelphia: J. B. Lippincott Co., 1972), p. 2.

3

catapulting them into positions of political influence across the country. The first is the continuing migration of blacks from the rural South to the cities, particularly in the North.

Census figures show jumps in the black populations of most major cities. In 1960 New York City's black population comprised 14 percent of the total, in 1970 21 percent; the proportion in Chicago vaulted from 23 to 33 percent, in Los Angeles from 14 to 18, and in Philadelphia from 26 to 34. Of the thirty largest cities only three, Indianapolis, Jacksonville, and Phoenix, failed to show increased black proportions between 1960 and 1970. Ten of the thirty are expected to have black majorities by 1985; two already have them, Washington, D.C. and Atlanta.[2] Similarly, many medium-sized communities across the country with populations between twenty-five and one hundred thousand showed comparable increases.

The larger black populations have expanded local electoral bases for black office-seekers. Along with heightened political consciousness rooted in civil rights activities and laws of the 1950s and 1960s, these bases have already marked an increase in elected blacks. Though black citizens are still underrepresented in proportion to their numbers, the trend is clear; the percentage of blacks at all levels of government is growing. In 1960 four blacks were members of the House of Representatives, in 1975 seventeen. There had been no black mayors of large cities, or even close contenders, until the mid-1960s. By early 1975 more than 3,500 blacks held elective office across the country, three times the number six years earlier. Black mayors had been elected in Atlanta, Cincinnati, Cleveland, Dayton, Detroit, Flint, Gary, Grand Rapids, Los Angeles, Newark, Raleigh, and Washington, D.C. Until 1968 no sizable city in New Jer-

[2] U.S. Bureau of the Census, *Statistical Abstract of the United States: 1972*, 93rd ed. (Washington, D.C.: U.S. Government Printing Office, 1972), pp. 21-23; *Report of the National Advisory Commission on Civil Disorders* (New York: Bantam Books, Inc., 1968), p. 391. The other eight cities are New Orleans, Baltimore, Jacksonville, Cleveland, St. Louis, Detroit, Philadelphia, and Chicago.

sey had ever had a black mayor; in 1972 there were four: Kenneth A. Gibson in Newark, William S. Hart, Sr., in East Orange, Matthew G. Carter in Montclair, and Walter S. Taylor in Englewood. The populations of these cities each numbered over twenty-five thousand, but there were also black mayors in two smaller New Jersey communities, Hilliard T. Moore in Lawnside and George J. Phillips in Chesilhurst.[3]

A second trend that has enhanced black electoral success arises from increasing white support. Incumbent blacks not only win reelection but often receive more white votes than at their first election. Mayors Carl B. Stokes of Cleveland and Richard G. Hatcher of Gary are examples, and so is Senator Edward W. Brooke of Massachusetts. Blacks running a second time in New Jersey communities have done the same. Isaac G. McNatt fell two votes short of becoming high man among seven when reelected to the Teaneck council in 1970; Matthew Carter led the five Montclair commissioners in 1968; in East Orange, Mayor William S. Hart's plurality of 45 percent in 1969 swelled to a 60 percent majority four years later.

Not all whites leave racial prejudices outside the polling booths. But for some, reluctance to support blacks diminishes once they have served. They answer a question raised by Howard N. Lee shortly after he was elected mayor of Chapel Hill, North Carolina. The first black mayor of a predominantly white southern city, he voiced concern about "those, both black and white, who constantly wonder whether a black man is really capable of handling the reins of municipal government."[4] As whites are exposed to black

[3] Sixty percent of Chesilhurst's 801 residents are black, as are all but a half-dozen of Lawnside's 2,757. Located outside Camden, Lawnside was a secret stop on the underground railway, and after the Civil War was settled by freed slaves. Since its creation as a town in 1926 it has been governed by blacks.

[4] Howard N. Lee, "The Black Elected Official and Southern Politics," in Mervyn M. Dymally, ed., *The Black Politician* (Belmont, Calif.: Duxbury Press, 1971), p. 83.

officials, the importance of a candidate's race as an electoral determinant appears to diminish.

The third trend arises from increased if still inadequate state and federal response to the plight of cities. The effort has been uneven. Federal expenditures for public housing, for example, were cut in 1973. But the longer view reveals that higher government is providing far more assistance than it did a decade ago. Expenditures by the Department of Housing and Urban Development climbed from about $250 million in 1965 to over $3 billion 400 million in 1972. Numerous programs from other federal and state agencies have been conducted with cooperative direction by local officials. The revenue sharing law passed in 1972 received bipartisan endorsement at all levels of government. Under the law between $5 and $6 billion are returned annually to state and local governments. Two-thirds go directly to local communities for uses they themselves determine. Many cities argue that their share is inadequate. Indeed it is questionable whether any amount of money unaccompanied by institutional changes can root out social miseries. But money is power, and as more comes into the cities, power and influence accrue to the local political leadership, which is black in increasing numbers.

The principal question addressed throughout this study is whether, apart from the race label, black elected officials differ from their white counterparts; and, as a corollary, whether white attitudes toward black officials are shaped principally by perceptions of race, or whether race is only incidental to other considerations.

In his study of *Negro Politics*, James Q. Wilson generalized that "in most cases, and for most purposes, the Negro politician acts as politicians do anywhere."[5] Chuck Stone

---

[5] James Q. Wilson, *Negro Politics* (New York: The Free Press, 1965), p. 15. A more cynical observation was made by Alcee Hastings: "Blacks are like everybody else in politics—selfish, practical, political and playing the money game," in Stephan Lesher, "The Short, Unhappy Life of Black Presidential Politics, 1972," *The New York Times Magazine*, June 25, 1972, p. 13.

argued contradictorily in *Black Political Power in America* that "the black politician walks on eggs throughout his whole career. . . . He must be willing to compromise far more frequently than white politicians because of the peculiarities of American racism, which demand that he not be too independent, too audacious, or too unpredictable."[6] Taking yet another view, Nathan Wright, Jr., in *What Black Politicians Are Saying*, glorifies them: "The Black politician is freed in a singular way from loyalty to repressive elements in our society. Primarily because of this, he is best equipped to provide the new leadership which realistically promises peace, integrity and the best possible life for all of our nation's citizens." He is "the present exemplar of humane values in our legislative halls."[7]

These and other studies veneered a methodological weakness. None examined a substantial body of elected blacks alongside an equivalent group of whites. Most suffered from a condition of their times. So few blacks had held elected positions that generalizations and analogies had to be drawn about the few who did, or about "politicians" never elected.[8]

[6] Chuck Stone, *Black Political Power in America*, rev. ed. (New York: Dell Publishing Co., 1970), p. 168.

[7] Nathan Wright, Jr., ed., *What Black Politicians Are Saying* (New York: Hawthorn Books, Inc., 1972), pp. viii, 203.

[8] Harold F. Gosnell's *Negro Politicians* (Chicago: The University of Chicago Press, 1935) preceded Wilson's *Negro Politics* by twenty-five years. It too was a landmark and based on Chicago. Because it was written so early, however, it suffered even more from the scarcity of elected blacks. Everett Carll Ladd, Jr.'s *Negro Political Leadership in the South* (Ithaca, N.Y.: Cornell University Press, 1966) repeats Wilson's emphasis on civic and non-elective leadership within the race. Other recent books are bland overviews, like Edward T. Clayton's *The Negro Politician* (Chicago: Johnson Publishing Co., Inc., 1964); or collected statements of black officials, like Richard W. Bruner's *Black Politicians* (New York: David McKay Co., Inc., 1971) and the works by Dymally and Wright cited above; or compilations of articles with scarce reference to elected officials, as in Lenneal J. Henderson, Jr., ed., *Black Political Life in the United States* (San Francisco: Chandler Publishing Co., 1972), Edward S. Greenberg, Neal Milner, and David J. Olson, eds., *Black Politics* (New York:

No earlier study confronted substantial numbers of black and white elected officials in close geographic proximity with the same questions during a limited period. Now the existence of many more elected blacks not only permits comparative analysis but allows for refinement of the question of their "differences." This study reveals the inadequacy of the facile generalizations of the past. In some ways blacks are very different, in some not at all. We shall examine the question from three perspectives. The first encompasses routes to office. Is there a difference in social and political backgrounds between white and black officials? Is the impetus to seek office different in one group from the other? Do they travel separate political roads to office?

Second, we shall examine behavior in office. Do blacks behave as a bloc on all issues, on none, or on those that pertain directly to race? Do they define the importance of an issue only in proportion to its racial implications? The remaining perspective, which is related to behavior, is that of perception, and to this we give the bulk of attention. As a New Jersey mayor quipped, "It's not what is that is, it's what people believe is that is." We shall emphasize the functions blacks perceive for themselves as elected officials among fellow office-holders and the general citizenry, and how their perceptions differ from those of whites.

"Ideas govern the world," said E. E. Schattschneider. "Ultimately we are governed by what we think. Government is a state of mind, a way of thinking, a way of seeing the world about us, something we believe about other people. Governing has much less to do with control of the bodies of people than it has with what is going on in their minds. Without some patterns of political ideas, government would be *unthinkable*."[9] Too often politics and gov-

Holt, Rinehart and Winston, Inc., 1971), and Harry A. Bailey, Jr., ed., *Negro Politics in America* (Columbus, Ohio: Charles E. Merrill Publishing Co., 1967).

[9] E. E. Schattschneider, *Two Hundred Million Americans in Search of a Government* (New York: Holt, Rinehart and Winston, Inc., 1969), p. 99. Italics in original.

ernment are drawn as a continuum of objective events, and the cultural history, prejudices, and psyche of participants are disregarded. Political issues are in fact molded by perceptions. The issue of school busing is a prime example.

Culminating earlier statements in opposition to "forced busing," President Richard Nixon on March 17, 1972, called for a moratorium on court-ordered busing intended to achieve racial balance. He implied that excessive busing was already under way and that "massive busing produces inferior education."[10] Demagogues like George Wallace had attacked busing earlier, but where busing for integration had been undertaken, most people had come to accept it with compliance, if not enthusiasm. Whatever his intention, the President's statement helped stir anxiety. Anti-busing fever gripped much of the nation. The issue affected several presidential primaries, and in two states, Florida and Michigan, it was virtually the only one. In November, Californians overwhelmingly supported a referendum to forbid busing. The New Jersey Commissioner of Education was denied reappointment by the state senate, largely on the issue. A filibuster by liberal senators at the end of the 1972 congressional session prevented the passage of legislation suspending busing for integration. The House of Representatives had already passed a bill, and most senators declared themselves in support. Busing opponents vowed they would pass a law next session or, if necessary, a constitutional amendment.

Busing was a national issue, kept prominent in part by the President's words. Yet by almost any barometer, historical, educational, statistical, the issue was a hoax, "the most phony issue in the country," according to Reverend Theodore M. Hesburgh, then chairman of the United States Commission on Civil Rights.[11] Not only has busing been a

[10] *Education for a Nation* (Washington, D.C.: Congressional Quarterly, Inc., 1972), p. 34; the quotation is from a transcription of a statement by Richard Nixon made on November 6, 1972, on NBC-TV, New York.

[11] *The New York Times*, November 17, 1972, p. 1. Father Hesburgh

part of American education in all parts of the country for over half a century,[12] but busing to *separate* the races has deep historical roots, as any American knows. While the educational benefits of an integrated education may be considerable or marginal (evidence conflicts), there is no debate over the fact that most schools attended by whites are superior to most of those attended by blacks: they have better teachers, better physical facilities, and more money is spent per child.[13] Finally, and most striking, twenty million of the forty-six million children who attended school were bused at public expense; but of the twenty million no more than three percent were bused to achieve desegregation.[14]

No one can gauge how many people opposed busing out of racial prejudice and how many genuinely believed that the convenience of neighborhood schools was the main issue. In either case the opposition leaned against flimsy struts. In no sense had busing per se been considered a threat to the American educational system in the past, nor is it today. Only when used to pander to other prejudices did it appear ominous. Thus can elections, national policies, even the alteration of the Constitution turn on people's perceptions, whatever the facts.

Political reality is a thin crust shaped by a core of hopes, beliefs, fears, and prejudices that it may often conceal. This

---

was forced to resign after President Nixon's reelection. Those who believe I exaggerate the President's role should recall the wave of opposition to the Supreme Court decisions in 1962 and 1963 to abolish prayers in public schools. The President (Kennedy, and then Johnson) stood behind the Court, and popular indignation melted. Similiarly when Presidents backed civil rights laws and court decisions, the laws and decisions were sustained. Hostility was hammered into lasting acceptance even when troops or federal marshals were required; examples are Little Rock's Central High School under Eisenhower, the Universities of Alabama and Mississippi under Kennedy, voter registration of blacks in the South under Johnson.

[12] *Education for a Nation*, p. 33.

[13] See Christopher Jencks, *Inequality* (New York: Basic Books, Inc., 1972), pp. 27-28.

[14] Figures from the U.S. Office of Education are cited in *Education for a Nation*, pp. 32-33.

study places a premium on the perceptions and attitudes of elected local officials, black and white. It is built largely around their words.

Method and Format

Among New Jersey cities with populations of twenty-five thousand or more, sixteen contain substantial black populations, at least 15 percent of each city's total. The sixteen cities are governed from 123 elected executive and legislative offices, and, in the course of 1972, 135 individuals filled these offices; 31 blacks served, though never more than 27 at one time.[15] Of the 135 elected officials—mayors and commissioners, councilmen, or aldermen, depending on the local form of government—127 were interviewed, including all 31 blacks.[16] The interviews were semi-structured, evoking scaled answers as well as open-ended discussion. Most ranged between thirty and sixty minutes, but some lasted a few hours. Substantial portions of almost all interviews were taped. Anonymity was promised to the extent that quotations would not be attributed by name.

The format engenders a paradox. While our interest centers on black officials, there are many more elected whites, and a comparative analysis unavoidably incorporates this imbalance. But though more whites than blacks were interviewed, 96 to 31, race is treated as an independent variable. Each group is evaluated as an entity unaffected by numerical difference.

In addition, 551 telephone interviews were completed from a random sample of the population. The number of

---

[15] Included is Councilman Charles H.L.D. Clark of Plainfield, an American Indian. Though proud of his own heritage, Councilman Clark represented a largely black constituency, was generally identified as black by the electorate, and saw his role as a spokesman for black interests.

[16] Board of education members were not included because in several municipalities they are appointed. Moreover, many limit their concern to education.

interviewees selected in each city was proportionate to the
city's population among all sixteen cities (see Appendix II).
Although these interviews were more limited than the interviews with the officials, several parallel questions were
asked.

Table I-1 lists the cities, their populations, the percentage
of blacks, the number of elected positions, and the largest
number and percentage of blacks in office at any time in
1972. In only five cities, East Orange, Englewood, Hackensack, Plainfield, and Teaneck, were the proportions of black
elected officials roughly equivalent to the cities' black populations; and in two, Elizabeth and Passaic, no elected
blacks served. Yet, compared to a dozen years earlier, this
representation was impressive; for in 1960, though the collective black proportion in the sixteen cities was 22 percent
(compared to 31 percent in 1970), there sat only two blacks,
Councilmen Irvine I. Turner in Newark and John W.
Wright in Englewood. Now, however, blacks were beginning to get their electoral due.

New Jersey is a fertile field for political study, especially
about city officials. It has no great cities, yet it is almost all
urban. It is the most urbanized state in America; 87 percent
of its 7,168,164 residents live in urban areas (population
2,500 or more) according to the 1970 census. Only three
states, California, New York, and Massachusetts, have more
communities of 25,000 or larger—New Jersey has 53—and
all three contain much more land area.

New Jersey is the obverse of ancient Athens, a state-city,
a sprawling land area more densely populated than any
other state, yet lacking a single cultural, economic, or political focal point. Lodged between New York City and Philadelphia, the state's geographic anomaly leads some to say
that it lacks its own identity.[17] Some attention of the north-

[17] Michael Barone, Grant Ujifusa, and Douglas Matthew, *The
Almanac of American Politics* (Boston: Gambit, Inc., 1972), p. 470.
In their 1974 revised edition, the authors say that New Jersey is no
longer obscure, but in view of recent convictions and indictments
of politicians it is "the nation's most corrupt state" (p. 602).

TABLE I-1: Sixteen Cities: Populations and Number of Elected Officials by Race

City	Pop. (1970)[a]	% Black	Number of Elected Officials	Black Elected Officials (maximum any one time in 1972)	% Black Officials
Atlantic City	47,859	44	5	1	20
Camden	102,551	39	8	2	25
East Orange	75,471	53	11	6	55
Elizabeth	112,654	16	10	0	0
Englewood	24,985	33	6	2	33
Hackensack	35,911	17	5	1	20
Jersey City	260,545	21	10	1	10
Montclair	44,043	27	5	1	20
Newark	382,417	54	10	4	40
New Brunswick	41,885	23	6	1	17
Orange	32,566	36	5	1	20
Passaic	55,124	18	7	0	0
Paterson	144,824	27	12	2	17
Plainfield	46,862	40	8	3	37
Teaneck	42,355	15	7	1	14
Trenton	104,638	38	8	1	13
Total	1,554,690	36	123	27	22

[a] City populations and black proportions were derived from U.S. Bureau of the Census, *General Social and Economic Characteristics, New Jersey*, Final Report PC(1)-C32 (Washington, D.C.: U.S. Government Printing Office, 1972), pp. 267-74, 347-54, 495-98.

ern and southern New Jersey counties gravitates to the mammoth out-of-state metropolises. But New York and Philadelphia are great equalizers. Nowhere within New Jersey does one metropolitan area overwhelm its smaller neighbors. Every city counts.

Politically New Jersey informs the nation. Its politics is watched closely, especially in presidential years, for "to do well in New Jersey is usually to do well nationally."[18] Presidents Kennedy, Johnson, and Nixon won in New Jersey by about the same margins as they won across the country. The two major parties are evenly balanced. Since 1958 when Harrison Williams, a Democrat, was elected to the Senate to join Clifford Case, a Republican, each has been reelected by huge margins. The present Democratic governor, Brendan Byrne, was preceded by a Republican, William Cahill, and before him by a Democrat, Richard Hughes. In 1974 eight of the fifteen New Jersey congressmen were Democrats, while control of the state legislature changed from Republican to Democratic the year before. New Jersey is a model two-party state, well-suited for a study of local officials.

Local pride abounds among city leaders. But officials function under a common umbrella of state guidelines, and the cities' proximity to each other reflects a similar regional outlook, history, economic base, and ethnic composition. Thus municipal borders, while important, are only one of many behavioral determinants. Heinz Eulau and Kenneth Prewitt found that even varying the sizes of city councils (from five to seven or nine members) affects the interrelationships of their members, and ultimately their behavior.[19] But few characteristics are as distinctive as race, and few are more likely to influence an individual's social and political consciousness.

Blacks as well as whites on Englewood's governing body are of course affected by constraints different from those affecting Newark's officials. Again, as Eulau and Prewitt point out, the "collective adaptations" of council members

18 See *The New York Times*, June 9, 1972, p. 36.
19 Heinz Eulau and Kenneth Prewitt, *Labyrinths of Democracy: Adaptations, Linkages, Representation, and Policies in Urban Politics* (New York: The Bobbs-Merrill Co., 1973), pp. 81-84.

are influenced not only by council size, but by the size of their city.[20] Indeed the social and economic problems of center cities make more pronounced their distinction from the suburbs; and this we examine in Chapter VIII. But a comparison of the attitudes, beliefs, and behavior of black officials with white beyond municipal boundaries confronts the question of race directly. We inquire whether the election of blacks, irrespective of council size or nature of municipality, makes a difference.

The racial pattern of New Jersey is the same as that of the country as a whole. Its 770,292 blacks constitute 11 percent of the total population, which is identical to the national proportion. And as Newark's Mayor Kenneth Gibson likes to say, "Wherever cities are going in America, Newark will get there first." If he is correct, Jersey City, Paterson, Trenton, Camden, and Elizabeth will not be far behind. While older than others across the nation, these cities share urban problems that are common to most, whatever their historical, ethnic, or earlier economic differences. Increasing concentrations of poor people (especially blacks), the exodus of middle-class whites, shrinking tax bases at a time when the need for services mushrooms, galloping crime rates, and heightened fear are problems in New Jersey's as in most metropolitan areas.

As the larger New Jersey cities are typical, so in their own right are their more modestly sized neighbors, the inner suburbs or "zones of emergence" like Plainfield, East Orange, Montclair, Englewood, and Teaneck. Though they are affected by problems common to cities, the problems are less severe. Moreover, some suburbs with substantial black populations have developed bold policies toward interracial harmony, as will be discussed in Chapters VIII and IX. Suburban integration is imperfect, fragile, possibly ephemeral. But as several inner suburbs have demonstrated, it is possible.

[20] *Ibid.*

Integration versus Separation

In New Jersey, as across the country, the desirability of integration has become an important issue. To the extent that a study of black elected officials can make the point, it is a thesis of this book that integration rather than separation will bring social, economic, and political benefits to blacks; and that black identity and black consciousness are not only compatible with policies designed to achieve integration, they can be beneficial to the process. In the concluding chapter the meaning of integration and separation will be reviewed in the perspective of the book's presentation; but first we present an overview.

Through most of the twentieth century, separation has rarely been regarded by blacks as an appropriate means of attaining equal rights. Only since the mid-1960s has black separatism found serious advocates, though most blacks still favor integration.[21] St. Clair Drake senses that rejection of "white values" is a response to the American experience of "limited integration rather than complete acceptance." Black nationalism, he says, is a proclamation of "psychological independence."[22]

If separation yields "psychological independence," why during the past hundred years of segregation was this not evident? The response of course is that separation then was forced by whites: segregation was hierarchical, a function of white dominance. Whites controlled the political, economic, and social destinies of blacks. Now, however, anti-integrationists argue that blacks can attain political, economic, and social benefits only through separation, but

[21] Angus Campbell and Howard Schuman, *Racial Attitudes in Fifteen American Cities* (Ann Arbor, Michigan: Survey Research Center, Institute for Social Research, the University of Michigan, July 1969), pp. 15-16. Only one black in eight, for example, favored residential separation.

[22] St. Clair Drake, "The Social and Economic Status of the Negro in the United States," in Greenberg, Milner, and Olson, *Black Politics*, pp. 47-48.

willed this time by blacks—voluntary "apartheid." Though recognizing that the political and economic base is weaker for blacks than whites, Stokely Carmichael and Charles V. Hamilton believe that only separation would enable the black to "stand on your own."[23]

This presents a troubling contradiction, however. For proponents of separation invariably hold that white racism and suppression continue unabated. But if their proposition is corrrect, how can separation in a society still dominated by whites enhance black lives any more than segregation did during the past hundred years? In rejecting integration, Carmichael and Hamilton say that it presupposes that "there is nothing of value in the black community," that white is "automatically superior," and that "black people must give up their identity, deny their heritage."[24] Black pride and black culture, according to the argument, are submerged in an integrated environment. Only by self-sufficiency through separation can black power develop.

Before assessing the validity of this argument here and in the concluding chapter, we inquire into its ascendancy. Separatist ideology emerged, paradoxically, when the legal impositions of segregation in the South were crumbling. The mid-sixties also capped two decades of unequaled activity by blacks (and whites) in the cause of civil rights—marches, sit-ins, picketing, lobbying, voter registration. What often is insufficiently recognized, however, is that the activity not only stimulated, but was in turn stimulated by, government action. As Matthew Holden indicates, integration as national policy began with President Truman's absorption of a civil rights plank into his 1948 campaign.[25] In the succeeding twenty years, executive, judicial, and ultimately congressional action aimed at dismantling discrimi-

[23] Stokely Carmichael and Charles V. Hamilton, *Black Power: The Politics of Liberation in America* (New York: Vintage Books, 1967), p. 81.

[24] *Ibid.*, pp. 53-55.

[25] Matthew Holden, Jr., "The Crisis of the Republic: Reflections on Race and Politics," in Henderson, *Black Political Life*, p. 127.

natory institutions. The government sought to eliminate state and local legal strictures against blacks and to stimulate political, economic, and social opportunities. The three branches of government prompted educational, labor, housing, and health programs designed to improve conditions for blacks and other minorities; and official efforts aroused further citizens' activity. The 1954 Supreme Court decision against segregated schools galvanized citizens' efforts against segregation in general. The years between the five major civil rights acts (1957, 1960, 1964, 1965, 1968) witnessed activity in response to the most recent act that helped generate the next.

But improvements, while measurable, were slow and incomplete. Benefits matured gradually, undramatically. The inadequacies of government policies fostered dissatisfaction, and the failure of government to correct injustices quickly was viewed by some as a failure of the civil rights movement. Malcolm X, Stokely Carmichael, the Black Muslims, and the Black Panthers argued the need for blacks to look to themselves exclusively. Whites were impediments, oppressors.

Heightened black consciousness prompted some to press harder within the system for government and institutional action. But for others it bred the frustration that seeded the urban riots of the late sixties. Rioting, the supreme rejection of the system, peaked by the end of the decade. At the same time, political participation—voting, lobbying, campaigning, office-seeking—expanded. The number of black voters in the South and the number of black elected officials across the country grew every year.

The two responses, rioting and political activity, emerged from the common root of dissatisfaction with the black condition. But one was a response of despair, the other of hope. In a sense they relate to the separation–integration conflict. Though separatists do not necessarily endorse violence, they, like the rioters, are guided by despair. They despair of the political system and of coalition politics as a means to gain justice. Integrationists, on the other hand, believe that justice and opportunity are possible within the system. They recognize systemic inadequacies, but despite frustration and doubts integrationists have not discarded conventional politics.

Seen in this way, integration is an extension of the pluralist interpretation of American politics, that power is dispersed among contending groups. Thus, as business, labor, and civic groups try to influence government actors, so do blacks.[26] Pluralism further infers that public policy is the outcome of bargaining and negotiation; change is incremental.[27] Some reject the pluralist model as inappropriate to black needs, contending that blacks do not have sufficient access to decision-makers, or that incremental change is inadequate in view of the seriousness of black problems.[28] Yet the behavior of the federal government in the fifties and sixties speaks for the influence of blacks on policy. The 1954 school segregation case was argued before the Supreme Court by the NAACP Legal Defense and Educational Fund. Presidents Kennedy and Johnson were in frequent contact with black leaders like Martin Luther King, Jr., Roy

[26] Robert A. Dahl, an exponent of pluralist theory, has written that "a central guiding thread of American constitutional development has been the evolution of a political system in which all the active and legitimate groups in the population can make themselves heard at some crucial stage in the process of decision" (*A Preface to Democratic Theory* [Chicago: The University of Chicago Press, 1956], p. 137). A substantial literature has developed over the pluralist versus elite theories of politics. Contending arguments are reviewed by William Spinrad, "Power in Local Communities," in Alan Shank, ed., *Political Power and the Urban Crisis* (Boston: Holbrook Press, Inc., 1971), pp. 170-200. The arguments need not detain us. Edward S. Greenberg dismisses both models as irrelevant to black needs ("Models of the Political Process: Implications for the Black Community," in Greenberg, Milner, and Olson, *Black Politics*, pp. 3-15). His criticisms of the pluralist model will be examined shortly.

[27] Greenberg, "Models of the Political Process," pp. 9-11.

[28] *Ibid.*, pp. 12-14; William A. Gamson, "Stable Unrepresentation in American Society," in Greenberg, Milner, and Olson, *Black Politics*, pp. 59-64; Theodore Lowi, "The Public Philosophy: Interest-Group Liberalism," in Edgar Litt, ed., *The New Politics of American Policy* (New York: Holt, Rinehart and Winston, Inc., 1969), pp. 13-38.

Wilkins, Whitney Young, Jr., Bayard Rustin, and A. Philip Randolph. Congress was lobbied by the NAACP, the Urban League, and the Southern Christian Leadership Conference.[29] True, integrationists had relatively easy access, and separatists like Malcolm X or the Panthers did not. But if polls reflect accurately the tenor of the black population of the sixties, blacks were well represented by spokesmen who did have access. In surveys by Brink and Harris, for example, black citizens approved of integrationist leaders overwhelmingly, of separatist spokesmen far less. In the mid-sixties Martin Luther King, Jr., was approved by 88 percent of the black citizenry, Roy Wilkins by 64 percent. But Stokely Carmichael was approved by only 19 percent, Elijah Muhammad by 12 percent.[30]

Expressing the view that incremental change is inadequate, Edward S. Greenberg holds that "the problem of Black people is their exclusion from social, economic, and political power, and a rectification of that situation requires fundamental change. Black economic and social advancement . . . is not amenable to incremental change."[31] But he fails to say what he means by "fundamental" as opposed to "incremental." Government cannot suddenly and "fundamentally" eliminate economic, political, and social deprivation by fiat. What government can and must do is to create conditions favorable to their elimination. It cannot provide everyone with a college education, but it *can* insure that blacks have equal and perhaps preferential opportunities of gaining an education. Government can stimulate or create training programs, jobs, anti-poverty programs, hous-

[29] The success of the NAACP in influencing laws and policies is summarized by Harry A. Bailey, Jr., "Negro Interest Group Strategies," in Henderson, *Black Political Life*, pp. 162-63.

[30] William Brink and Louis Harris, *Black and White* (New York: Simon and Schuster, 1967), p. 54. See also William Brink and Louis Harris, *The Negro Revolution in America* (New York: Simon and Schuster, 1969), pp. 116-17, and Gary T. Marx, *Protest and Prejudice* (New York: Harper and Row, 1967), pp. 26-27.

[31] Greenberg, "Models of the Political Process," p. 14.

ing. It can help insure that black candidates run with legal restrictions no greater than for whites. All this it has tried, though with uneven success. But on balance there has been progress, "incremental" perhaps, but measurable.[32]

As he deplores the conditions of many blacks, Greenberg recognizes that change in a pluralist system is unlikely to be abrupt. But however one may wish differently, amelioration will not be sudden, not measurable in weeks or months. If blacks are to gain a larger and fairer portion of society's resources, others will receive proportionately less. In a pluralist system this change will not be abrupt, because the vast majority of whites will not tolerate it. Whites, however, have increasingly recognized that blacks have been deprived and now deserve at least equal treatment.[33]

Thus after one hundred years whites have reached the point where they see blacks almost the same way as other ethnic or religious groups. Racism has not disappeared; nor

[32] Progress was slowed, in some cases reversed, during the Nixon administration. The median income gap between black and white families narrowed between 1964 and 1970 (50% to 39%), though in 1973 it had widened again (42%). But this reflected a national economic slowdown and a decreased proportion of black working wives, as well as lower priority for civil rights under the administration. See *The New York Times*, July 24, 1974, p. 10. The extent of black progress was debated in *Commentary* by Ben J. Wattenberg and Richard M. Scammon, "Black Progress and Liberal Rhetoric," 55, no. 4 (April 1973), 35-44, and in letters to the editor, 56, no. 2 (August 1973).

[33] Increasing tolerance is confirmed in several studies. Surveys by the National Opinion Research Center between 1942 and 1970 reveal a trend "distinctly and strongly toward increasing approval of integration," unaffected by the racial turmoil of the sixties. Andrew M. Greeley and Paul B. Sheatsley, "Attitudes toward Racial Integration," *Scientific American*, 225, no. 6 (December 1971), 13. Campbell and Schuman, *Racial Attitudes*, found only one in five whites seriously disturbed by the prospect of a black "with about the same education and income" as himself living next door (p. 33). By comparison, Gertrude J. Selznick and Stephen Steinberg in their study on anti-Semitism reported only 7 percent of respondents would "prefer not to have any Jewish neighbors" (*The Tenacity of Prejudice* [New York: Harper and Row, 1969], p. 39). One can hardly imagine Irish or Italian immigrants when they came to the New World scoring better than blacks today.

does black migration to cities and suburbs replicate earlier immigrations of Irish, Italians, and Jews. The history of the American black, his color, the timing of his migration, are unique. But two fundamental features of the earlier immigrations characterize today's black experience. The first is a burgeoning group consciousness. For, as Oscar Handlin points out, earlier immigrant groups necessarily became conscious of their identity, developed "a shared heritage, presumed or actual," in response to conditions in the New World.[34] The second is the continuing abatement of racial discrimination, which in reference to the earlier immigrants Handlin called a "precondition for opening the group to the influence of the broader society."[35] Indeed, the increasing number of black elected officials from racially mixed constituencies is testimony to a developing white enlightenment concurrent with black political consciousness.

This study, then, while not one of unleashed optimism, is one of hope. The focus on black elected officials, their remarkable and continuing increase, their skill at representing black interests while attracting white support, affirms the best possibilities of the American political system. In the context of the black condition in general, however, they represent only one cause for hope among others for despair. Yet the implications are powerful. For black elected officials are at the meeting point of conflicting currents. Uniquely they embody the power to respond to black pride and white fear, and to implement programs toward eliminating racial injustice. It is unreasonable to expect that any group could fully satisfy such divergent interests. But this generation of elected blacks offers surprising promise.

[34] Oscar Handlin, "Historical Perspectives on the American Ethnic Group," in Harry A. Bailey, Jr., and Ellis Katz, eds., *Ethnic Group Politics* (Columbus, Ohio: Charles E. Merrill Publishing Co., 1969), p. 11.

[35] *Ibid.*, p. 16. For other perspectives on blacks and the earlier immigrants see Nathan Glazer, "The Peoples of America," in Shank, *Political Power*, pp. 98-107; and Irving Kristol, "The Negro Today Is Like the Immigrant Yesterday," *ibid.*, pp. 108-123.

Local Government and Blacks

A comment remains to be made about the power of local government and the role of blacks. Whether black officials represent the "true interests" of black people is a continuing argument. It relates of course to an individual's perceptions, and we shall examine the question in the course of the book. But it is important now to note that black candidates of any political hue are supported by black voters across the spectrum. By definition a public official thinks the system can work. Yet even militant critics who scorn the system have flirted with electoral politics. Bobby G. Seale and Erica Huggins ran for office, while Imamu Amiri Baraka and Huey P. Newton supported black candidates.[36] This reflects in part the recent political success of blacks. Chuck Stone, a critic of the system, understands the implications: "In a nation that owes its viability to politics, black politicians will grow in prestige and numbers. . . . The age of demonstrations has passed, and the age of the ballot box is upon the black man. It is the tool of survival. . . ."[37]

Whatever the shortcomings of the American political system, the argument that local officials are unimportant is specious. They do face red tape and bureaucratic roadblocks; they are often sandwiched between an abusive electorate and unconcerned state and federal officials. But at every level of government, from the presidency to that of municipal councilman, complaints about the limits of power are legion. Power is fractionalized, and even the man with

[36] Studies conducted in Los Angeles indicate that the black electorate substantially trusts black elected officials in general; and militants, while not necessarily renouncing violence, "endorse all conventional civil rights activities." See T. M. Tomlinson, "Ideological Foundations for Negro Action: Militant and Non-Militant Views," in Nathan Cohen, ed., *The Los Angeles Riots* (New York: Praeger Publishers, 1970), p. 372, and David O. Sears, "Political Attitudes of Los Angeles Negroes," *ibid.*, pp. 683-84.

[37] Stone, *Black Political Power*, p. 10.

the most, the president, sometimes seems shorn.[38] Of course his powers arch across the citizenry, and in the nuclear age the president can uniquely affect the survival of the nation. But at the same time there *is* power within local government. The power to tax, to zone, to create and administer services lies with local government. Day-to-day activities of an individual are affected more by his city's government than any other locus of political power. The kind of home he lives in, where it is located, the proximity of shopping areas, the location, cost, and quality of schools, the effectiveness of police, fire, and garbage services, the type of business or industry he lives near, ultimately the kind of people his neighbors will be, are more related to policies of local executives and legislators than to those of the president and Congress. However oblivious of it we may be, "municipal government directly affects more people at more points and more frequently than any other type of government."[39]

Further, municipal office is a tempering crucible for higher positions. Many state and federal legislators first attained elective office at local levels. Some of the local officials interviewed contemporaneously held office in county and state governments; two were preparing to contend for seats in Congress. In a word, local government and the people who hold its reins matter.

In particular it matters that blacks should hold office. Not only should they share in the administration of their own people's affairs, but they should be in a position to affect racial attitudes among all citizens through their political

[38] Only recently, since the Vietnam War and Watergate, has presidential power been broadly attacked. Earlier, many suggested it was too restricted, particularly in domestic affairs. See Louis W. Koenig, *The Chief Executive*, rev. ed. (New York: Harcourt, Brace and World, Inc., 1968), p. 12, or Richard E. Neustadt, *Presidential Power* (New York: John Wiley and Sons, Inc., 1960), pp. 192-93.

[39] Stanley N. Worton, Wilbur E. Apgar, David Jacobson, and Abraham Resnick, *New Jersey: Past and Present* (New York: Hayden Book Co., 1964), p. 134.

visibility. When there were no black elected officials, as when there were no black major league baseball players, many simply presumed they could not do a decent job. But blacks are proving as politically talented (or untalented) as whites, and there is evidence that racial significance fades as blacks serve in office. Of course race will remain a political consideration no less than religion and ethnic background. We may hope, however, that it will become no more significant.

Black elected officials in this first contemporary wave carry a special burden. Not only do they affect affairs of government, but they also create standards for their successors. They orchestrate the expectations of the entire citizenry.

II

Historical Overview: New Jersey and the Nation

Blacks have been denied political equality since colonial times, but ours is not the only generation in which they have reached office. The earliest black immigrants, arriving in Jamestown, Virginia, in 1619 and after, were not necessarily slaves; several came as indentured servants. They paid for passage, as did many whites, by working a specified number of years, after which they were free. They were then "accorded substantially the same rights as freed whites. They voted in eleven of the thirteen original colonies. And some of them became the first black office-holders in America by filling the minor posts of *beadle* and *surety*."[1]

Slavery did not appear in any colonial statutes until the 1660s, though in some places blacks were "being set apart and discriminated against" compared to Englishmen as early as the 1630s.[2] By the end of the seventeenth century it is doubtful whether blacks held office in any of the colonies. In 1705, Virginia formalized the restriction by forbidding any Negro, mulatto, or Indian to "bear any office" or "be in any place of trust or power."[3] Until the Revolu-

[1] Mervyn M. Dymally, "The Black Outsider and the American Political System," in Mervyn M. Dymally, ed., *The Black Politician* (Belmont, Calif.: Duxbury Press, 1971), p. 15.

[2] Carl N. Degler, "Slavery and the Genesis of American Race Prejudice," in August Meier and Elliott Rudwick, eds., *The Making of Black America* (New York: Atheneum, 1969), p. 95.

[3] Cited in Emil Olbrich, *The Development of Sentiment on Negro Suffrage to 1860* (New York: Negro Universities Press, 1969), p. 8.

tion, blacks were denied suffrage by law only in North Carolina, South Carolina, Georgia, and Virginia, though a few freedman might have been permitted an occasional ballot. But the presence of slavery in every colony and "the general deep-seated prejudice against Negroes" militated against their electoral participation everywhere.[4]

After the Revolution, most states continued to limit the ballot to whites by practice if not by statute. The issue stimulated debate at state constitutional conventions, notably in New York, Pennsylvania, and Massachusetts.[5] But electoral participation of blacks generally changed little when the colonies became states.

New Jersey was an exception. Its constitution of 1776 stipulated voter qualifications relating only to age, residence, and property. Otherwise "all inhabitants" could vote. Subsequently women as well as free blacks voted, though in modest numbers. Freedmen in any case constituted less than 20 percent of New Jersey's fourteen thousand or so blacks.[6] But thirty years later the legislature became unnerved by the mistaken impression "in regard to the admission of aliens, females, and persons of color, or negroes to vote in elections." It passed a law in 1804 requiring that every voter be "a free, white, male citizen."[7] In 1844, while some northern states were relaxing their racial qualifications, New Jersey enshrined the "free, white, male citizen" clause in its constitution.

Nor was this inconsistent with the views of New Jerseyans toward blacks in general. New Jersey was part of the "underground railway," but "both slaves and their conductors breathed more freely when a shipment left New Jersey. This state, alone among all Northern states, supported en-

---

[4] *Ibid.*, pp. 8-9.   [5] *Ibid.*, pp. 11-20.

[6] U.S. Bureau of the Census, cited in *The Negro in New Jersey*, report of a survey by the Interracial Committee of the New Jersey Conference of Social Work (Trenton: New Jersey Conference of Social Work, 1932), p. 77.

[7] Olbrich, *Negro Suffrage*, pp. 23-24.

forcers of the Fugitive Slave Act and offered no opposition when slaves were seized."[8]

Most New Jerseyans "completely ignored the question of slavery," and through 1860 industrialists and factory owners were dismayed by the prospect of war "over anything so incidental (to them) as slavery."[9] Southern markets for New Jersey goods, a seasonal flow of southern vacationers to the Cape May area, and bastions of Democratic party strength contributed to New Jersey's lack of sympathy for blacks. The attitude carried through the Civil War and after.

The question of enfranchising blacks became an "outstanding political issue" in the 1867 campaign for the legislature.[10] The Democrats, who opposed granting blacks the vote, were elected by an overwhelming margin. They promptly rescinded New Jersey's earlier ratification of the Fourteenth Amendment. Congress rejected the New Jersey act, calling it "scandalous."[11] Three years later the legislature voted against ratification of the Fifteenth Amendment giving blacks the right to vote. Ultimately a Republican-dominated legislature approved the Fifteenth Amendment; but not until 1875 was the state constitution amended to remove the word "white" as a voting qualification.

At about this time black political participation in the South reached a zenith. After the Civil War barriers were dismantled. Blacks held office at most levels of government in the South. Between 1867 and 1877 they served in the legislatures of every southern state. From 1867 until the end of the century twenty blacks were elected to the House of Representatives, as many as seven serving at one time in 1873-74. Two black men were elected to the United States Senate from Mississippi, and one served as governor of

8 John T. Cunningham, *New Jersey—America's Main Road* (Garden City, New York: Doubleday, 1966), p. 171.

9 *Ibid.*, pp. 154, 170-71.

10 *The Negro in New Jersey*, p. 17.

11 Cunningham, *New Jersey*, p. 189.

Louisiana.[12] But the number of elected blacks at all levels declined sharply after Reconstruction ended in 1877. As federal troops withdrew, southern states imposed legal and illegal obstacles to black electoral participation. By the end of the nineteenth century blacks in most of the South were disfranchised. The last black Congressman, George H. White of North Carolina, left the House on January 29, 1901, parting bitterly "in behalf of an outraged, heart-broken, bruised and bleeding, but God-fearing people, full of potential force." But he prophesied that "Phoenix-like" they would rise some day and return to the Congress.[13]

Not until 1929 did a black man, Oscar S. DePriest from Chicago, again serve in the House. During the next twenty-five years only three other blacks were elected, Arthur W. Mitchell and William L. Dawson from Chicago, and Adam Clayton Powell from New York. Except for Powell, each was subordinate to a white-controlled city political organization.[14] Indeed city machines across the country dominated politics within their suzerainties. The few blacks elected to office at any level until the decade after World War II owed their positions largely to the suffrance of and cooperation with machines. But in the fifties and sixties the power of political bosses and city machines was waning. Corruption was increasingly exposed, while welfare services replaced the traditional machine function of dispensing "favors." In northern cities where black populations mushroomed, party machines yielded to black influence or were bypassed by blacks who built their own political organizations.[15] The stage was set for the entry of elected blacks.

[12] Dymally, "The Black Outsider," pp. 16-17.

[13] Quoted in Edward T. Clayton, *The Negro Politician* (Chicago: Johnson Publishing Co., Inc., 1964), p. 37.

[14] On the contrasting styles of Dawson and Powell see James Q. Wilson, "Two Negro Politicians: An Interpretation," *Midwest Journal of Political Science*, 4, no. 4 (November 1960), 346-69.

[15] Hanes Walton, Jr., *Black Politics* (Philadelphia: J. B. Lippincott Co., 1972), pp. 189-91.

In the South, the Voting Rights Act of 1965 and concurrent civil rights activities shattered institutional resistance to black participation. Rearguard segregationists tried to prevent blacks from attaining office. They attempted to abolish offices, extend terms of white incumbents, and make elective office appointive. But sustained pressure under the laws and by the civil rights movement overcame most obstacles. As barriers were eliminated, more and more blacks attained office. Thus, as Hanes Walton points out, "convergence was taking place. Blacks took control of the party organizations in the North at the same time southern blacks broke the long standing control of white supremacy and segregation."[16]

New Jersey's part in the convergence was preceded by a modest shift to enlightened policies after World War II. Previously, however, sensitivity and policies toward blacks went little beyond New Jersey's dismal record after the Civil War. An irony in the state's history, as well as the nation's, was Woodrow Wilson's racial insensitivity. Elected governor in 1910, "he achieved nearly all the reforms that progressives of both parties had been pursuing for twenty years."[17] Yet, influenced by his southern background, he could write of his sympathy with removal of the "incubus" of the "ignorant and hostile" Negro vote in the South; and refer to West Coast Chinese as Orientals with "strange, debasing, habits of life."[18] Through the twenties and thirties racist groups like the Ku Klux Klan and the German–American Bund flourished in many parts of the state. Their influence was uneven, but in one community, for example, robed Klansmen were welcomed to church services and credited with forcing theaters to segregate blacks.[19] A study

[16] *Ibid.*, pp. 193-94.

[17] Cunningham, *New Jersey*, p. 263.

[18] Cited in Henry Wilkinson Bragdon, *Woodrow Wilson, the Academic Years* (Cambridge, Mass.: Harvard University Press, 1967), pp. 221, 249.

[19] Joseph Brandes, *Immigrants to Freedom* (Philadelphia: University of Pennsylvania Press, 1971), p. 286. See also E. Frederic Morrow, *Way*

in 1928 concluded that school segregation was not only common throughout the state, but, unlike in other northern states, segregation of blacks in New Jersey was brought about "artificially in cases where natural means do not do the trick."[20]

New Jersey enacted a civil rights law in 1921 providing for equal treatment of all persons in places of public accommodation. Laws against racial discrimination in life insurance transactions and in matters of exclusion from public schools followed. But after eleven years a state-supported investigation could find only one decision taken under any civil rights law. In 1932 the committee that prepared *The Negro in New Jersey* concluded:

Although civil rights are guaranteed by law to Negroes in New Jersey, their personal privileges are increasingly more limited. Segregation instead of lessening has increased. Thus, because of a tremendous increase in population, the Negro group has noted tendencies toward an increasing social separation in housing, theatres, restaurants, hotels, swimming pools, beaches and other public accommodations.[21]

By the early thirties a few blacks in New Jersey had attained elective office as an occasional county freeholder or member of the state assembly. But the investigative committee held that "there are frequent evidences of the exploitation of the Negro vote by both white and Negro politicians." In Newark's third ward, for instance, where blacks comprised over 80 percent of the population, they registered "no influence beyond having a few district leaders."[22] Black political participation in New Jersey had developed

---

Down South Up North (Philadelphia: United Church Press, 1973), p. 95.

[20] From a study by E. George Payne, quoted in *The Negro in New Jersey*, p. 39.

[21] *The Negro in New Jersey*, p. 65.

[22] *Ibid.*, p. 64.

at best into an instrument of selfish, usually white, advantage. So it went until World War II.

The postwar record is less tarnished. In 1945 New Jersey became one of the first states to create a Division against Discrimination. Its authority covered racial discrimination in employment, and after 1949 in places of public accommodation.[23] In 1947 New Jersey desegregated its national guard by mandate in the state constitution, and was the first state to do so.[24] In laws enacted in 1954, 1957, and 1961 discrimination was forbidden in public housing and much privately financed housing. In 1970 the Division on Civil Rights (formerly the Division against Discrimination) received 1,368 cases and resolved 1,090, most of them by conciliation, some through a hearing examiner. The Employment and Public Accommodations Bureau of the division held seventeen public hearings at which complainants were awarded over $10,000 in compensation.[25] The division's activity has prompted some to applaud its handling of "hundreds and hundreds of complaints in which citizens found that the law and the bureaucrats were on the side of open housing and equal opportunity in employment."[26] Still the privations nurtured by centuries of discrimination festered. In 1960 only two blacks held elective office in the sixteen cities of this study, though black proportions of the population were over 20 percent in nine of the sixteen.

In the late sixties, riots tore several New Jersey cities, as they did others across the country. George Wallace, running for president in 1968 on a racist platform, received 9 percent of New Jersey's popular vote—the highest percentage of any state's in the Northeast. But five years later an

[23] Stanley N. Worton, Wilbur E. Apgar, David Jacobson, and Abraham Resnick, *New Jersey: Past and Present* (New York: Hayden Book Co., 1964), p. 104.

[24] Cunningham, *New Jersey*, p. 302.

[25] New Jersey, *Department of Law and Public Safety Annual Report 1970*, George F. Kugler, Attorney General (Trenton: Office of the Attorney General, May 1971), p. 31.

[26] Editorial in *The Record* (Hackensack, New Jersey), Nov. 28, 1972, p. 26.

impressive trend could be recorded. While in 1969 there
were only 55 black elected officials at all levels of government in New Jersey, by 1973 there were 134.[27] New Jersey
was moving faster than most states, for only six states had
more elected blacks, though fifteen had larger black populations. Indeed five of the six, Alabama, Illinois, Michigan,
Mississippi, and New York, had larger black populations
than New Jersey's (Arkansas did not). When Matthew G.
Carter received the highest popular vote among Montclair's
commissioners in 1968, he became the first black mayor of
a sizable New Jersey community. In 1972 six New Jersey
cities were led by black mayors, more than in any other
state except Arkansas. Black electoral opportunity began to
flower in New Jersey no less than elsewhere across the
nation.

Thus for the second time in American history blacks in
substantial numbers surged to political office. One must
wonder whether their tenure will be more permanent than
after the Civil War. Certainly a national policy of repres-
sion could reverse electoral gains as quickly as they were
achieved. Even a laissez-faire attitude in Washington might
encourage reversals, particularly in the South. Some believe
that the Nixon administration's passive attitude toward civil
rights slowed, if it did not reverse, black gains toward equal
treatment. Patricia Roberts Harris, former dean of the
Howard University Law School, lamented in 1972 that
blacks no longer believed that the government was "on our
side and the side of the courts."[28] Nevertheless, conditions

[27] New Jersey, Bureau of Education [sic], Civil Rights Division, "1969
Elected Black Officials of New Jersey" (Trenton: mimeographed, n.d.);
National Roster of Black Elected Officials, Vol. 3 (Washington, D.C.:
Joint Center for Political Studies, May 1973). The figures must be con-
sidered approximate. The Joint Center's New Jersey list omitted several
officials (Councilman Howard Gregory of Hackensack, Commissioner
Horace J. Bryant, Jr., of Atlantic City, Aldermen Odis B. Cobb, and
Junius C. Sturdifen of Paterson), and included others no longer serving
(Commissioner Karlos R. LaSane of Atlantic City, Councilmen Betty
Dean of East Orange, and Sam Perry of Passaic).

[28] Quoted in *The New York Times*, December 12, 1972, p. 28.

now compared to those of a century ago favor black electoral advances, even if government policy becomes less
supportive.

Virtually all black office-holders during Reconstruction
were in the South. Their support came from ex-slaves,
docile, uneducated, with little political consciousness. They
were surrounded by a sea of hostile whites who did not
usurp authority only because of federal control and the
presence of troops.

Today, however, the South is generally reconciled to
black political participation. The black vote has been un-
dergirded by federal legislation, and were these laws weak-
ened there might be slippage toward earlier patterns of
denial. But in the meanwhile white political leadership frequently seeks black support. Moderate whites have prevailed increasingly over outspoken racists. Hardened resistance to the black vote and to black officials has receded.

Even more important is the organization and political
consciousness of blacks. Southern blacks would not yield
gracefully to a reimposition of political sterility. Unlike the
period after the Civil War, for the past two decades black
people themselves have been principals in unfurling the
carpet to political power. Beside southern-based civil rights
groups like the Southern Christian Leadership Conference
and the Student Nonviolent Coordinating Committee, new-
ly formed political organizations have pressed for electoral
opportunities. Largely black organizations like the Mississippi Freedom Democratic Party and the Lowndes County
Freedom Organization in Alabama were created in the mid-
sixties. Despite early frustrations, their efforts were vital in
accomplishing present levels of black participation.[29] It is
hard to imagine they would accede to a reversal, especially where blacks constitute majorities.

In the North the spurt of black officials has relied not

[29] With respect to early disappointments, see Stokely Carmichael and
Charles V. Hamilton, *Black Power: the Politics of Liberation in America* (New York: Vintage Books, 1967), chaps. 4 and 5.

only on increased numbers of blacks and successful organization; liberal whites have also contributed to black electoral successes, often comprising the margin of victory. In New Jersey many elected blacks serve predominantly white constituencies, yet remain responsive to the needs of the black community. Biracial electoral bases for black incumbents often swell at reelections. Thus large-scale disaffection by white supporters would impair the electoral chances of some black candidates. But there is little to suggest impending defection. Moreover, the constituencies of about half the black officials in this study were at least 50 percent black. Consequently, short of forced disfranchisement, a substantial number of blacks will continue to get elected.

Less certain than the number of black local officials will be the level of power left to local government. The possibility of regionalization, or "administrative metropolitanism," is seen by some as a threat to budding black political power.[30] A city and its government could be largely black, yet control over revenue and services might be co-opted by a predominantly white higher regional authority. Such a challenge should not be underestimated, though regionalization is not necessarily an electoral liability to blacks, as will be discussed. Moreover, in New Jersey thus far there has been little diminution of the powers of local government. Challenges have been made against community autonomy over zoning and school districting, and court decisions are pending. But the actions were instituted by civil rights sympathizers. They argue that white suburban areas ought to share the social and financial burdens of the inner cities, that communities should be denied the right to exclude low- or middle-income housing. To undermine the power of black officials would be the least of their intentions. If the courts support the plaintiffs, deprived minorities

[30] Frances Fox Piven and Richard Cloward, "Black Control of Cities," in Edward S. Greenberg, Neal Milner and David J. Olson, eds., *Black Politics* (New York: Holt, Rinehart and Winston, Inc., 1971), pp. 118-130.

should benefit. The ultimate effects on the power of local government, and local black officials, is less predictable. Most black officials interviewed, however, did not feel threatened by the prospect of a regional zoning authority; they welcomed it. But more will be said of this in Chapter IX.

The election of substantial numbers of blacks, especially at local levels, will in any case almost certainly continue. We turn to a closer look at them.

III

Roads to Office, I:
Social and Political Backgrounds

Social Background

Anyone who meets the constitutional requirements of age and citizenship can be president of the United States, as long as he is of proper race, sex, religion, wealth, education, occupation, and residential location. Perceptive observers recognize that "the idea that any boy can rise to high national office is one of the most pervasive myths in American politics."[1] The social background of elected officials at the highest levels of government is remarkably unrepresentative of the citizenry. Congress is a middle and upper class organization. Fathers of senators and representatives tend to be professionals, businessmen, or farmers rather than industrial workers or farm laborers. Members of Congress are better educated: four-fifths have college backgrounds, compared to one-fifth of the population as a whole; about half are lawyers. They are disproportionately white Protestant men. Blacks, women, Jews, Catholics, and other minorities are underrepresented.[2]

But at local levels of government, economic and ethnic barriers have been more easily breached. Local leaders more nearly reflect the social composition of their constituents. Heinz Eulau and Kenneth Prewitt found that the

[1] James MacGregor Burns and J. W. Peltason, *Government by the People*, 8th ed. (Englewood Cliffs, N. J.: Prentice-Hall, Inc., 1972), p. 329.
[2] *Ibid.*

37

socioeconomic status of council members in eighty-two cities around San Francisco varied in proportion to a municipality's socioeconomic characteristics. While the councilmen's status was higher than their constituents' in general, high-status communities tended to be governed by high-status councils, lower-status communities by lower-status councils.[3] The political history of cities across the country may be written as a parade to power of successive ethnic groups, Irish, Italians, Jews, and now blacks.

Similarly, the social characteristics of mayors and councilmen in this study resemble those of their constituents more closely than do those of federal officials. White Anglo-Saxon Protestant officials are scarce, as are financial and business magnates. Yet local officials are an elite group. They tend to be better educated than the general population, with higher occupational and professional status. In effect there are qualifications for office beyond those codified in law. The differences we seek, however, are not only those between citizen and leader, but between white leader and black leader, the differential "requirements" for the election of blacks. It is important to reiterate that the modest number of black and white officials in this study, thirty-one and ninety-six, is not merely a random sample. They comprise virtually all the elected municipal officials in 1972 serving the sixteen New Jersey cities with moderate-to-large black populations.

Sex

Despite a greater tendency toward matriarchy in black family structure than in white,[4] men overwhelmingly out-

---

[3] Heinz Eulau and Kenneth Prewitt, *Labyrinths of Democracy: Adaptations, Linkages, Representation, and Policies in Urban Politics* (New York: The Bobbs-Merrill Co., 1973). The authors emphasize that the pattern is not a statistical artifact, that in the lowest status communities "there are more than a sufficient number of high-status individuals . . . so that a city council could include only the very wealthy, best-educated, and prestigious persons" (p. 267).

[4] A voluminous bibliography on black family structure is cited in

number women among politicians in both races. Yvonne
Brathwaite Burke and Barbara C. Jordan were elected to
the House of Representatives in 1972, Cardiss Collins to her
deceased husband's seat the following year; together with
Shirley Chisholm they comprised a quarter of the 16 black
congressmen serving in 1974. This was far higher than the
proportion of women in the House—14 out of 435, or about
3 percent. In New Jersey the lone black state senator was
a woman, Wynona M. Lipman. But across the country few
black women have contended for office. Almost all mayoral
aspirants, North and South, have been males. Of the 2,630
black elected officials in the United States in 1973, 337 were
women.[5] All 6 blacks in the New Jersey assembly were men.
Among the 31 blacks in this study just one is a woman, Nellie F. Suratt, a member of the Plainfield council. Similarly,
only 6 of the 96 whites are women, though one was a mayor,
Patricia Sheehan of New Brunswick.

Age

Table III-1 reveals few differences in age concentrations between black and white officials. One might have expected blacks to be younger, since electoral opportunities
in earlier decades were closed. Blacks during those years
would have pursued fields other than politics, and their interest would have been permanently diverted. To some extent this supposition is borne out. At the time of the interview in 1972, 16 percent of the whites were over fifty-nine,
compared to 3 percent of the blacks, and 32 percent of the
blacks were under forty, compared to 27 percent of the
whites. But most striking is the preponderance of officials

James M. McPherson, Laurence B. Holland, James M. Banner, Jr.,
Nancy J. Weiss, and Michael D. Bell, *Blacks in America* (Garden City,
New York: Anchor Books, 1972), pp. 364-72.

[5] Herrington J. Bryce and Alan E. Warrick, *Black Women in Electoral
Politics* (Washington, D.C.: Joint Center for Political Studies, August
1973), p. A.

TABLE III-1: Age of Elected Officials by Race[a]

Age	Whites %	Blacks %
22-29	2	3
30-39	25	29
40-49	29	29
50-59	28	36
60-69	14	3
70 plus	2	0
Total	100 (96)	100 (31) [b]

[a] Age is recorded as of interview date in 1972.

[b] Percentages are rounded off and totals may not come to 100 percent.

in their thirties, forties, and fifties. The distribution in these age categories is fairly even for both races.

Religion

One of the largest but least surprising discrepancies is in religious background. The predominant religion among black officials is Baptist, though it is embraced by less than half (see Table III-2). Most American blacks trace their forebears to the antebellum South. Religion was encouraged among slaves by their masters, and Baptism and Methodism were the principal denominations. The roots are still firm. Three of the black officials were ordained Baptist ministers. Baptists, Methodists, and non-denominational Protestants accounted for 68 percent of the elected black officials.

James Q. Wilson observed in his 1960 study that most black "civic leaders" in Chicago were members of "the Negro upper-class churches—Episcopalian, Presbyterian, Congregational, Lutheran, and Roman Catholic."[6] On the

[6] James Q. Wilson, *Negro Politics* (New York: The Free Press, 1965), pp. 11-12.

TABLE III-2: RELIGION OF ELECTED OFFICIALS BY RACE

Religion	Whites %	Blacks %
Catholic	73	10
Jewish	13	0
Protestant (non-denominational)	1	16
Presbyterian	4	3
Episcopalian	3	13
Methodist	1	10
Baptist	1	42
Seventh Day Adventist	0	3
Other	2	0
None (or would not specify)	2	3
Total	100 (96)	100 (31)

other hand, the black rank and file was largely Baptist, as were several politicians. The religion of the contemporary black elected official, however, appears to be more in harmony with that of the black population. (Of the blacks in our citizens survey 58 percent were Baptists.)

In contrast, 73 percent of the white officials were Catholic, 13 percent Jewish. Barely 12 percent were Protestant. Fewer than 25 percent of the whites in the citizens survey were Protestants; 57 percent were Catholic, 11 percent Jewish. Among whites, therefore, Catholics were overrepresented in elective office at the expense of Protestants. Out of the entire sample of 127 officials, just 10 percent were white Anglo-Saxon Protestants.

Education

The difference in formal educational background is impressive. Table III-3 reveals that black elected officials are distinctly better educated than white fellow officials.

TABLE III-3: EDUCATION OF ELECTED OFFICIALS BY RACE

Highest Level Completed	Whites %	Blacks %
Elementary school	2	0
Some high school	4	3
Graduated high school	23	7
Some college	18	29
College degree	12	10
Some post-degree studies	10	16
Advanced college degree	31	36
Total	100 (96)	101 (31)

Twenty-nine percent of the whites went no further than high school, compared to 10 percent of the blacks. Sixty-two percent of the blacks had college degrees, compared to 53 percent of the whites.

The educational achievement of black officials is more remarkable in relation to the general population. According to the 1970 census, 12.5 percent of New Jersey's urban whites over twenty-five completed four years or more of college, compared to 4.1 percent of the blacks.[7] The black officials' educational high-jump implies a requirement to be "better" than whites to reach equivalent levels. Further, broadened political opportunity attracts more blacks. Though they were previously denied electoral opportunity, educated blacks now see fewer obstacles to success in politics than in other fields. This view is supported by an examination of occupational backgrounds.

Occupation

Table III-4 indicates that, except for lawyers, members of professions account for a small percentage of white

[7] U.S. Bureau of the Census, *General Social and Economic Characteristics, New Jersey*, Final Report PC (1)-C32 (Washington, D.C.: U.S. Government Printing Office, 1972), p. 229.

TABLE III-4: Occupation of Elected Officials by Race

Occupation	Whites %	Blacks %
Health professional (doctor, dentist, therapist)	2	3
Lawyer	20	3
Accountant	1	10
Engineer	2	10
Teacher or administrator in elementary or high; social worker	4	16
Teacher, administrator, or researcher in college	3	7
Business, industrial, or banking executive or manager	19	13
Salesman, broker, adjuster, public relations	9	10
Small business owner or manager	14	10
Policeman or fireman	5	3
Other civil service	8	3
Skilled laborer	5	3
Semi-skilled laborer	1	0
Union official	2	3
Industrial scientist	1	0
Clergyman	0	7
Housewife	1	0
None	2	0
Total	99 (96)	101 (31)

elected officials. Health professionals like physicians and dentists, accountants, engineers, teachers, and researchers comprise only 12 percent of the total. Among black officials, however, professionals exclusive of attorneys make up 46 percent.

Their attraction to office suggests an anticipation of greater fulfillment in politics than in their original professions. At the least, success in politics—and the fact of being elected means some success—can provide lateral fulfillment

when vertical opportunities appear restricted in their field.[8]
A few years ago a black dentist from a community in this
study told me that he had once aspired to a specialty in oral
surgery. But since oral surgeons depend on referrals from
general dentists, most of whom are white, he saw little hope
of success. He became reconciled to general practice. He
has since sought elective office and become increasingly active in politics, perhaps satisfying a need frustrated in his
first profession.

The fact that professional frustration may influence
blacks in their decision to enter politics does not imply that
they lack a sense of social or racial obligation. A belief that
more can be done for people through politics than through
other professions clearly affects the decisions of many, as
will be shown shortly.

Twenty percent of the white elected officials are attorneys. They comprise the largest single category, undoubtedly for the same reasons that attorneys are everywhere found in government. An attorney's interest is the
law, while the function of government is to create and administer law. There is thus a kindred relationship. Moreover, the nature of a legal practice allows for outside
activities more than do other fields. A lawyer's schedule,
especially if he is in partnership, is more flexible than a doc-
tor's or teacher's or engineer's. Indeed, the prestige and
income of a law practice may be enhanced if one of the
principals holds political office. Heinz Eulau and John D.
Sprague hypothesize further that many who were originally
interested in political careers studied law before they entered politics. Law was an intended vehicle toward political
advancement.[9]

    [8] Joyce Gelb similarly found that "because so many avenues have been
closed to Negroes, . . . politics has been seen as a major route to upward
mobility." See "Black Republicans in New York," *Urban Affairs Quarterly*, 5, no. 4 (June 1970), p. 468.
    [9] Heinz Eulau and John D. Sprague, *Lawyers in Politics* (New York:
The Bobbs-Merrill Co., 1964), p. 83.

In view of the attraction between the legal and political professions, one might wonder why there was just a single attorney among the elected blacks. The primary reason is scarcity. Only 125 blacks are members of the New Jersey Bar, compared to about 9,000 whites.[10] Furthermore, several older attorneys enjoy material and personal fulfillment in their own practices. They spurned politics earlier because they could not have risen higher than district party leader, and this, according to a young black attorney, was "beneath their dignity." But the number of black lawyers in politics will probably increase before long. At the end of 1972 some fifteen were admitted to the New Jersey Bar. One of them told me that several intended to become active politically.

Few other occupational distinctions between black and white officials are prominent. There are three black ordained ministers, including one who now classifies himself as a business executive. This modestly reflects the leadership assumed by many black clergymen in political and civil rights activities.[11] White officials with business or sales backgrounds outnumber blacks by 42 to 33 percent. But racial implications still run deepest among the professionals. Nevertheless, the impetus of blacks toward political activity owes less to social background than to a political consciousness acquired during the past decade.

[10] The New Jersey Bar Association keeps no record of ethnic composition of its membership. The number of blacks was provided by an officer of the Concerned Legal Associates, Inc., which maintains a file on black attorneys in the state. The list is unofficial and must be considered approximate.

[11] See Gary T. Marx, "Religion: Opiate or Inspiration of Civil Rights Militancy Among Negroes?" in August Meier and Elliott Rudwick, eds., *The Making of Black America* (New York: Atheneum, 1969), pp. 362-75. Clergymen including Martin Luther King, Ralph Abernathy, Jesse Jackson, Andrew Young, and Adam Clayton Powell were national leaders in the civil rights movement. Powell was first elected to Congress in 1945, Young in 1972.

Political Background

Blacks by and large approached elective office out of concern for the welfare of the black citizenry. Many entered politics from a base provided by the civil rights movement. As one black mayor said typically, "I was involved in traditional civil rights activities in the late fiftes and early sixties —education, housing, employment—and we found that if you were to have any effect on these issues, to improve the quality of services, you have to influence most people who hold elective office, or become the people who hold elective office." Or a councilman who had held office nearly a decade: "I was approached by both parties several years before I ran, but refused. It was during the black social revolution, the work of Dr. Martin Luther King, SNCC [the Student Nonviolent Coordinating Committee], and the whole bit that I changed my mind. I decided that here is one place [i.e., politics] I could make a contribution."

Whites on the other hand were more general in their expressions of civic interest. Unlike blacks, they were recruited for office from auxiliary government or civic leadership.[12] When asked, "What led you to seek public office in the first place?" whites were far more likely to recite a chronology of civic or political participation, a step-by-step progression of activity in the PTA, the Boy Scouts, the zoning board, perhaps a political party, and ultimately elective office. Several traced life-long political interest to forebears: "My father was a candidate for office on many occasions—he served as a clerk in the Senate and was associated with the Presidential elections of Roosevelt. More or less it's in the blood, so to speak. . . . I've been associated with the Democratic party in [city] since 1946. I ran for office on numer-

---

[12] Auxiliary government includes public bodies like library boards, planning commissions, and local agencies. Civic leaders have been officers in chambers of commerce, service clubs, community chests, and similar organizations. See Eulau and Prewitt, *Labyrinths of Democracy*, p. 273.

ous occasions, and decided to seek public office because I felt that a different viewpoint was perhaps needed in this city."[13]

Blacks had no such family histories, and were less involved in general community activities. Although their springboard to elective office was usually related to the struggle for civil rights, after attaining office they became concerned with a spectrum of civic issues.

White officials frequently expressed "love" for their cities. Their comments were embroidered with pleasant memories, often going back to childhood. This was rarely true of blacks, not only because their experiences may have been less pleasant but because their residency tended to be shorter. Forty-two percent of the black officials lived in their cities less than twenty years, compared to 10 percent of the whites. Many whites wanted to serve their memories —"to make this town the great place it once was." Blacks never remembered its being great.

Kenneth Prewitt shows the importance of friends and acquaintances on the decision of San Francisco area councilmen to seek office. But the relationship was reciprocal. He observes that prospective candidates, while influenced by small groups, sought out in the first place "groups which accord with their values."[14] In our study, blacks were far more reluctant than whites to seek office. Forty-eight percent, compared to 23 percent of the whites, insisted that they were entreated by friends or associates or "the community." Thus: "Several people in the community presented my name and more or less propelled me into becoming a candidate. I didn't seek it on my own." Or from another black councilman: "Well, I was prevailed upon by a num-

[13] Kenneth Prewitt found that half of the councilmen interviewed in the San Francisco area dated their initial preoccupation with politics in childhood or early adolescence (*The Recruitment of Political Leaders: A Study of Citizen-Politicians* [New York: The Bobbs-Merrill Co., 1970], p. 63).

[14] *Ibid.*, p. 111.

ber of people in my community . . . and my general feeling
along with them was that change was needed." The hesitant
transition to candidacy is drawn typically in this sketch:

> It was kind of strange. I didn't really seek it. Others
> sought me for it. I was sought out by, I guess you
> could say, a consensus of the black community—and by
> some of the white community also. The town was
> certainly long overdue for black representation in the
> city government.
>
> I wasn't politically oriented. I was active in a civil
> rights organization and doing anything I could to help,
> you know, right what I considered basic injustices all
> over—everywhere, in terms of employment and what
> have you. . . . I was doing a threefold thing: something
> for my company, for myself and my family, and also
> for minorities—not all just blacks you know, Spanish-
> speaking people, and what have you.
>
> When this thing became apparent that I might be
> the one, there was another fellow in contention that I
> went to see who was also active in the civil rights
> organization. In fact he happened to be the president
> at that time. I was a member of the executive board,
> and told him that perhaps it might be better if he took
> it because I thought I was doing my job where I was.
> He declined, and that was it.

The reluctance of many blacks to seek office must have
related to doubts about winning, doubts that were realistic
in view of the past record. Indeed most blacks in this study
were pioneers. Seventeen of the thirty-one were the first
blacks ever elected to their positions (four mayors and thirteen councilmen or commissioners). As Table III-5 indicates,
most were Democrats. Eighty-seven percent of the blacks
and 65 percent of the whites were members of or generally
supported the Democratic party. But few blacks had been
members for long. Thus a major vehicle of candidate re-

TABLE III-5: PARTISANSHIP OF ELECTED OFFICIALS BY RACE[a]

Party	Whites %	Blacks %
Democratic	65	87
Republican	31	7
None (independent)	4	7
Total	100 (96)	101 (31)

[a] "Which political party are you a member of, or do you generally support?"

cruitment and confidence, especially in cities with partisan elections, bypassed blacks. Though 44 percent of the blacks and 59 percent of the whites said they were active in a political party, the black percentage can be misleading. Several blacks became active when they became interested in office. Many whites were party workhorses for years, even decades, before they sought or were offered office. Thus party linkage and political experience, common to many white officials, were novelties to blacks. Inexperience, however, was not necessarily deemed a liability. Howard N. Lee, the first black mayor of Chapel Hill, North Carolina, believes "in some ways it is better to go into the office without previous experience, it eliminates the problem of bringing old attitudes onto the job. Furthermore, it frees the black elected official not to be connected to the 'establishment'; it allows him to be as unconventional as he likes without feeling any responsibility to persons of the previous establishment group . . . Although experience has been billed as providing a great advantage for the black elected official, it can also enslave."[15]

Despite limited political experience before election, by the time they were interviewed most blacks had held office sufficiently long to formulate views about tenure. Seventy-

[15] Howard N. Lee "The Black Elected Official and Southern Politics," in Mervyn M. Dymally, ed., *The Black Politician* (Belmont, Calif.: Duxbury Press, 1971), p. 82.

one percent had served for 2 years or more; the mean number of years was 3.7, compared to 4.8 for whites. Officials responded to the question: "Are your aims and expectations being fulfilled?" on a scale of "very much," "some," "not much," or "not at all." Table III-6 reveals several patterns.

TABLE III-6: Fulfillment of Aims and Expectations in Political Office by Race[a]

	Whites %	Blacks %
Very much	29	16
Some	43	68
Not much	20	13
Not at all	5	0
Don't know, no opinion, etc.	3	3
Total	100 (96)	100 (31)

[a] "Are your aims and expectations being fulfilled?"

Most officials felt "some" or "very much" fulfillment, 72 percent of the whites and an overwhelming 84 percent of the blacks. But more whites expressed near-complete satisfaction. Twenty-nine percent felt "very much" fulfilled, compared to 16 percent of the blacks. The crux is to know the aims and expectations. Perhaps blacks expected so little that any accomplishments loomed large.

In fact, few officials, black or white, entered office with a programmatic set of aims and expectations. Thus it is hard to find a barometer of fulfillment. Only one black official whose aims were "very much" fulfilled cited a campaign goal realized during his term. "My great aim was to bring to [city] the Model Cities program, the demostration program, and in 1967 I campaigned on that issue. As soon as I was elected we did pass that. That was my major objective. The year before it was turned down. The city council wanted nothing to do with it." Another with a less clear-cut program felt "good fortune to have been assigned to the departments that relate to the people—welfare, recreation, and health. Through these departments we've made substantial changes, and provided a broader and more effective service to the people who need it most." Others were vague, even cryptic: "We've broken ground, and the sun is coming up over the horizon."

Among whites who felt "very much" fulfilled the pattern is similar. Few spoke in terms of specific issues. Rare were accomplishments listed like "the new fire house . . . that was needed for the last ten years or so." Several gauged fulfillment by "progress" in housing, education, recreation, and the like, but in general terms. Most were vague: "I'm very happy with the experiences I've had. . . . My answer is just based on the overall approach that I've enjoyed my six years in politics. I think I've been on the right side of most of the issues."

The preponderance of general rather than specific responses carries through among whites who felt "some" fulfillment. But among blacks about half who were somewhat fulfilled were quite specific. A few were clearly goal oriented when they decided to run: "When I sought public office I basically was concerned about attempting to involve more people in government and finding out just what's going on. This has always been an apathetic city, particularly among black people. But due to the efforts of a lot of [us] political activists in the city, more people have gotten involved." Others derived fulfillment from programs articulated only during the course of their terms:

We've had some accomplishments, and we've made pretty good progress.

Q. In what areas?

Well, in any area you can think of. I mean, the physical area of the city; we've improved the condition of our parks, public properties, and we've encouraged private

COLLEGE OF THE SEQUOIAS

LIBRARY

development. We've made some progress in the area
of social problems. We've given minorities a greater
voice under this administration in policy-making right
on to the Board of Adjustment, principal of the junior
high school, captain of the police force. They've been
appointed to just about every board that we have, and
in numbers too—not just one minority member on the
board of seven.

A quarter of the white officials felt little or no fulfillment
of their aims and expectations. One unwitting councilman
cast a virtual self-indictment: "For ten years I've been in
here and we haven't had anything going." Others would
castigate bureaucratic inefficiency, red tape, insufficient
funds, political opponents. But not a single black official felt
totally devoid of fulfillment, though 13 percent answered
"not much." This turns us again to the question of what was
expected in the first place.

Contrasting sentiments enliven the dilemma. A white
councilman had low expectations: "My aims and expectations are basically fulfilled. I expected what I received. I expected some of the problems we have in city government,
people not talking to each other, not being able to realize
what's going on, not being able to subdue some of their
prejudices—their petty interests for the sake of the larger
picture." Reconciled to the worst even before he took office,
he appeared cynical throughout his evaluation. A black
councilman, on the other hand, was pleasantly surprised:
"I didn't come in with any high expectations. I came in with
the idea of being able to do a job and introduce a few new
ideas. . . . In the time I've been in government I've come to
realize that there are a heck of a lot of things that can be
done if people want to do them." But another black, who
thought he understood the political process before reaching
office, saw his aims and expectations barely trickling out of
the political faucet. "I realize the fact that the legislative

process is very slow and all the rest," but it worked even "at a much slower pace than I had anticipated." One thoughtful white official was impatient with the question itself. "I don't know what you mean by my aims or aspirations. My aims are to serve the town the best I can as long as I am in office. I have been doing that; but what my aspirations are or expectations, I don't know. I would not focus on it that sort of way at all. The job in [city] is to do the best you can with what you have to operate with, and do it consistently at your best, and you don't start with any preconceived ideas of being able to save the world or not."

Thus aims and expectations vary greatly from individual to individual. A handful of officials used fulfillment of specific campaign promises as barometers. Several enumerated programs undertaken after entering office that were not part of pre-election schemes. This was true more for blacks than whites. But about half the blacks and most whites did not articulate any issues as criteria of fulfillment. A variety of reasons could account for this.

First, the officials did not know the questions in advance. Inquiries elicited a scaled "gut" response. But in-depth supportive argument could be difficult to muster on momentary notice. Second, some officials undoubtedly interpreted the question as a measure of enjoyment. Their translation of "fulfillment of aims and expectations" meant pleasure in holding power or public recognition. Similarly, a need to justify their tenure probably played a part. Robert E. Lane relates political consciousness to psychological needs: political thought is framed by the need to feel moral, to be liked, to overcome feelings of inadequacy.[16] It would be difficult for many officials to admit to themselves, let alone to an interviewer, that nothing they wanted had been accomplished after several years in office. Finally, there might have been legitimate fulfillment from intangibles—from a feeling that

[16] Robert E. Lane, *Political Thinking and Consciousness* (Chicago: Markham Publishing Co., 1969), chaps. 6, 7, and 10.

citizens' fears had lessened or business morale improved. Thus even if an official did not list specific issues, his claim of "general" progress might be valid.

The variety of interpretations came from blacks as well as whites. Blacks were more specific in explaining their fulfillment, but the patterns of the groups were similar. Variation among blacks was as extensive as among whites.

Summary

The typical black elected official emerged from a social and political background containing sharp differences from those of his white counterpart. Both were likely to be males in their early to middle years, the white official being somewhat older. But the black was better educated. He probably retained antecedent ties to the Baptist or Methodist churches or to non-denominational Protestantism. The white official on the other hand tended to be Catholic. Both officials were almost certainly professional men, if not from business or sales backgrounds, the white a lawyer, the black anything but a lawyer.

The white official was likely to be a Democrat, and the black almost surely was one. Nevertheless, the white official's history of party activity as well as residency in his city was far longer than the black's. The white leader probably came from a background of general civic or party participation; the black entered politics with a sense of social injustice nurtured in civil rights activity. Each, especially the black, felt at least some fulfillment of his aims and expectations in elective office; but neither could readily define his aims and expectations. The black official, however, more often specified accomplishments as criteria for fulfillment, while the white generalized. But blacks, like whites, rarely entered office on a platform of specific programs.

One of the preconditions insisted upon by Carmichael and Hamilton before blacks join coalitions with whites is that "the coalition deals with specific and identifiable—as

opposed to general and vague—goals."[17] Black elected officials have largely ignored this advice. While they have successfully entered coalitions, their programmatic aims have
developed after they attained office. Though we delay until
later chapters discussion of programs, the next chapter con-
firms the value of coalitions in electing blacks.

[17] Stokely Carmichael and Charles V. Hamilton, *Black Power: The
Politics of Liberation in America* (New York: Vintage Books, 1967),
pp. 79-80.

Roads to Office, II: Structural Determinants[1]

Governmental form, electoral structure, and party arrangements vary among New Jersey's 567 municipalities. Though the options from which municipalities may choose their form and structure are limited by the state legislature, within the limits diversity is considerable. Governmental form, moreover, describes not only administrative apparatus, but is commonly seen as a determinant of the kind of individuals who seek office, their bases of political loyalty and obligation. Paterson's "strong" mayoral form was blamed for attracting to its board of aldermen "an ineffectual collection of political stumblebums."[2] And non-partisan systems were regarded a liability to "opportunity for the ethnic minorities and the poor to participate and to be represented in government."[3]

Recent successes of blacks in citywide, non-partisan elections where the black electorate is a minority confound traditional expectations. Such occasions, according to the literature, ought to be rare: only in partisan elections, with ward representation and a majority black electorate, would

[1] This chapter appeared as an article, "Electing Blacks to Municipal Office: Structural and Social Determinants," in *Urban Affairs Quarterly*, 10, no. 4 (September 1974), 17-39, and is reprinted by permission of the publisher, Sage Publications, Inc.

[2] *The Record* (Hackensack), July 9, 1972, p. D-2.

[3] D. Bennett Mazur, "How Nonpartisan Do We Want It?" *ibid.*, February 1, 1972, p. A-19.

blacks be likely to gain office.[4] Yet in most of the nation's major cities where blacks have become mayors since 1967, the system has been non-partisan, the electoral majority white.[5] New Jersey municipalities reflect the national pattern.

Table IV-1 lists the form of government of each of the sixteen municipalities, the type of elections (partisan or non-partisan), and the system of representation (ward or at-large). Moreover, the cities are ranked by their proportions of black elected officials relative to their black populations. (The proportions of black elected officials and residents in each community were listed in Table I-1.) Thus, since one of Hackensack's five elected officials was black, black political representation amounted to 20 percent. But since 17 percent of the city's population was black, blacks were over-represented by 3 percent. Trenton's blacks, at the other extreme, were under-represented by 25 percent. Thirty-eight percent of Trenton's population, but only 13 percent

---

[4] Edward C. Banfield and James Q. Wilson, *City Politics* (New York: Vintage Books, 1966), pp. 158-59, 303-308; Joyce Gelb, "Blacks, Blocs and Ballots," *Polity*, 3, no. 1. (Fall 1970), 62-69; Leonard E. Goodall, *The American Metropolis* (Columbus, Ohio: Charles E. Merrill Publishing Co., 1968), pp. 48-50; Willis D. Hawley, *Nonpartisan Elections and the Case for Party Politics* (New York: John Wiley and Sons, 1973), p. 128; John H. Kessel, "Governmental Structure and Political Environment: a Statistical Note about American Cities," *American Political Science Review*, 56, no. 3 (September 1962), 615-17; Robert L. Lineberry and Edmund F. Fowler, "Reformism and Public Policies in American Cities," *American Political Science Review*, 61, no. 3 (September 1967), 715-16; Harry M. Scoble, "Negro Politics in Los Angeles: the Quest for Power," in Nathan Cohen, ed., *The Los Angeles Riots* (New York: Praeger Publishers, 1970), p. 662; Murray S. Stedman, Jr., *Urban Politics* (Cambridge, Mass.: Winthrop Publishers, 1972), pp. 119-27.

[5] Of the eleven largest cities with black mayors, nine had non-partisan systems. Only Gary and Cleveland had party elections (though filing as an independent in Cleveland allows a candidate to bypass party primaries). Eight of the eleven had majority white populations according to the 1970 census, but all had majority white electorates. The eleven cities and their black populations are: Atlanta (52%), Cincinnati (28%), Cleveland (38%), Dayton (31%), Detroit (44%), Flint (28%), Gary (53%), Grand Rapids (11%), Los Angeles (18%), Newark (54%), Raleigh (23%). The first mayoral election in Washington, D.C. (71% black), held in 1974, was won by the appointed black incumbent.

TABLE IV-1: GOVERNMENTAL AND ELECTORAL FORMS IN MUNICIPALITIES
RANKED ACCORDING TO EQUITABILITY OF BLACK REPRESENTATION

City	Population (1970)	Equitability (difference between % black population and % black officials)	Form of Government	Type of Election	Type of Representation
Hackensack	35,911	+ 3	city-manager	non-partisan	at-large
East Orange	75,471	+ 2	mayor-council	partisan	ward
Englewood	24,985	0	mayor-council	partisan	ward[a]
Teaneck	42,355	− 1	city-manager	non-partisan	at-large
Plainfield	46,862	− 3	mayor-council	partisan	ward
New Brunswick	41,885	− 6	mayor-council	partisan	at-large
Montclair	44,043	− 7	commission	non-partisan	at-large
Paterson	144,824	−10	mayor-council[b]	partisan	ward
Jersey City	260,545	−11	mayor-council	partisan	ward
Camden	102,551	−14	mayor-council	non-partisan	at-large
Newark	382,417	−14.1[c]	mayor-council	non-partisan	ward
Elizabeth	112,654	−15.5	mayor-council	partisan	ward
Orange	32,566	−15.8	commission	mayor-council	at-large
Passaic	55,124	−18	city-manager	non-partisan	ward
Atlantic City	47,859	−24	commission	non-partisan	at-large
Trenton	104,638	−25	mayor-council	non-partisan	ward

[a] Type of representation was listed as ward, though in some municipalities with ward or district representation a few councilmen were elected at large.

[b] Paterson's ward representatives were called aldermen.

[c] Decimals were used to rank when rounding off gave two municipalities the same percentage.

of its elected officials, were black. Thus Table IV-1 ranks in order of equitability of black representation among elected officials. The ranking ignores differences in power of the offices, since our concern is with the office-holder as an expression of the voter and electoral structure.

After relating numerical equitability to form, type of election, and system of representation, we shall compare community socioeconomic features. Finally, the elections of black mayors in Montclair, East Orange, Newark, and Englewood will be examined in the context of their cities' social and electoral characteristics.

Form of Government

New Jersey's municipalities, like most of the nation's, are governed by one of three forms. In mayor–council governments, the power of the mayor relative to the council varies in different communities; but the two work in tandem to provide legislative and administrative leadership. Since early in the twentieth century communities have adopted one of two alternative forms with the hope of enhancing efficiency and accountability. The first, commission government, places responsibility for departments with individually elected commissioners. In council–manager arrangements, however, the mayor and council set general policy, but they appoint a professional manager to oversee day-to-day affairs.[6]

Others have correlated forms of government with community size, growth rate, ethnic composition. John H. Kessel indicates that city–manager forms have been adopted by a slight majority of cities with populations between twenty-five thousand and a quarter million. Mayor–council forms predominate in the largest cities (populations over half a million) and in smaller communities (populations less than twenty-five thousand). The commission form, rarest of the three, is found in none of the largest cities and fewer than 10 percent of the smallest.[7] Beyond size, Kessel

---

[6] League of Women Voters, *New Jersey: Spotlight on Government* (North Plainfield, N. J.: Twin City Press, 1969), pp. 82-91.

[7] Kessel, "Governmental Structure," pp. 615-16.

shows that cities with small growth rates and with high percentages of the foreign-born are more likely to have mayor–
council forms. The mayor–council form is suited to the ap-
peasement of long-standing rivalries, according to Kessel,
and is therefore optimal for non-expanding, ethnically diverse communities.[8] A rapidly growing community, on the
other hand, requires more street, sewer, garbage, and other
services. The new population, he suggests, is likely to be
politically amorphous, and a "professional administrator is
less likely to face organized opposition."[9]

Lineberry and Fowler relate forms of government to
socioeconomic cleavages. They find that cities with manager
forms are more likely to have homogeneous populations
than those with mayor–council forms. And city–manager
governments, according to the authors, are less responsive
to class, racial, and religious cleavages than mayor–council
forms.[10] They conclude that the manager form tends more
than the mayor–council to "seek the good of the community
as a whole" and minimize the impact of social cleavage on
policy-making.[11]

But the inferences of Kessel and Lineberry and Fowler
are unsupported by the data in this study. In the first place,
none of the sixteen municipalities exhibited much growth;
indeed half had slightly lower populations in 1970 than
1960. Therefore, according to Kessel, mayor–council forms
should have predominated; and ten of the sixteen do have
mayor–council structures. Kessel's inferences, however,
suggest that most of the nine communities with populations
between twenty-five thousand and one hundred thousand
would have mayor–council forms. But the contrary is true.
Not only did six of the nine have reform structures (three
city–manager, three commission), but all except one had reduced populations or negligible increases as well. Only
Hackensack's grew by more than 1 percent.

[8] *Ibid.*, pp. 616-17.   [9] *Ibid.*, p. 617.
[10] Lineberry and Fowler, "Reformism and Public Policies," p. 715.
[11] *Ibid.*, p. 716.

Moreover, besides slow growth rates, the sixteen municipalities should have had mayor–council governments because of the factionalism built into our criteria for selection. Since each city has a substantial black population, heterogeneity and racial cleavage are inherent. Thus, if Lineberry and Fowler are correct, governments with reform structures should not have been expected on that count either. Yet not only are six of the sixteen governments reform, but their equitability in terms of elected black officials is not appreciably worse than in mayor–council forms. For while three of the four cities with the least equitability are city– manager or commission forms, so are three of the seven with the most favorable proportions.

Type of Election

By the mid-1960s, 66 percent of American cities with populations of more than twenty-five thousand held non-partisan elections: the party system was forbidden.[12] In keeping with the reform approach that government and administration be "above" party politics, most reform governments (city– manager or commission) are non-partisan. But non-partisanship, critics suggest, is not necessarily salutary. Robert Wood holds that it encourages the naïve assumption that political problems have "a single right answer."[13] Fred I. Greenstein believes it a liability to candidates' exposure because traditional party financing and organization are unavailable.[14] Virtually all students of local government contend that minority-group candidates are disadvantaged by non-partisan systems. Edward C. Banfield and James Q. Wilson say characteristically:

[12] Phillips Cutright, "Nonpartisan Electoral Systems in American Cities," *Comparative Studies in Society and History*, 5, no. 2 (January 1963), 212.

[13] Robert C. Wood, *Suburbia* (Boston: Houghton Mifflin Co., 1959), p. 155.

[14] Fred I. Greenstein, "The Changing Pattern of Urban Party Politics," *Annals of the American Academy of Political and Social Science*, 353 (May 1964), 11.

If a Negro is known politically to the public at all, it is
likely to be only on account of his race. But in a
partisan system, being a member of a minority group
may be a positive advantage. The party runs a "ticket"
or "slate" which it "balances" with candidates who
represent the elements within the party in due
proportion to their voting strength. A minority-group
member "adds strength to the ticket." . . . In some non-
partisan elections, to be sure, a "slate" is made up and
endorsed by a local party or party-like organization.
Although the slate-makers may try to balance it, their
effort is likely to be futile for lack of one indispensable
element—party loyalty.[15]

Our data, however, support this affirmation only modestly (Table IV-1). Of the nine cities whose blacks are under-
represented by margins of 10 percent or greater, six held
non-partisan elections; and of the seven whose under-representation was less than 10 percent, three were non-partisan.
But, despite the tendency, the figures negate rigid asser-
tions that blacks cannot do well in non-partisan elections.
Indeed two of the four communities with the most favorable margins of black representation, Hackensack and Teaneck, hold non-partisan elections.

Type of Representation (Ward or At-Large)

At-large arrangements, it is commonly believed, are less
favorable to the electoral chances of blacks than ward representation. In districts where blacks numerically predominate, blacks will likely win. But at-large or citywide elections reduce the impact of black districts and, according
to the argument, black electoral chances.[16] Daniel R. Grant,

[15] Banfield and Wilson, *City Politics*, pp. 158-59. This view is commonly held by authors cited in n. 4.

[16] *Ibid.*, pp. 307-308; Lineberry and Fowler, "Reformism and Public
Policies," pp. 715-16.

however, examined the metropolitan government formed of the fusion of Davidson county and Nashville, Tennessee, in 1963. He cited fears "commonly suggested by political scientists" that black voting strength and influence would be diluted by creation of the larger governmental unit. But he found "no instance in which a candidate supported by the overwhelming majority of Negroes was defeated because of the white voters added to the local electorate by metro."[17]

Our data make evident that at-large or citywide voting has not precluded the election of blacks. Of the twenty-seven offices held by blacks in 1972, thirteen were at-large. Beyond that, six of the ward-elected blacks represented districts whose electorate was less than 50 percent black. Thus about 70 percent of the black officials were elected by constituencies with black voters in the minority, though in some a substantial minority.[18] This does not deny the advantage for a black political aspirant from a largely black ward. But the assumption must be questioned that blacks will rarely be elected unless they constitute "at least fifty percent of the electorate," or unless a party organization seeks to offer a "balanced ticket."[19] Thus neither at-large representation, non-partisan elections, nor forms of government are rigid determinants of black electoral opportunity.

[17] Daniel R. Grant, "A Comparison of Predictions and Experience with Nashville 'Metro,'" *Urban Affairs Quarterly*, 1, no. 1 (September 1965), 52.

[18] This includes blacks elected citywide in East Orange and Newark whose black populations were 53 and 54 percent. But the proportion of black voters to the black populations was considerably lower than for whites. Similarly, three of the ward councilmen estimated that blacks in their wards comprised 50 percent, but voting blacks much less—because there were more children among blacks, and because eligible blacks voted less frequently than whites. On this see James Q. Wilson, "The Negro in American Politics: The Present," in John P. Davis, ed., *The American Negro Reference Book* (Englewood Cliffs, N. J.: Prentice-Hall Inc., 1967), pp. 431-32.

[19] *Ibid.*, p. 444.

Beyond Governmental Structure

If we look beyond forms and styles of government, it becomes apparent that the number of blacks in a municipality
does not necessarily determine the number in office. The
black populations of East Orange and Plainfield, 53 and 40
percent, are equitably represented by black elected officials. But blacks in Newark and Atlantic City, 54 and 44
percent, are under-represented. At the same time some
communities with smaller black populations, Hackensack
(17 percent) and Teaneck (15 percent), have equivalent
proportions of elected blacks, while others, Elizabeth (16
percent) and Passaic (18 percent), do not.

The size of the cities, on the other hand, does appear to
be related to the proportions of elected blacks. Blacks in the
largest cities are numerically less well represented than in
the smaller. The seven communities with the most equitable
proportions of elected blacks, i.e., the smallest differentials
between the proportions of elected blacks and the black
population, have populations under one hundred thousand.
The six with populations over one hundred thousand have
less equitable black representation. But further analysis
suggests that size is less a determinant than socioeconomic
characteristics.

Residents of the larger cities generally are of lower socioeconomic status than those of the smaller municipalities.
In socioeconomic categories an impressive relationship
emerges. Figure 1 relates median school years completed
by males over twenty-five to the sixteen cities.[20] The munici-

---

[20] U.S. Bureau of the Census, Census of Population: 1970, *General
Social and Economic Characteristics,* Final Report PC (1)-C32 New Jersey (Washington, D.C.: U.S. Government Printing Office, 1972), pp.
283-90, 445-54. The figures are given separately for males and females,
though in each municipality they are nearly identical. Because of
Teaneck's peculiar designation as a "township," it was not listed among
New Jersey "places" in this census report. The figures were derived
instead by averaging education medians of adults over twenty-five years
of age reported in Teaneck's six census tracts in U.S. Bureau of the
Census, *1970 Census of Population and Housing,* PHC (1)-156, Census

palities are ranked in order of equitability of black electoral representation. Without exception the seven municipalities with the most equitable proportions contain the best educated populations. Their number of school years completed range between a median of 11.5 for New Brunswick and 12.8 for Montclair and Teaneck. The nine with less equitable black representation range from a median of 9.4 for Camden to 11.2 for Orange.

Figure 2 illustrates median annual earnings for families and unrelated individuals of each city.[21] The seven with the most equitable black representation are in the most favorable earnings categories—though earnings in Elizabeth, with no elected blacks, exceed those in New Brunswick and East Orange. Nevertheless, the tendency is linear. The lower the annual income of a city's residents, the less likely are the city's blacks to be proportionately represented in their government. Finally, Figure 3 relates the size of each community's business and professional class to its equitability of black representation.[22] As with education and earnings, people at higher occupational levels are found in greater numbers in communities with the most favorable proportions of black elected officials. In the seven municipalities with the best proportions, professionals and business managers comprise at least 22 percent of the popula-

Tracts, Paterson-Clifton-Passaic, New Jersey (Washington, D.C.: U.S. Government Printing Office, March 1972), p. 26. Teaneck comprises tracts 0541 through 0546. Subsequent information on income and occupation as it relates to Teaneck is derived from these tracts.

21 U.S. Bureau of the Census, *General Social and Economic Characteristics*, pp. 331-38, 485-94; U.S. Bureau of the Census, *1970 Census of Population and Housing*, p. 58.

22 U.S. Bureau of the Census, *General Social and Economic Characteristics*, pp. 307-14, 465-74; U.S. Bureau of the Census, *1970 Census of Population and Housing*, p. 42. Occupations are listed in the census reports in a hierarchy based on skills. Those under the two highest categories, "professional, technical, and kindred workers" and "managers and administrators, except farm," comprise our professional and business class.

Figure 1

Median Number of School Years Completed by
Males Over Twenty-Five, and
Equitability of Black Electoral Representation[a]

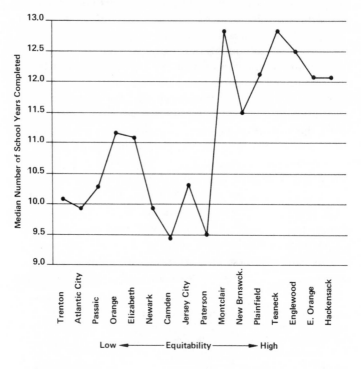

[a] See note 20.

tions, topped by Teaneck with 39 percent. But professionals
and managers in eight of the other nine comprise no more
than 17 percent. (Orange contains slightly over 21 percent.)

The data here tie in with earlier research relating racial
tolerance to socioeconomic levels. Several studies have
scaled people's education, income, and occupational levels

Figure 2

Median Annual Earnings (For Families and
Unrelated Individuals), and
Equitability of Black Electoral Representation[a]

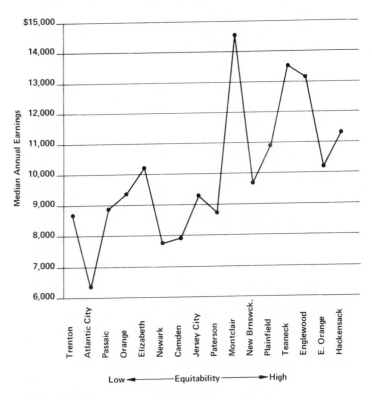

[a] See note 21.

with the likelihood of their holding liberal social attitudes.[23]
The higher a person's socioeconomic level, the less likely
will he exhibit racial bigotry.

[23] V. O. Key, Jr. *Public Opinion and American Democracy* (New
York: Alfred A. Knopf, Inc., 1964), p. 135; Seymour Martin Lipset,

Figure 3

Percent Business and Professional Class, and Equitability of Black Electoral Representation[a]

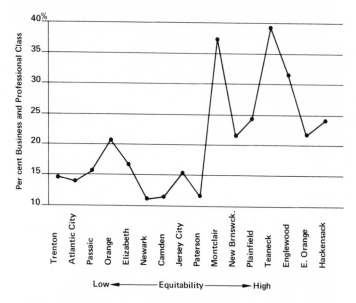

Low ◄———— Equitability ————► High

a See note 22.

Of course high socioeconomic levels assure neither freedom from prejudice nor election of blacks. Moreover, the importance of governmental structure as an electoral determinant, though traditionally exaggerated, cannot be ignored[24]—any more than campaign organization, financial

Political Man (Garden City, N.Y.: Doubleday and Co., 1960), pp. 101-102; Angus Campbell, Philip E. Converse, Warren E. Miller, and Donald E. Stokes, *The American Voter* (New York: John Wiley and Sons, Inc., 1960), pp. 512-15.

24 Lee Sloan describes an exceptional case in which a municipality's electoral structure was changed specifically "to cope with the black minority," in " 'Good Government' and the Politics of Race," *Social Problems*, 17, no. 2 (Fall 1969), 173.

resources, voter turnout, or personal attributes of candidates. But neither is there any justification for rhetoric that urges blacks "to consider using any means necessary to resist if and when there are proposed schemes to change to nonpartisan at-large elections. Further, in cities like Detroit they should fight with a missionary zeal to change at-large systems to small ward-based ones."[25]

Socioeconomic considerations have been given little weight in black electoral studies. Chuck Stone does glance at support for black mayoral candidates from "Los Angeles's wealthy and influential Jewish community," and Chapel Hill's "professors and employees of the traditionally liberal University of North Carolina," and James Q. Wilson cites the importance of the liberal suburban white to black electoral success.[26] Moreover, Thomas F. Pettigrew found that, irrespective of local issues, white supporters of black candidates for mayor in Cleveland, Gary, Los Angeles, and Newark were disproportionately upper-status, college educated, Democratic, Jewish, and non-bigoted.[27] Discussions devoted to electoral and governmental structure have been more common, however.

A review of the elections of black mayors in four of New Jersey's principal municipalities minimizes the significance of formal structure. Rather it shows that, coupled with distinctive local issues, dependence on white electoral support was common. Moreover, this support appeared more forthcoming from populations with higher socioeconomic characteristics.

[25] Ernest Patterson, *Black City Politics* (New York: Dodd, Mead and Co., 1974), p. 63.

[26] Chuck Stone, *Black Political Power in America*, rev. ed. (New York: Dell Publishing Co., 1970), pp. 277, 280. James Q. Wilson, "The Negro in Politics," in Talcott Parsons and Kenneth B. Clark, eds., *The Negro American* (Boston: Houghton Mifflin Co., 1966), p. 437.

[27] Thomas F. Pettigrew, "When a Black Candidate Runs for Mayor: Race and Voting Behavior," in Harlan Hahn, ed., *People and Politics in Urban Society* (Beverly Hills, Calif.: Sage Publications, 1972), pp. 99-105.

The Mayors[28]

Matthew G. Carter, Montclair

It is symbolically appropriate to the argument that governmental form plays less part in determining equitability than socioeconomic features that in May 1968 Matthew G. Carter became the first black mayor of a sizable New Jersey municipality. For not only did Carter become mayor in a non-partisan, commission form of government, but the socioeconomic characteristics of Montclair's residents were among the highest of the sixteen communities.

Carter first attained office in 1964 at the age of forty-eight when he received the most votes among eleven candidates for the town commission. He became director of public works, and was chosen vice-mayor by his four fellow commissioners. Though he was an ordained minister, his principal occupation, that of executive for the YMCA, brought him to Montclair in 1958 after years in Richmond, Virginia, and Columbus, Ohio. He had been active in civil rights efforts since his early adult life, but was broadly seen in Montclair as a negotiator, not a demonstrator.[29] Moreover, he made clear that his concern was not just for Negroes but for "the total population."[30] His endorsement by Montclair's community committee lent credentials to his townwide appeal.

Though Montclair's elections are non-partisan, since 1952 a community committee has been organized in advance of each municipal election to support a slate of five. The quadrennial committees, operating in a reform spirit, are com-

[28] See Jeffrey K. Hadden, Louis H. Masotti, and Victor Thiessen, "The Making of the Negro Mayors 1967," *Trans-Action*, 5, no. 3 (January-February 1968), 21-30, for contrast. The authors' conclusions that "the possibility of coalitions (with whites) to elect other Negro candidates appears, except in a handful of cities, remote," is contrary to the evidence presented here.

[29] *The Sunday News* (Newark), May 17, 1964, p. 40.

[30] *Ibid.*

posed of representatives of most of the town's interests—business, sectional, religious, ethnic. They screen and promote candidates and ultimately endorse a slate, most of whose members win election. Carter was designated by the committee in 1964 from among three blacks proposed by the Montclair Council of Negro Men and affiliated black organizations. Four years later he was endorsed again.

When Matthew Carter ran in 1968, not only was he again the highest vote-getter, but he received over a thousand votes more than the first time. His support among blacks and whites was solid as he increased his margin in four of Montclair's five wards. His mandate was respected by the town commission, which unhesitatingly selected him as mayor as well as director of the department of public affairs.

Though the power of the mayor in a commission form of government is little greater than the other commissioners'—his functions are largely ceremonial—the symbolic importance was not to be underestimated. "I am proud that Mayor Carter is my mayor," said a resident; "I am a Negro."[31] Carter himself interpreted his election as a confirmation of "hope and faith in America and the American dream."[32]

But he also sensed that his landmark election was made possible, or at least more likely, because Montclair was not just any town with a 70 or 75 percent white majority. Upon election he cited Montclair's "sense of style . . . tradition of excellence . . . and unusual blend of intellectual, esthetic and emotional qualities."[33] He campaigned on a platform of social integration, affirming his commitment to integrated schools and housing. He led at the polls.

Carter chose not to run again in 1972. No blacks were elected to the town commission that year, but Mayor Carter's tenure was applauded widely. The local newspaper lauded him as "a man who earned universal respect," and

[31] *Montclair Times*, May 23, 1968.
[32] *Ibid.*   [33] *Ibid.*

praised his "aim to give leadership to all the people, on the one hand urging intelligent rather than emotional weighing of items, while spearheading the fight for human rights and justice on the other."[34] Some criticized his lack of militance, but he was broadly seen as having blended the needs of blacks with those of the entire community.

William S. Hart, Sr., East Orange

The election of William S. Hart, Sr., as mayor of East Orange in November 1969 contrasts sharply with Carter's. East Orange is governed by a mayor–council form, and unlike in Montclair, the mayor is elected independently, appoints boards and commissions, and can veto resolutions and ordinances passed by the ten-member city council. Elections are partisan, and while the Republicans and Democrats house intra-party factions, no one has been elected to city government in recent memory without a major party label.

Hart's victory climaxed a long partisan effort. He had been active in Democratic party affairs in East Orange since he moved there in 1957, and in 1960 he became the first black to be elected to the city council. He took office in 1961 at the age of thirty-five, and when his term ended the following year he was appointed executive assistant to Democratic Governor Richard J. Hughes and later director of the New Jersey State Youth Division. A professional educator, Hart became a Junior High School principal in Elizabeth in 1968; but upon election he assumed full-time responsibilities as mayor.

In 1958 Hart's predecessor, James W. Kelly, Jr., became East Orange's first Democratic mayor in forty-four years. But the council remained dominated by Republicans until the mid-sixties. By the end of the decade, however, not only was the council under solid Democratic control (seven Democrats to only three Republicans); but, with five blacks

34 *Ibid.*, March 16, 1972.

on the council, the election of Hart marked the first time a major city in New Jersey, and perhaps anywhere in the North, was governed by more elected black officials than white.

Hart had designs on the mayor's office long before his election. He announced his candidacy in February 1968, over a year and a half before the election. Unlike many blacks who had to be entreated to seek elective office, Hart was his own tactical chief from the start: "I had enough political awareness to know there would be a change in government here the next time around. If I could get early backing, I felt I could win."[35]

Though 53 percent of East Orange's population was black, black voters were in the minority. Hart made a pointed appeal to whites. He sought to allay apprehensions about race from his opening announcement ("I will not run as a Negro mayor, but as a mayor for all the people"[36]) through the eve of the election ("I will be mayor of everybody and not only a segment of the community"[37]). He reviewed his campaign in "both white and black homes" as having "dealt with issues—education, housing and how both of these affect the tax problem—and this is what brought me a sizable white vote."[38]

Hart became the Democratic nominee by winning the June primary. But the incumbent, James Kelly, would not yield, and ran in November as an independent. Thus Hart faced two white opponents, Kelly and the Republican nominee. Though he won with a plurality of 45 percent, he probably would have won even if Kelly had not contested. By 1969 the city was clearly Democratic. Kelly, however, could count on a personal loyalty nurtured during ten years in office, and he received 19 percent of the vote. Certainly if Kelly had not run some of his support would have defected

35 *The Evening News* (Newark), November 6, 1969, p. 21.
36 *Ibid.*, November 5, 1969.
37 *East Orange Record*, November 6, 1969.
38 *The Evening News* (Newark), November 6, 1969, p. 21.

to the white Republican candidate. But among Kelly's supporters, presumably Democrats, hardly more than a quarter would have been necessary to give Hart a majority.

Hart's mandate was not as decisive as Carter's. But he
had reason to believe that in a two-man partisan race he
would have won. Most of the city's voters were not only
Democratic but placed high on the socioeconomic scale;
and, as indicated, residents in such communities appear less
likely to manifest racism in their political selections.

Kenneth A. Gibson, Newark

Kenneth A. Gibson's campaign for mayor of Newark,
New Jersey's largest city, bore implications deeper than
Carter's or Hart's. Though Newark's elections are non-
partisan, the structure of government provides for a
"strong" mayor and council. The mayor is elected independently of the council, as in East Orange. But since he was
unable to achieve victory by plurality like Hart, Gibson ultimately had to oppose a single white opponent, the incumbent Hugh Addonizio. At the election on May 17, 1970, Gibson received the most votes of seven candidates, but less
than a majority. Since Newark's law requires the winner to
obtain a majority, he faced the runner-up, Addonizio, the
following month. But while Newark's population was 54
percent black, blacks comprised a minority of voters. Nevertheless, on June 16, 1970, Gibson was elected with 56 percent of the vote.

Gibson, unlike Carter or Hart, had lived in his city since
childhood. His family had moved to Newark in 1940 when
he was eight, and he had attended its public schools and
later graduated from the Newark College of Engineering.
He was a civil rights activist in the NAACP and CORE, and
a leader of a Business and Industry Coordinating Council
dedicated to finding jobs for blacks. Through his work on
the Coordinating Council he became a public figure in
Newark, and at the urging of several black community lead-

ers he ran for mayor in 1966. He finished third in a field of six.

Realizing "that a black candidate can get votes from all segments of the community," Gibson decided to "run for the next four years."[39] Though Newark's elections are non-partisan, its politics are influenced by the Essex County Democratic organization. Moreover, Addonizio, mayor since 1962, had created a powerful personal machine. Thus Gibson's four-year campaign sought to bypass the machines.[40] He went to countless house parties, social gatherings, factories, even bus stops. His ultimate success, however, was intertwined with his opponent's legal troubles.

Mayor Addonizio had been indicted for conspiracy to extort money from contractors working for the city. Throughout his campaign he divided time between court appearances in Trenton and soliciting votes in Newark. Though the election took place before the trial ended, undoubtedly the suspicion of guilt alienated many voters (he was ultimately found guilty). Addonizio's trial was one of two atypical features that enveloped the campaign. The other tended to work against Gibson, though the net result still left him the winner.

Many whites were disconcerted by some of Gibson's supporters. Some feared Gibson's association with, and perhaps dependence on, the black nationalist writer, Imamu Baraka. Baraka organized a black and Puerto Rican political convention in 1969 that nominated Gibson, and criticism followed that Gibson was the product of a racist convention. Addonizio flayed him as a "radical revolutionary."[41] But Gibson refused to disavow Baraka's support, arguing that it was better to have him working inside than outside the

[39] Quoted in Richard W. Bruner, *Black Politicians* (New York: David McKay Co., 1971), pp. 54-55.

[40] For a discussion of ethnic loyalty as a replacement for party loyalty in Newark's non-partisan elections see Gerald Pomper, "Ethnic and Group Voting in Nonpartisan Municipal Elections," *Public Opinion Quarterly*, 30 (Spring 1966), 79-97.

[41] *The Evening News* (Newark), June 17, 1970, p. 11.

system. Moreover, he continued to appeal across racial lines, insisting that unemployment and taxes were problems facing whites as well as blacks.[42] He scoffed at attacks that called him racist: "I am seeking and have received the support of all the people of Newark without regard to race or ethnic consideration. Charges that I am a racist or that I exclude whites from my campaign are false and without substance."[43] In the final election he received almost all the black vote and about 20 percent of the white.

Addonizio's machine could not overcome the taint of corruption; and fears about Imamu Baraka's influence did not warp Gibson's image as a man who had concern for the entire population. By 1974 Gibson and Baraka were political antagonists. Gibson, however, won re-election with 55 percent of the vote in a five-man contest.

Walter S. Taylor, Englewood

The last of the four mayors, Walter S. Taylor of Englewood, was elected in November 1971. Like Mayor Hart in East Orange, he won by a plurality against two white opponents. He received 38 percent of the vote in a partisan, mayor–council system. But unlike East Orange, which had become securely Democratic before Hart became mayor, Englewood still leaned toward the Republican party. For the first time in sixty-eight years, a Democratic mayor and three Democrats among five councilmen were elected in 1967. But Democratic dominance was short-lived. Two years later the Republicans regained a council majority, while their party's nominee was elected mayor. But in 1971, the pendulum swung once more. Not only was Taylor elected, but the single at-large council seat was won by a Democrat, again giving the party control. The Democratic victory was abetted by a divided opposition. The Republi-

[42] Bruner, *Black Politicians*, p. 57.
[43] *The Evening News* (Newark), April 16, 1970, p. 19.

cans were fragmented during the election; the incumbent mayor, unable to retain his party organization's endorsement, ran as an independent.

Taylor, a Methodist minister, came to Englewood in 1952 at the age of thirty-five to assume appointment to a church. Like Carter and Gibson, his party ties were nebulous before his mayoral candidacy; and like the other three black mayors he had been active in the civil rights movement for much of his adult life. In the 1950s, as local president of the NAACP, he was a leader in the fight to integrate Englewood's public schools. He argued before a public hearing in which the Board of Education was found guilty of gerrymandering school districts. Townwide integration followed. In the years before his election, as president of the Greater Englewood Housing Corporation, Taylor led a successful campaign to build a racially mixed housing project.[44]

Taylor was never inclined to seek political office, however, and rejected repeated overtures by Democratic leaders in early 1971. But he relented shortly before the filing deadline for the June primary. Like the other black mayors, he pointedly campaigned for white as well as black support; this was especially realistic in a community that was two-thirds white.

About a fourth of Taylor's votes were cast by whites. But while it is possible that the 1971 election portended a permanent citywide shift toward the Democrats, it is doubtful that Taylor would have won against a single Republican candidate. His 38 percent edged his Republican opponent by three points. Moreover, though the incumbent mayor, Ned Feldman, failed to regain the Republican nomination because party regulars deemed him too liberal, he was still identified as a Republican.

Ironically, each party thought Feldman's independent candidacy would hurt their man. The Democrats feared that Feldman would attract liberals, the Republicans their

[44] *The Press Journal* (Englewood), November 4, 1971, pp. 1, 3.

own regulars.[45] But the Democrats, to their good fortune, misjudged the tide. Some liberals, even a few black leaders, announced for Feldman.[46] Yet the June primary was a comment on Feldman's viability among Republicans. Having decided to run independently when the organization denied him endorsement, he was not listed as a Republican candidate. But he attracted over 10 percent of the Republican primary vote by write-ins, and built his November vote around this core. Thus even if race had no influence (hardly conceivable in itself), the Republican designee would probably have drawn more of Feldman's votes in a two-man context than would the Democratic candidate.

While Taylor sought white votes, some worried that he would focus unduly on Englewood's poorer blacks, most of whom were packed into the fourth ward. But upon election Taylor attempted to draw perspective: "We've been stressing the fourth ward because there's an urgency about it. When you've got a human body with a cancer on it, you have to cure the cancer before you attend to the rest. But there's no area of this city that need worry about neglect."[47] Thus Taylor, like the other black mayors, reiterated to whites that their interests would be heeded.

The salient features of the elections of the black mayors may be summarized:

1. Three of the four (all but Gibson) were elected in communities with high socioeconomic levels.
2. Two (Carter and Gibson) were elected in non-partisan systems.
3. Three were new to politics when they first ran for office; only Hart had a history of party activity.
4. The same three were more or less pushed by others to seek candidacy.

[45] *The Record* (Hackensack), September 9, 1971, and November 3, 1971, pp. C-1, C-5.
[46] *Ibid.*, September 24, 1971, p. C-3.
[47] *Ibid.*, December 31, 1971, pp. B-1, B-2.

5. All four had histories of considerable public involvement in civil rights causes.
6. All received overwhelming electoral support from the blacks in their cities.
7. All were generally perceived as moderate rather than militant.
8. But all enunciated policies before and after election concerned with civil rights and black needs (like supporting school integration, better housing, appointments of blacks to city positions).
9. All appealed to whites for support during their campaigns and after election.
10. All depended on the white vote for their margins of victory.
11. Three of the four attained between 15 and 25 percent of their cities' white vote; Carter received over 50 percent.

The elections of the black mayors flesh out the suggestion that neither a majority black electorate nor a particular form or style of government are necessary for the election of substantial numbers of blacks. They may contribute, in some case centrally, but in this study they are frequently unrelated to electoral success.

When one examines them individually, one is tempted to attribute the non-partisan elections of black mayors in the nation's major cities to local idiosyncrasies: Kenneth A. Gibson's success in Newark may be attributed to the fact that his opponent was under indictment, Theodore M. Berry's in Cincinnati to a compromise in the city council, and Thomas Bradley's in Los Angeles to the withering of a twelve-year incumbent's popularity. But whether in national urban overview or among New Jersey municipalities black success in white majority, non-partisan systems has become common. It cannot be dismissed as an aberration arising from local conditions. Moreover, explanations obviously lie beyond form of government. The New Jersey experience suggests that socioeconomic characteristics of local populations are essential considerations.

James Q. Wilson has suggested that, unfashionable as it may be, effective political strategy for blacks requires political alliance with white liberals.[48] This chapter demonstrates the viability of the thesis. But implicit is a requirement that blacks who reach office maintain goals, philosophies, and moral sensitivity compatible with liberalism. We examine the question in the next chapter.

[48] James Q. Wilson, "The Negro in Politics," in Talcott Parsons and Kenneth B. Clark, eds., *The Negro American* (Boston: Houghton Mifflin Co., 1966), p. 437.

V

Philosophy and Ideology

The political behavior of an elected official is determined in part by his values, experiences, and assumptions about the political process and the citizenry. A comprehensive inquiry into an official's behavior requires knowledge of his psyche as well as the political culture and legal forms of his system. Yet such a complex mixture is generally beyond the access, if not the expertise, of investigators. Patterns of behavior and attitude, however, can be traced, if from less complete information.

Most typologies of black leaders, nevertheless, obscure even these patterns. Attitude and behavior are blurred into categories of "political style," with every study suggesting a new typology. Everett Carll Ladd, Jr., summarized race leadership typologies by other scholars. None used the same labels and criteria. Gunnar Myrdal examined "accommodationists" and "protestors," James Q. Wilson "moderates" and "militants," Daniel C. Thompson "Uncle Toms," "race diplomats," and "race men."[1] Ladd himself preferred a continuum of "conservatives," "moderates," and "militants."[2] Joyce Gelb more recently wrote of "old timers" and "new breeders."[3] Mack H. Jones, supported by Hanes Walton, Jr., classified black politicians as "integrationist," "accommoda-

[1] Everett Carll Ladd, Jr., *Negro Political Leadership in the South* (Ithaca, N.Y.: Cornell University Press, 1966), pp. 146-50.

[2] *Ibid.*, p. 150.

[3] Joyce Gelb, "Blacks, Blocs and Ballots," *Polity*, 3, no. 1 (Fall 1970), 57.

tionist," prone to "black consciousness," "black nationalist," or "revolutionist."[4]

A typology of black officials alone is of little concern to this study. The emphasis is comparative between blacks and whites, and vocabulary applicable to both must be employed. Thus, intra-racial labels like "Uncle Tom," "race man," and "black nationalist" are not useful. Moreover, we seek typicality of each race within the category "elected official." While recognizing differences within each racial group, we are principally concerned with determining whether predominant characteristics differ between black and white.

Additionally, the order of inquiry in this work is different from that in others. In emphasizing perception as a determinant of behavior, we separate attitude from action and examine them in sequence. Philosophical shorelines are mapped in this chapter and the next. Their contours direct the flow of behavior that will be discussed later. Now we inquire broadly into the political philosophies of the officials —their sense of political morality and responsibility to their constituencies. In seeking a common measure that crosses racial lines, we compare blacks and whites on a left-right spectrum. Finally, attitudes toward the slogan "black power" again demonstrate the importance of perception in understanding reality.

Government by Consent

Whether an elected official should reflect his constituents' convictions or express his own when they are contrary to theirs remains a long-standing question. E. E. Schattschneider summarizes the dilemma by citing two famous phrases in American history: "government by the people" from

[4] Mack H. Jones, "A Frame of Reference for Black Politics," in Lenneal J. Henderson, Jr., ed. *Black Political Life in the United States*, (San Francisco: Chandler Publishing Co., 1972), p. 15; Hanes Walton, Jr., *Black Politics* (Philadelphia: J. B. Lippincott Co., 1972), p. 204.

Abraham Lincoln's Gettysburg Address, and "government by consent of the governed," Thomas Jefferson's words in the Declaration of Independence. Confusion arises, says Schattschneider, when people fail to recognize the profound differences between the phrases.[5] "Government by the people" implies that the people (presumably most of them) pass on every public decision. But this would be unwieldy, impossible. There are too many citizens even at local levels of government. Neither in theory nor practice can the American political system be understood as a raw democratic arena. Rather, "the heads of the government accept responsibility for doing public business, take the initiative in making decisions, furnishing leadership, and so on. Then they go to the people for approval or disapproval in an election in which they may be turned out of office."[6]

Phrases like "the public interest," "will of the people," "power to the people" gush from protagonists who claim theirs as the voice of the people. But most officials interviewed, black and white, appeared to understand their roles as governors by consent. Some balked at drawing distinction between their own positions and their constituents'. Hardly any, however, said they would "always" give way to their constituents' positions when in conflict with their own—only 7 percent in either racial category (Table V-1). More black officials than white, 23 percent to 13 percent, would "usually" go along with the people. But 68 percent of the blacks and 76 percent of the whites said they usually or always acted on their own convictions irrespective of their electors'.

Comments could not be categorized along racial lines. White councilmen who reduced their roles to conduits for their constituents said: "My duty is to educate them to my way of thinking, or to vote the way they tell me to if I can-

---

[5] E. E. Schattschneider, *Two Hundred Million Americans in Search of a Government* (New York: Holt, Rinehart and Winston, Inc., 1969), pp. 58, 62-63.

[6] *Ibid.*, p. 73.

not educate them." Or: "If there is a difference of opinion I make it known to my group how I came about arriving at my feelings. However, if I could not convince them that I was right, being an officer who represents the people, I would definitely go by their view." And from a black: "I never vote my conviction; I vote for the people's conviction. There are times I disagreed with certain positions, but if it was the majority opinion of those citizens who elected me, I believe it was my job to reflect their thinking, their inter-

TABLE V-1: RESPONSES OF ELECTED OFFICIALS TO THE QUESTION: WHEN YOUR PERSONAL CONVICTION DIFFERS FROM THAT OF THE PEOPLE YOU REPRESENT, WHAT POSITION DO YOU TAKE?

	Whites %	Blacks %
Personal conviction, always	31	23
Personal conviction, usually or with qualification	45	45
Usually go with the people's conviction	13	23
Always go with the people's conviction	7	7
Don't know, no opinion, etc.	4	3
Total	100 (96)	101 (31)

ests and their goals. Sometimes I have been a devil's advocate, arguing for something that I did not agree with."

Those who would stick to their own convictions also spoke without racial implications. The first three of the following excerpts were spoken by white officials, the last three by black:

I feel that I am elected to use my best judgment, and within my own set of values I make my decisions based on what I think is best for the community. The

fact that there are people who do not want a swimming
pool because they believe they're going to have to pay
a little more, or that they don't want to swim with
blacks—it doesn't make any difference to me that the
majority of people feel that way. Although, I recognize
their right to get rid of me at the next election.

. . .

They have elected me to give them the benefit of my
best thinking, and they've elected a particular man.
And I follow my judgments on what I feel is the best
decision. I do not feel I should be pressured. If they
do not like my thinking, when I run again they'll tell
me.

. . .

I've always tried to tell it the way it is, and I find after
being in office six years that many people don't want
to hear the truth. But I think in the long run you'll
have these people believe in you. I never tried to take
the middle of the road on any issue or any question
that's fired at me. I tell them the way I feel; and I stick
to my convictions.

. . .

I hold to my personal convictions. I think every
politician does, though I don't believe most of them
will admit it. But it's true, because most politicians do
not have the day-to-day contact with their constituents.
Of course an official on a lower level of politics would
have more involvement with his constituents than
those higher. But even in my case politics is just part-
time, because I must make a living. I don't have the
time to devote to day-to-day involvement with my
constituency.

. . .

I have to follow my personal convictions. I have to
weigh the facts and make a decision. It may be
unpopular, but if in my opinion it is going to be more

to the overall good of the city as opposed to any
particular group, or even my ward, then I'll have to go
with my opinion.

    . . .

I think the people entrusted me with a vote of
confidence to make decisions and determinations. I'm
able to go to sleep at night because I make my
decisions on what I think is best in behalf of the city.
So if I differ with them, and I have—for instance when
I voted for the police and firemen's contract before a
predominantly black audience that was by nature
anti-police—it is because I feel I'm right. In that
instance we could not have afforded a police action or
strike.

Thus most officials regarded it as their duty to follow
their own judgment when it conflicted with their constituents'. This contrasted with the views of the rank and file,
however. In our citizens survey, only 27 percent of the
whites and 44 percent of the blacks believed that "when an
elected official feels differently about a particular issue than
the people who elected him [he should] stick to his own
belief." Sixty-one percent of the whites and 44 percent of the
blacks thought an official should "take the position of the
people who elected him" (Table V-2).

TABLE V-2: Responses of Citizens to the Question: When
an Elected Official Feels Differently about a Particular
Issue than the People Who Elected Him, Should the
Official:

	Whites %	Blacks %
Stick to his own belief?	27	44
Take the position of the people who elected him?	61	44
Don't know, no opinion, etc.	12	13
Total	100 (411)	101 (140)

The discrepancy between white officials and white citizens is much greater than that between black officials and black citizens. Most officials of both races agreed that they should hold to their own beliefs, while most rank and file disagreed. But the views of blacks—officials and citizens—were far more congruent than those of whites.

In fact, neither alternative sufficiently describes officials' behavior. Joseph A. Schlesinger ascribes a politician's behavior to his "office goals." Ambition, he believes, is the cornerstone of every political decision.[7] In formulating a theory of representation, Eulau and Prewitt broaden Schlesinger's interpretation. Like him, they reject the proposition that representatives either disregard public opinion totally or obey a continual flow of instructions from the public. Rather, they suggest that local representation be evaluated on a scale of responsiveness and accountability. Responsiveness emerges from a "multitude of council-public interactions," governed by parameters of accountability. The parameters include the number of candidates contesting an office, the likelihood of incumbent loss at the next election, voter turnout, perceived electoral sanctions, and career ambitions.[8]

Officials in our study, however, rarely mentioned these subtleties affecting their decisions. Regardless of race, most believed they made judgments on the merits of issues, apart from self-interest. An examination of their philosophical and moral perspectives, therefore, should help reveal their perceived bases for judgment.

Philosophy and Morality

As indicated earlier, many officials did not campaign on specific issues (Chapter III). They tended toward generali-

[7] Joseph A. Schlesinger, *Ambition and Politics: Political Careers in the United States* (Chicago: Rand McNally and Co., 1966), p. 6.

[8] Heinz Eulau and Kenneth Prewitt, *Labyrinths of Democracy: Adaptations, Linkages, Representation, and Policies in Urban Politics* (New York: The Bobbs-Merrill Co., 1973), chaps. 21-22.

ties. In that light the question of overall political philosophy
assumes particular importance. For even if an array of programs was not enunciated, an official's philosophical or
moral views help provide insights into expected behavior. An
open-ended question was asked at each interview: "What
philosophical or moral views about politics affect your decisions as an office-holder?" Before the answers are discussed,
three caveats must be mentioned. First, the non-directional
nature of the question led to divergent answers. Quantifica-
tion thus becomes difficult, generalizations loose. Second,
there is a tendency toward defensiveness in answering a
question about one's philosophical or moral values. Some
officials postured self-righteously, defending their integrity.
To what extent this affected the answers is uncertain.
Finally, whether enunciated or not, all officials, all people,
have philosophical and moral views that condition their
sense of priorities and ultimately their choice of alternatives. Thus it was logically contradictory for an official to
answer: "None. I have no philosophy. I just believe what is
supposed to be right based on forty-five years of life, and
from there I make a decision." This demonstrates that the
question is as much a measure of self-awareness as of expected behavior. But self-awareness and self-image are
themselves constructs of behavior. How the officials related
to specific issues will be discussed in later chapters, but
here we discuss perceptual foundations.

It is intriguing to find only 15 percent of white and 13
percent of black officials relating their philosophical and
moral bases for action to narrow considerations like race,
class, party, ideology. Of those who did, whites referred to
party, class, or ideology, blacks to race. Thus, from whites:
"I think in terms of a liberal"; "I'm a Nixonian Republican"; "My philosophy is based on economy in government";
"I believe in the liberal causes . . . one of my goals is to have
a totally integrated society"; "You might consider me a conservative Democrat . . . both parties seem to be going quite
liberal these days—I don't go that far out." But the few

blacks with narrowly defined philosophical bases referred implicitly to race: "I think the great thing that affects my decisions is the people I represent—low income, poor housing, high crime, under-skilled, poor education." "Generally I try to function as a steward for the community that hasn't been represented in the past." "If you are a minority person you know what's needed. And what you do is go about the business of trying to fill the need. It's that simple. You don't have to look for a basic philosophy as such. It's just there day to day. You live it."

But such answers were scarce. Eighty-seven percent of the black officials and 72 percent of the whites related their political philosophies to general concerns or claimed no philosophical or moral bases. Again, differentiation by race as well as by party, class, or ideology was indistinct. A white conservative Republican replied: "I believe citizens should be made to accept responsibility—that with rights goes responsibility." No one could argue with that any more than with the philosophical underpinnings of a black, self-proclaimed radical Democrat: "Politics is neither good nor bad; it is simply the art and science of governing people. It's everybody's business. I think as many people ought to be involved in politics as possible."

Most of the officials reached into the casket of political clichés for moral and philosophical responses. But two characteristics predominated. The remarks of black and white officials could be virtually interchanged, and they embraced the common theme of responsibility to *all* the people. The first four of the following responses were from whites, the last four from blacks:

I see myself as a person who has no political ambitions
. . . this frees me from a showcase approach. We're all
affected by group pressures . . . and the process of
learning to be a good councilman requires deliberate
consciousness beyond group interests.

　　　·　·　·

Well, there's really nothing morally that affects my
decisions because we get plenty of back-up material
on every issue, and on every ordinance or resolution.
If I can't understand it, and I'm not a lawyer, I do go
to a friend that's a lawyer, or to the particular person
in that field, and get opinions. And then I'll go back
into the community and get the community's opinions.

· · ·

Oh, I have deep moral views—moral views that have
led me over the years to fight the politicians who are
deeply mistrusted by the electorate. . . . There has
been a pervasive feeling that corruption has existed,
and I've been yelling that for many years, and
subsequent events have proven it to be true. I'm
gratified even at this moment that I had a major part
in electing the reform mayor.

· · ·

While I am absolutely one hundred percent bound to
be honest, and to try to make this a better place in
which to live, I am not sure that those are moral
considerations—maybe they are. Philosophically, I
believe that all people who have elected an official
have the right to speak through that official, and that
the official should not necessarily be speaking
for himself.

· · ·

Historically before coming into public office the
opinion I'd always heard was that there's no such
thing as an honest politician. It was always alleged
that a politician had to be someone who was near-
corrupt or just corrupt. Now, before making a
decision, I first try to make sure that it is based on the
facts, that it's an objective decision—and more
important, that it's not one of any corrupt nature, but
is a people's decision.

· · ·

Any decision that I make is based primarily upon the
good it will do for the greater number of people,

without hurting anyone if possible. I know that sounds broad to a lot of people. But even with the big push towards blackness and what have you, I try to temper all of my decisions based on the needs of people. . . . When it appears that an office-holder who happens to be black is emphasizing his effort towards problems that may be black oriented, it's being oriented primarily because that's what the problems are, not because he happens to be black.

. . .

Well, my views have always been ones of honesty, integrity. It's my upbringing. And I know what the stigma of politics carries. . . . Basically people felt to be a politician you've got to be crooked, this kind of thing. Philosophically I've always felt that a politician . . . should represent the people fairly and honestly, and I think that basically they do.

. . .

The belief that public officials ought to be honest— that they make decisions and hold to them, and to win support for them rather than swing back and forth. I believe we are moving into a period where the integrity of people is being looked at more closely, and that the moral position of a man is going to be questioned more and more, rather than simply electing people and letting them go along.

Though they were given unlimited latitude to discuss philosophical and moral influences, their responses revealed little about how officials decided particular issues. Thus it would be futile to try to match typologies of earlier studies with these replies, and difficult to guess about expected behavior. But familiarity with politics means familiarity with the ideological spectrum. Somebody is seen to be to the "right" or "left" of somebody else. In seeking philosophical parameters we employ the left-right spectrum as a measuring rod.

Left-Right

"I'd say liberal, probably, but I've never really thought about it. Liberal is a concept to me that's sort of been applied to white political interests as opposed to black. A black being a liberal or a black being a conservative, you know, it's hard to think of it that way. In my opinion, really, the black masses view it as a white kind of thinking." Thus did a black councilman wrestle with a request to place himself on the left-right political spectrum. (Which of the following terms best describes your political tendencies: radical; liberal; middle-of-the-road; conservative; reactionary?)

The councilman was correct. Liberalism-conservatism, born in eighteenth-century Europe and America, was a "white kind of thinking." The terms have been twisted during three centuries and their original essence—the liberal's belief and the conservative's disbelief in man's natural goodness and the instinctive rightness of the masses—has been blurred.[9] But liberal philosophy enunciated classically by Jean-Jacques Rousseau and Thomas Paine and conservative philosophy articulated by Edmund Burke were spawned in white political experience.

Whether the terms supersede Western institutions, whether they describe universal man, is here irrelevant. In the first place, labeling has been inconsistent, even in the narrow channel of American political history. Thomas Jefferson's "strict construction" of the Constitution rested in the faith that the common man was wiser than the central government.[10] Conversely, Alexander Hamilton, distrustful of the masses, was a "loose constructionist" who favored strong central government.[11] But in recent years the terms have been shuffled. Richard Nixon appointed "strict con-

[9] Peter Viereck, *Conservatism from John Adams to Churchill* (Princeton, N. J.: D. Van Nostrand Co., Inc., 1956), p. 13.

[10] See letters of Thomas Jefferson in Henry J. Silverman, ed., *American Radical Thought* (Lexington, Mass.: D.C. Heath and Co., 1970), pp. 12-15.

[11] Viereck, *Conservatism*, p. 119.

structionists" to the Supreme Court to reverse the liberal "loose-construction" decisions of the Warren Court that had emphasized minority and individual rights. Thus, a "strict constructionist" was now a conservative, a "loose constructionist" a liberal.

Moreover, the difficulty of left-right labeling is compounded when it is applied to blacks. For blacks have been the have-nots of the system. Abstract ideologies for "all mankind" mean less to them than filling voids created by oppression. How does one philosophically label Marcus Garvey, who in the 1920s urged a "central nation" in Africa for all blacks? Was his movement, as he alternately suggested, "liberal and helpful" or conservative—designed "to conserve the rights" of blacks?[12] Further, neither black nationalism nor integration perch comfortably on a left-right spectrum. In much of the North black separatism is equated with radicalism, integration with conservatism; in the South, the reverse.

Nevertheless, labels bob about the sea of political words. They are buoys that guide, flotsam that confuse, but ever-present. While few politicians like to reduce their images to a single category, every politician knows the terms. Moreover, most responded to the request for self-labeling, if reluctantly, and with the exception of "radical" understood the terms in their current usage. Before the responses are reported, contemporary meanings should be summarized. Radicalism holds that the political system is not responsive to all the peoples' needs and that drastic change is necessary. It often implies that revolution, perhaps violent, is required to alter power arrangements. Liberalism emphasizes that within the existing system man's life can and should be enhanced by government programs, by government innovation and planning. Conservatism, to the contrary, stresses that people can and should take care of them-

12 Marcus Garvey, "The Negro's Place in World Reorganization," in John Hope Franklin and Isidore Starr, eds., *The Negro in Twentieth Century America* (New York: Vintage Books, 1967), pp. 111-12.

selves; that government ought not to foster programs that help the citizenry, except perhaps as a last resort. Reaction carries self-contradictory implications—a return to the "old" values of individualism and self-reliance is to be accompanied by an authoritarian leadership to guide (perhaps press) the citizenry to these "earlier" virtues. (The confusion need not detain us, since no official labeled himself reactionary.) The definitions, I recognize, are not beyond challenge; none could be. But they establish a gauge against which responses can be measured.

Table V-3 reveals a marked leftward orientation of the

TABLE V-3: SELF-PLACEMENT OF ELECTED OFFICIALS AND CITIZENS ON AN IDEOLOGICAL SCALE, BY RACE

	Elected Officials		Citizens	
	Whites	Blacks	Whites	Blacks
	%	%	%	%
Radical[a]	0	16	1	5
Liberal	34	52	26	21
Middle-of-the-road	42	7	30	25
Conservative	14	0	27	26
Reactionary	0	0	2	5
Other or none	10	26	14	19
Total	100 (96)	101 (31)	100 (411)	101 (140)

[a] Respondents were read the categories and asked to choose one that "best describes your political tendencies." Officials were then asked to elaborate.

black officials. The 16 percent who labeled themselves radical and 52 percent liberal contrast with no radical and 34 percent liberal among whites. Fifty-six percent of the whites were middle-of-the-road or conservative, but only 7 percent of the blacks called themselves middle-of-the-road and none conservative. Significantly, none of the "radicals" spoke of circumventing the system. Their positions were bold and impatient, but hardly threatening to the political order. Thus:

> I am radical from the point of view that I express what I believe in, what I think is right. . . . I don't play political games, because every time you trade off, my community loses. I expose areas of wrong regardless of who it might be, so radical from my point of view, yes.
>
> . . .
>
> If I have to take a choice, radical. I'm not inclined to be patient with educating for change. I'm not inclined to believe in the benevolence of anybody running the show to offer benefits to all the people. I feel it has to be taken. If there is a pie to be divided, I'd rather take a chance on taking my slice and determining what size it would be than to wait and see if I get an appropriate portion.
>
> . . .
>
> I'm radical for the simple reason that my ideas are way, way past what is occurring today. It's in the future. And I raised a lot of hell about things because people don't understand. Well, maybe it's too early for them to understand.

Thus "radical," as understood by blacks who so labeled themselves, implied none of the violent, destructive, anarchic stereotypes often inferred from the label. The other categories evoked conventional interpretations. A black councilman who called himself a liberal said typically: "I'm not too tight fisted with respect to dollars, but I want to know where they're going, and see that they've been applied to good use. I'm concerned about what goes on all over the city as opposed to certain segments of it. I'm more apt to take a chance and vote for something that I feel might work as opposed to knowing whether it would work or not." Another black was "probably liberal. I like to give, but I don't feel I can throw up my hands and say 'whatever you say, that's what we should do.' . . . But we've come to a time in history when we can't be rigid and not move from traditional things."

Among whites who designated themselves liberal, there was an undercurrent of defensiveness. The meaning of the term was not in question, just the firmness of conviction: "There was a time in my career when I was a lot more liberal. I'm still a liberal, but toward the middle-of-the-road. I used to say hang the expense—spend it. But this is not a very practical position any more with the present cost of administration and government. . . . I'm still an arch-liberal as far as social matters. I mean I'm not way out in orbit, but I like the city because it does have a good balance of the races." Tentativeness in accepting the label was further exemplified by a mayor who was

probably more liberal than anything else, although I
find myself to be conservative on issues from time to
time. I have a concern for equal representation for
minority groups, for housing, for quality education.
What I'm really attempting to promote whatever way
I can is a fair shake for everyone based on his
individuality, and not where he happens to live or
what color he or she happens to be, sex or religion or
anything else. . . . I think we have a problem in
defining each person as a particular one-word thing,
whether liberal or conservative, hawk or dove,
reactionary, hard hat, or whatever. I believe that each
of us is a good deal more complicated.

Thus white liberals cast toward the middle. In rejecting ideological extremes, many joined the 42 percent who termed themselves middle-of-the-road. This comports with the traditional model of American politics—an institutional and cultural pressure cooker that fosters accommodation

within a consensual political culture.[13] Middle-of-the-road
was the dominant theme among whites: "I go either way";
"Programmatically, socially I'm a liberal, but fiscally a conservative"; "Many times I am conservative, but when we
can afford it I like to be liberal." The tensions in trying to
categorize are summed up by a white councilman:

A liberal is an individual who will cheer for [black
radical] Angela Davis, but forget the judge that was
shot. . . . the liberal will tell us [contradictorily] that
killing is bad, but that abortion is good. Now, a
conservative will not provide for any better housing
or education—they're against anything that I feel is in
the interest of the people. . . . I would like to say that
I'm a middle-of-the-roader.

More blacks than whites resisted categorization. But
blacks who rejected labels nevertheless spoke to the question. "I've never heard a good description of radical or liberal and I don't know what they are. I'm definitely not
middle-of-the-road or the others. Truthful—and I guess
many of the things that I express as truthful would be considered radical by some people." An angrier response: "Personally I think that those are just terms that the news media
find very attractive for selling papers. I like to describe myself as a person who knows what some of the problems are,
and I work like hell to get those problems solved. . . . I'm
fiercely independent when I know that I'm right, and I
couldn't care less who thinks otherwise."

Thus, despite tentativeness among officials, despite wari-
ness of labels, blacks placed themselves unmistakably to the
left of whites. But officials of both races are further left than
their constituents. Table V-3 indicates that more white officials than citizens are in radical and liberal categories, and

13 Fred W. Grupp, Jr. and Marvin Maurer, eds., *Political Behavior
in the United States* (New York: Meredith Corporation, 1972), pp. 9-11.

fewer in conservative and reactionary ones; the same applies to blacks. Moreover, congruence between black officials and black citizens is lower than between whites.

Black Power

Few slogans gripped national attention more quickly and provocatively than "black power." Within days of its enunciation by Stokely Carmichael in 1966, its definition, its conceptual validity, and its utility were being nationally debated. Black power in its various interpretations rallied supporters and opponents of the civil rights movement. The words snaked through election campaigns, discussions of the urban riots and race relations, and became the subject of scores of books and articles.[14]

Carmichael used the term to chart a departure from the civil rights movement. After years of involvement, he rejected coalition with whites as a means of fulfilling the needs of blacks, and integration as an end. Now he sought "the coming together of black people" to change "patterns of oppression through pressure from strength—instead of weakness."[15] "Black Power," he said with Charles V. Hamilton, "is a call for black people in this country to unite, to recognize their heritage, to build a sense of community. It is a call for black people to begin to define their own goals, to lead their own organizations and to support those organizations. It is a call to reject the racist institutions and values of this society."[16] Of more concern to many than the rejec-

[14] An incomplete bibliography through 1970 lists thirty-seven works whose titles alone include the words black power. James M. McPherson, Laurence B. Holland, James M. Banner, Jr., Nancy J. Weiss, and Michael D. Bell, eds., *Blacks in America, Bibliographical Essays* (Garden City, N. Y.: Anchor Books, 1972), pp. 383-86.

[15] Stokely Carmichael, "Black Power," in Thomas R. Dye and Brett W. Hawkins, eds., *Politics in the Metropolis*, 2nd ed. (Columbus, Ohio: Charles E. Merrill Publishing Co., 1971), p. 69.

[16] Stokely Carmichael and Charles V. Hamilton, *Black Power: The Politics of Liberation in America* (New York: Vintage Books, 1967), p. 44.

tion of white alliances, however, was an allowance for violence: "Those of us who advocate Black Power are quite
clear in our own minds that a 'non-violent' approach to civil
rights is an approach black people cannot afford and
a luxury white people do not deserve. . . . White people
must be made to understand that they must stop messing
with black people, or the blacks *will* fight back!"[17]

So stated, black power was immediately rejected by civil
rights leaders. Roy Wilkins called it "a reverse Mississippi,
a reverse Hitler, a reverse Ku Klux Klan. . . . We of the
NAACP will have none of this. We have fought it too
long."[18] Martin Luther King, Jr., insisted: "We must never
seek power exclusively for the Negro, but the sharing of
power with the white people. Any other course is exchang-
ing one form of tyranny for another. [Black power] falls on
the ear as racism in reverse."[19] Bayard Rustin, long committed to a liberal-labor-civil rights coalition, disdained
Carmichael's "extravagant rhetoric."[20] He deplored the

suggestion that non-violence be abandoned. The
reasoning here is that turning the other cheek is not
the way to win respect, and that only if the Negro
succeeds in frightening the white man will the white
man begin taking him seriously. The trouble with this
reasoning is that it fails to recognize that fear is more
likely to bring hostility to the surface than respect;
and far from prodding the "white power structure"
into action, the new militant leadership, by raising the
slogan of black power and lowering the banner of

17 *Ibid.*, p. 53.
18 Quoted in Joel D. Aberbach and Jack L. Walker, "The Meanings
of Black Power: A Comparison of White and Black Interpretations
of a Political Slogan," *American Political Science Review*, 64, no. 2
(June 1970), 367.
19 *Ibid.*
20 Bayard Rustin, "'Black Power' and Coalition Politics," *Commentary*, vol. 42, no. 3 (September 1966), reprinted in Alan Shank,
ed., *Political Power and the Urban Crisis* (Boston: Holbrook Press, Inc.,
1969), pp. 253-54.

non-violence, has obscured the moral issue facing the
nation, and permitted the President and Vice President
to lecture us about "racism in reverse" instead of
proposing more meaningful programs for dealing with
problems of unemployment, housing, and education.[21]

But black power had "no direct, generally accepted
meaning," as Aberbach and Walker reported, based on a
survey conducted in 1967.[22] Rather, like other slogans, the
words evoked "associative meanings, . . . ambiguities that
permit them, like Rorschach ink blots, to suggest to each
person just what he wants to see in them."[23] Thus, while
most whites in the Aberbach and Walker study equated
black power with violence, racism, or black supremacy, few
blacks did. And while 42 percent of the blacks viewed the
slogan favorably, only 10 percent of the whites did.[24] By
1971, the authors found, favorable inferences by blacks had
risen to 53 percent, by whites to 22 percent.[25]

The question first asked of the citizenry by Aberbach and
Walker in 1967 was asked of officials in this study: What do
the words "black power" mean to you? In the five interven-
ing years little progress was made toward establishing a
common definition. Though the crescendo of the debate
was lower, the meaning remained unresolved. But the slogan's prominence was timed to the quantum increase of
elected blacks, and with years to digest the phrase, to observe its effects on black political aspirations, interpretations could be tempered by experience. Moreover, ideologies of elected leaders affect their governing. As liberals
and conservatives govern differently, so would advocates
and critics of black power.

[21] *Ibid.*, p. 256.
[22] Aberbach and Walker, "The Meanings of Black Power," p. 386.
[23] *Ibid.*; Robert E. Lane, *Political Thinking and Consciousness* (Chicago: Markham Publishing Co., 1969), p. 316.
[24] Aberbach and Walker, "The Meanings of Black Power," pp. 370-71.
[25] Joel D. Aberbach and Jack L. Walker, *Race in the City* (Boston:
Little, Brown and Co., 1973), p. 109.

The words "black power" elicited largely favorable responses from black officials, unfavorable from white (Table V-4). Only 7 percent of the blacks viewed the term unfavorably, in contrast to 53 percent of the whites. Not one black

TABLE V-4: RESPONSES OF ELECTED OFFICIALS TO THE QUESTION: WHAT DO THE WORDS "BLACK POWER" MEAN TO YOU?

	Whites %	Blacks %
Favorable	24	61
Unfavorable	53	7
It depends who says them, the context, etc.	12	13
Don't know, no opinion, etc.	12	19
Total	101 (96)	100 (31)

official associated the term with racism or violence. The few unfavorable inferences drawn by black officials were expressed as an undefined "dislike," the feeling that in "trying to balance for the past . . . you have to step on people and this I don't exactly agree with." Or: "It runs off me like water. I'm concerned with green power."

But the dominant interpretation among black officials related to getting a "fair share" of society's benefits. "Black power" as a slogan would bring black people together; as an end it would insure that they received fair proportions of goods, services, and opportunities.

I guess more than the word power I think it means black representation—the opportunity that blacks should have to be represented in government, in employment, in social affairs, in all aspects of living, if they are qualified and capable.

   • • •

It means that black people would like to have a slice of the political and economic pie of the country. It doesn't mean overthrow or riots or things of that

nature. Black power means that black people would
like to have a share of jobs, opportunities, decent
housing, religious institutions, playgrounds, all kinds
of recreational facilities, senior citizens housing. We
would like not to be denied anything.

    . . .

My personal reaction is that black power means that
we have enough involvement, enough political muscle
to get what anyone else is getting; that we are fully
represented in government, education, business, or
what have you. You know, we as black people have the
same American dream that any white would have.

    . . .

It means a need for black people to unite. . . . It means
the ability of the smallest black man to pull the lever
in the voting booth, or to come to city hall and voice
his opinion. It shouldn't be a threat to anyone; it's just
something that's necessary.

    . . .

It means that blacks have adopted a slogan that's
trying to bring some togetherness and understanding
among each other; and where they're trying to get a
piece of the action. They're not trying to take over the
country or overthrow the government, as so many
people think.

    . . .

It depends on who uses it. If an extremist utters black
power, it means physical power. If it's uttered by a
group with a history of genuine representation of
black people, struggling for progress, I would think
in terms of black economic power, education, unity
among black people.

Fewer than a quarter of the white officials interpreted the
term favorably, and most of these with restraint. Only a few
said without qualification that "it means blacks working together to develop an economic and social base for political

power"; or, "it is an attempt at ethnic identification, a rally-
ing point for political solidarity." Rather, even favorable
inferences were strained:

> It has two meanings: black people getting their fair
> share economically and politically. . . . On the other
> hand it can be equated to a militant who would rather
> disrupt or destroy the system, and that I find very
> distasteful. . . . I'm trying the best I can to see things
> of the past remedied, to have a more integrated
> society, and that's why I think black power has
> meaning in the right sense as far as I am concerned.
>
> • • •
>
> Black power was something willed on them because of
> being subject to a life of misery for so many years and
> centuries. I hope it doesn't cause problems in the
> future, but I think they have to have something to
> impress upon the whites in this country.
>
> • • •
>
> I'd like to think of black power in the good
> philosophical sense that means blacks are going to
> assert themselves politically, and gain through the
> ballot box. I think that black power is a very real
> factor if it's properly used. Of course I don't support
> any of the militant actions—I couldn't do that and I
> wouldn't. But I do think black power should relate
> itself directly to the ballot box.

Most white officials, however, perceived the term as hostile, dangerous ideology. Some gestured toward concern for
blacks, but in no way accepted black power. "I can see their
reasons for sometimes fighting the establishment, but again
we're back to the radical and militant groups who use the
term 'black power' in their own sense, for complete take-
over"; "I want to see the blacks make as much progress as
they can, but I don't like to see this attitude—fist in the air,
progress overnight." The usual unfavorable response, how-

ever, yielded nothing to sympathy. Disapproval was swift, angry, uncompromising: " 'Black power'? Hate, contempt, revolution"; "It means that people believe in everything for the blacks"; " 'Black power' to me denotes power through violence"; "I wouldn't want to tell you . . . personally I think it's un-American"; "Communism. Very similar to the type of internal political situation that has bred all the revolutionary movements in this world, from fascism on back."

Thus, the chasm between white and black officials as they interpret the meaning of black power is deep, shocking. Alone, the officials' comments appear so rigid as to preclude cooperation. But the problem is mellowed by several features. First, whites who disdain the slogan are hardly adamant about the interpretation placed on it by blacks. Who, after all, denies anyone's claim to a "fair share"? Second, black officials who embrace black power recognize the anxieties the expression conjures. As one said defensively, it does not mean "trying to take over the country or overthrow the government, as so many people think." Consequently, while black officials may act out their interpretation, they avoid unnecessary antagonism. They do not flaunt the slogan.

Finally, "black power" must be understood with reference to overall philosophy and ideology. The slogan, accordingly, could not be envisaged as an ideological bulldozer. Rather, as perceived by black officials it is largely an extension of liberal philosophy. It gives direction to an assumption that government can actively respond to the needs of its citizens. Black power is an expression of interest group pluralism. It is a call for people of like interest to exert pressure on the system—to coalesce, to lobby, to demonstrate, to vote, to become part of government.

In the distinctiveness of their interpretations, black and white officials underline the importance of perception. Fears and prejudices shape people's understanding of words, what they hear, to whom they listen. Racism and violence are real definitions of black power to whites, as fair share and unity are to blacks. Neither is right or wrong. But

in understanding the term functionally, ought not the bear-
er rather than the critic be given credence? As defined by
black elected officials, black power is not only legitimate;
it should be welcomed by critics who have heretofore
heeded rhetoric rather than action.

VI

Perceptions on the Importance of Race

"Nothing could be more important in the life of this nation and determinative of the future of Western civilization than Negro Americans becoming politically aware," said Martin Luther King, Jr., in 1964.[1] While his prose was exaggerated, he anticipated the surge of black political consciousness and ultimately elected officials. But the new consciousness leads to questions about the functions of black elected officials— as role models, as custodians of black interests, as orchestrators of racial harmony. In this chapter we shall examine the views of officials and citizens, their perceptions of the functions of elected officials in the context of race.

A stubborn American myth holds that people vote for the "best man," that party counts for little. The contrary is true. Most voters not only identify with one of the two major parties, but "a change of candidates and broad alteration in the nature of the issues disturb very little the relative partisanship . . . of voters."[2] The "best man" theme arises from historical suspicion by Americans of politics and its offspring, political parties.[3] The theme is reflected as well in requisites beyond partisanship.

[1] Edward T. Clayton, *The Negro Politician* (Chicago: Johnson Publishing Co., Inc., 1964), p. vii.

[2] Angus Campbell, Philip E. Converse, Warren E. Miller, and Donald E. Stokes, *The American Voter* (New York: John Wiley and Sons, Inc., 1960), p. 121.

[3] Sprinkled throughout the interviews were denials by elected officials that they were "politicians." No textbook on American politics fails

Though a candidate "happens" to fill regional, ethnic, or religious requirements, often these are recognized with discomfort, even denied. Thus in 1969 when President Nixon failed to nominate a Jew to succeed Abe Fortas on the United States Supreme Court, the "Jewish seat" disappeared. For the first time in fifty-three years no Jew sat on the Court. In the aftermath, retired Justice Arthur J. Goldberg disappointed many Jews when he argued against ethnic or religious qualifications. The nation, he asserted (contrary to reality), had reached a point where judicial and political offices could be filled on the basis of "individual merit," not with regard to a "so-called racial balance."[4]

But the assumption that "individual merit" determines *a* best man is a fallacy. An official's political experience, his affability, his knowledge of foreign language, not to mention ethnic or religious background may make him the best candidate in one situation, the worst in another. As the question pertains to communities with substantial black populations, individual merit and race become inseparable as qualifications for office. If half of a community's residents are black, but none of its elected officials, ought not a prerequisite for the "best" candidate at the next election include color? Ethics make the question rhetorical. But others have recognized, in addition, unpleasant tangible effects of black under-representation. A sense of political powerlessness was cited by state and national investigators as a principal cause of civil disorders in the late sixties and early seventies.[5] Several New Jersey cities suffered serious dis-

---

to recall the suspicion of partisan politics among the nation's founders, including George Washington, John Adams, James Madison. See, e.g., Dennis J. Palumbo, *American Politics* (New York: Appleton-Century-Crofts, Meredith Corporation, 1973), pp. 432-33.

[4] *The New York Times*, May 19, 1969, p. 12.

[5] See the Governor's Select Commission on Civil Disorder, State of New Jersey, *Report for Action* (Trenton, N. J., 1968), p. 162. Also see *Report of the National Advisory Commission on Civil Disorders* (New York: Bantam Books, 1968), pp. 137-39.

order, and the question of black representation became poignant.

Cognition

As blacks attained office, it was assumed, black citizens would feel less estranged from government.[6] Moreover, black mayors and councilmen would stand as proof that blacks *could* attain elective office and thus become role models for the citizenry. This suggests, however, that black citizens could identify black officials at least as readily as white officials. The question was tested by asking citizens to identify their mayors and either United States senator from New Jersey. Interviews were conducted around the time of the 1972 election, which afforded unusual prominence to Senator Clifford P. Case, then engaged in a successful reelection effort. Nevertheless, few blacks could identify either Case or Senator Harrison A. Williams, Jr., both white.

Table VI-1 reveals that white citizens were twice as likely as blacks to know the name of either senator. Twenty-nine

TABLE VI-1: PERCENTAGE OF CITIZEN RESPONDENTS IN SIXTEEN MUNICIPALITIES WHO IDENTIFIED ONE OF THE UNITED STATES SENATORS FROM NEW JERSEY AND THEIR MAYOR[a]

	Whites (411) %	*Blacks* (120) %
Identified either Senator	61	29
Identified their Mayor	78	82

[a] "Do you know the name of either United States Senator from New Jersey/your Mayor? (If yes, what is it?)"

[6] The contention is supported by a study of black citizens in Los Angeles who expressed greater trust in black than white officials. David O. Sears, "Political Attitudes of Los Angeles Negroes," in Nathan Cohen, ed., *The Los Angeles Riots* (New York: Praeger Publishers, 1970), p. 683.

percent of the blacks could identify one of the two, compared to 61 percent of the whites. Yet the number of black citizens who could identify the mayors of their cities leaped beyond the whites, though both exhibited remarkably high proportions. Eighty-two percent of the blacks and 78 percent of the whites knew the names of their mayors.

The figures show that New Jersey citizens are highly aware of the identity of their local leadership. The awareness crosses color lines and holds true regardless of the race of the mayor. But the suggestion that blacks become role models is also supported. Blacks in municipalities led by black mayors knew the names of their mayors more frequently than blacks in municipalities with white mayors. Eighty-seven percent of the black respondents in the four communities with black mayors in 1972 (East Orange, Englewood, Montclair, Newark) could identify their mayors. In the other twelve communities, 72 percent of the blacks could name their (white) mayors. Table VI-2 indicates simi-

TABLE VI-2: PERCENTAGE OF CITIZEN RESPONDENTS, DIVIDED BY THEIR MAYOR'S RACE, WHO IDENTIFIED THEIR MAYOR

| | Could Identify Mayor | |
	Whites %	Blacks %
Municipalities with White Mayors	75 (219)	72 (44)
Municipalities with Black Mayors	86 (102)	87 (69)

lar though less differentiated patterns for white respondents. In communities with black mayors, 86 percent of the whites could identify them; but the figure fell to 75 percent where whites were mayors.

The presence of a black mayor obviously heightens chances of recognition and, inferentially, the interest of all. The ability of black citizens to recognize black more readily than white mayors, however, is impressive not only because the differential is greater than for white citizens but also because blacks ordinarily would be expected to exhibit less political cognition than whites. Their lower socioeconomic status militates against high cognitive as well as participatory levels.[7] Thus it is not surprising when whites prove more likely to know the name of either senator. But the impact on a black citizen of having a black mayor overrides socioeconomic characteristics. True, black citizens recognize their white mayors almost as frequently as white citizens. This is probably explained by the heightened sensitivity among all citizens to the services their municipality provides, or ought to provide. Municipal services—police, fire, education, recreation, housing—are of uppermost concern to blacks and whites. Nevertheless, the ability of nearly 90 percent of black citizens to name their black mayors supports the argument that the presence of blacks in office does make a difference: a step toward identifying *with* a leader is taken when a citizen can identify him.

The Importance of Black Elected Officials

Officials and citizens of the sixteen municipalities were asked if it were important in the affairs of their city that blacks hold elective office. Substantial majorities in all categories believed that it was (Table VI-3). Black elected officials registered the highest proportion and intensity of agreement. Ninety-three percent agreed with the proposition, 77 percent strongly. Sixty-seven percent of the white officials agreed, though only 35 percent strongly. The black electorate overwhelmingly affirmed the importance of blacks in office, though at a surprisingly moderate intensity. Of the 82 percent who agreed, only 13 percent did so strongly. As with white officials, about 66 percent of the white electorate agreed, but only 8 percent strongly.

Among the 29 percent of the white officials who dis-

[7] V. O. Key, Jr., *Public Opinion and American Democracy* (New York: Alfred A. Knopf, Inc., 1964), pp. 185, 195-97.

TABLE VI-3: Responses of Elected Officials and Citizens to the Question: Some People Say It Is Important in Your City that Blacks Hold Elective Office. Do You:

| | Elected Officials | | Citizens | |
	Whites %	Blacks %	Whites %	Blacks %
Strongly agree that it is	35	77	8	13
Agree	32	16	58	69
Disagree	26	3	24	15
Strongly disagree	3	0	3	0
Don't know, no opinion, etc.	3	3	8	4
Total	99 (96)	99 (31)	101 (411)	101 (140)

agreed, virtually all professed that color should not count in electing a candidate. "First, somebody must be qualified. I don't believe you should select somebody because he happens to be black." From another: "I feel that the biggest blunder America is making today is to separate people by race, color, creed, whatever. . . . A man is elected to public office to serve the people. If he doesn't serve the people, then these ethnic groups have the prerogative of removing the man from office and getting someone in there to serve them." Or: "If you have a white who is not going to legislate on a white basis, but is going to legislate on a 'people' basis, then it doesn't make any difference."

White officials who felt it important that blacks hold elective office divided along two lines. The first believed that whites were capable of representing blacks, but that blacks might not agree. In consequence, black officials were "necessary only for one reason: that blacks *feel* they have representation. Otherwise it doesn't make a difference." Similarly: "I think we're open-minded enough that we would not necessarily need black spokesmen on the council; but from the black community's standpoint, there definitely needs to be representation." The other theme among white officials who thought it important that blacks hold office suggested that whites could not understand black thinking. Not only "should they have someone of their own race they can call upon when they need help. Also it's difficult many times for white people to understand the blacks' philosophies. They differ from ours, and you have to be involved to a great extent with the blacks before you understand their philosophy." A more sensitive response: "Most whites don't understand the thinking of blacks. Not that there is any difference in human beings—but there is an experience the white has not gone through and doesn't understand. So a black has to know there's someone there who understands." Empathetic remarks like this from whites were rare, however. A few were crass: "I think it's important so that they understand what we're all doing. The quicker the blacks get away from the idea that they're black and try to be Americans, the better." But most white officials were matter-of-fact in their agreement that black electoral representation was important.

Black officials, on the other hand, attended the question thoughtfully, some passionately:

I am sure it would be better to have a good white man than a bad black; but a good black man who knows his people, who is able to stand up and fight for them, I think helps them. It gives them a sense of belonging. And of course for our young people it is so important when all their lives they've seen whites in the role of the ruler, the boss. . . . The role model is very important, and it is equally important for white kids.

     • • •

Blacks should be represented like other ethnic groups —it gives them a voice in the direction the city takes. But blacks should be represented particularly, because their problems constitute some of the major areas which the city has to grapple with—in terms of welfare, housing, crime, narcotics and so forth. Then too, psychologically, you have to provide something to which young people can aspire, blacks as well as whites.

. . .

Assuming there's a direct relationship between a guy in public office and a guy on the street, if there aren't any visual images of blacks in power, then there's nothing for blacks to strive for. It's the way the Irish and others made it. The whole concept of ethnic recognition in politics is important.

. . .

The only way any group of people is able to share in the good life is to get control of part of the machinery of power in the community. Elected officials run the power house, and unless you can get men in there helping to dispense this power, it's not too much of a good life you can expect to enjoy. You then become part of the people who make the laws and determine how they're kept. And I think this is essential for any group of people who intend to rise.

The comments by blacks, insistent and uncompromising on the need for black officials, are nevertheless not simply self-serving. They exude a sense of responsibility beyond the normal duties of elected officials. Black officials seem conscious of their special burden as models for others, particularly young people. They believe they are examined for performance as whites are not, but they welcome the responsibility. Their view of themselves as models for the entire community is complemented by their rejection of the proposition that they care about blacks but not whites.

Eighty-seven percent of the black officials disagreed, 26 percent strongly, that black elected officials put the interests of the black community ahead of those of their entire city (Table VI-4). White officials, on the other hand, divided evenly on the question, 45 percent agreeing and 47 percent

TABLE VI-4: Responses of Elected Officials and Citizens to the Question: Some People Say Black Elected Officials Mainly Represent the Interests of the Black Community ahead of the Entire City's. Do You:

| | Elected Officials | | Citizens | |
| | Whites | Blacks | Whites | Blacks |
	%	%	%	%
Strongly agree that they do	15	0	7	4
Agree	30	10	35	23
Disagree	35	61	34	56
Strongly disagree	12	26	2	4
Depends on the individual	7	3	9	6
Don't know, no opinion, etc.	1	0	13	8
Total	100 (96)	100 (31)	100 (411)	101 (140)

disagreeing. The citizenry differed by race as did the officials. Sixty percent of the black electorate disagreed with the proposition, but only 36 percent of the white. Yet while more whites than blacks believed black officials cared principally for blacks rather than their entire city, their conviction was rarely strong. Moreover, it was held by a minority of whites—officials and citizens.

Among white officials who agreed with the proposition, a few were sympathetic toward blacks' placing black interests ahead of their city's. Said a mayor: "Like any other politician, it depends on the base from which he is elected, whether black, Irish, or Italian. . . . I think in some cases it's very necessary that the narrow base be represented." Most, however, were unsympathetic. "If you're going to live in the city without any attempt to polarize, then I think you should cast your vote for what is best for the city as a whole, not for any individuals. It can work the reverse, you know. A white councilman could vote strictly for a white situation without concern for others." From another: "They [black officials] are biased for the black community, and this really disturbs me, because I try always to call them the way I see them, very objectively. And I do not find this with the black leaders. I vote on issues sometimes that my community frowns on because I placated the black or dealt objectively. It's not reciprocal with the black leaders, and that really disturbs me."

White officials who disagreed with the proposition felt that was the way it should be, that blacks ought not to represent black interests first. "In my experience with a black commissioner, I think his interest for the city is paramount. Though he does look out for black interests, they are subordinated to those of the entire city. . . . The interests that I represent together with the interests that minority commissioners would have, should be subordinated to the overall good. But they and I would look out secondarily for groups that we may represent." Or: "As a general rule they represent all interests, and they should. They should represent the whole city just as I should. They should be elected officials who happen to be black rather than black officials." Some patronized: "We have no problems at all with our Negroes, and we've had at least one on the council for the past ten years. They represent the whole city, and they are always careful about saying that too."

Responses from black officials were consistent. Almost all recognized special needs of the black community, but fused them with their responsibility to the entire city. They were solid in their view that concern for blacks neither superseded nor displaced concern for the overall community:

I strongly disagree that most black elected officials believe they should exclusively represent black interests, but I strongly agree that they are sensitive to needs of the black community. They're sensitive to the

deprivation that has been there for years. It may
appear on the surface that they're favoring blacks,
because many times they're trying to uplift the total
community, and it's just like a human body. If you
have a cancer in one section you try to cure it—so the
real thing they're trying to do is uplift the total
community by bringing up the section.

Others spoke similarly: "Because of the circumstances of
the black individual in most communities he's coming from
behind, and if he gets more attention at a given moment, it's
an attempt to balance." "As a mayor, I certainly see my first
responsibility to the total community; but I must always be
aware of the inequities that exist within the black community and move toward creating a climate where blacks can
upgrade themselves." "I think we should be accountable to
the black people; that's one of my first tenets. But in seeking
the interests of black people, quite naturally it's going to be
for the benefit of all people." "I have to be concerned with
the total city, but I also have an obligation of making a better tomorrow for black folks. The problems of [city] are
such that when you talk about uplifting the city as a whole,
it's going to uplift blacks. But in terms of job opportunities
and better education, it's going to benefit whites too."

The following response searches the question at length,
revealing the delicacy of the issue:

I have an opinion, but I don't know whether it's going
to end up agreeing or disagreeing. As far as an elected
official is concerned, if he comes from a district that
is 85 percent black, then he can appear to be more
concerned about the problems of the black community
than someone who comes from a district that is 15
percent black. I heard Senator Brooke speaking in
Washington. He said, "Nobody in Congress has a
better record on civil rights than I have, but I have to
be concerned about other areas of my state, because

only 4 percent of the people in my state happen to be black.''

Well, naturally, if the only concern I have is for the problems in my community, and I don't show any concern for [city] in its entirety, then I'm not going to be around to be concerned about the problems of the black community. So although I am black and I am proud of it, and I feel very deeply about the problems of the black community, I also feel deeply for the problems of [city], not only for political expediency, but because this is my town. In other words, if we allowed the problems of [city] to continue and just concentrated on the black problems, then sooner or later [city] would be all black anyway. And we would not really have solved the problems.

So I look at it as a broader thing. I think I have the ability to lead white people, as white people have been leading black people. I think I have the ability to lead or represent everybody. So why should I concentrate my efforts on only one segment of the community? I have a loyalty to my heritage, so definitely I am concerned about that. When I see Joe Frazier fight Jerry Quarry, I root for Joe Frazier. I mean that's natural for me, just as it's natural for some Irish guy to root for Jerry Quarry. But nevertheless I'm interested in seeing Jerry Quarry get a fair shake too.

[As far as representing the interests of the black community ahead of the entire city's] how can you separate the two? If we don't have a proper educational system and blacks get the worst of it, is it representing the black community or is it representing [city] to seek better education? How do you separate it? If taxes are raised, that has an effect on black home owners. If you have an insufficient police force and therefore more crime is committed—most is against the black community

anyway—you try to make it sufficient. So when you
talk about the well-being of the town, you're also
talking about the well-being of the black community.
As long as everything is together like this, you can't
separate it.

Thus black officials expressed black consciousness and
sensitivity, but not at the expense of the overall needs of
their cities. They recognized an inseparable connection between the welfare of black residents and the city as a whole.
Whether based on morality or pragmatism, the attitudes of
black officials recall their subscription to coalition politics,
to accommodation.

Accommodation is the thread of the political system. Its
tension registers the system's viability. Suspended between
contending interests it remains taught, vibrant as long as no
interest tugs beyond reason. Conversely, if an interest
yields too much it slacks, enervated; the interest is ignored.
Black officials have largely maintained a viable tension,
neither snapping the thread nor loosening the grip. Whites
suspect that black political leaders favor black interests
ahead of theirs, but neither in numbers nor conviction is the
suspicion overbearing. Most believe that blacks ought to be
elected to office, and black elected officials consequently
enjoy legitimacy and leeway among whites. But black officials have not yielded their black consciousness to obtain
this legitimacy. Virtually all understand their roles as
spokesmen for black claims, who must also meet the needs
of their cities. A study of San Francisco officials drew similar conclusions, that black politicians appear "responsive
not only to the political system of [their] city as a whole,
but also to the demands of the Negro masses as articulated
by the Negro protest groups."[8]

[8] Richard Young, "The Impact of Protest Leadership on Negro Politicians in San Francisco," *Western Political Quarterly*, 22, no. 1 (March
1969), p. 110.

Perceptions on Black Interests in Government

The perceptual gap between races widens over the question of representation of black interests in city government. Whites believe black interests are adequately represented; blacks do not (Table VI-5). Fifty-nine percent of the white

TABLE VI-5: RESPONSES OF ELECTED OFFICIALS AND CITIZENS TO THE QUESTION: HOW DO YOU FEEL ABOUT THIS STATEMENT: THE INTERESTS OF BLACKS ARE ADEQUATELY REPRESENTED AT OFFICIAL LEVELS OF THE CITY GOVERNMENT. DO YOU:

| | Elected Officials | | Citizens | |
| | Whites | Blacks | Whites | Blacks |
	%	%	%	%
Strongly agree	42	13	7	1
Agree	42	26	52	33
Disagree	13	42	20	37
Strongly disagree	2	20	2	10
Don't know, no opinion, etc.	2	0	19	19
Total	101 (96)	101 (31)	100 (411)	100 (140)

citizenry, but only 34 percent of the black, felt the advocacy of black interests sufficient in their city's government. The differential between officials was larger. Eighty-four percent of the white officials thought black interests adequately represented, 39 percent of the black. The gap among officials holds even in municipalities where the proportion of black elected officials is about the same as the black population's. In the four municipalities with the most equitable proportions, Hackensack, East Orange, Englewood, and Teaneck, 85 percent of the white elected officials agreed with the proposition but only 45 percent of the black.

Most white and virtually all the black officials interpreted "adequate representation of black interests" in terms of the number of blacks in government. Since the question referred to city government in general and not only to elected positions, officials reviewed with me the number of blacks in appointive as well as elective office. Interpretations diverged, however. Blacks emphasized proportional deficiencies, whites the contrary. Within a single municipality, responses from officials could be 180 degrees apart. A white councilman's view that "the administration and the city council try to do everything we can for *all* the people," was contradicted by a black fellow councilman: "The chief powers in the city have not responded adequately." In another city a white official pondered aloud: "All right, just say for the police department we certainly have a number of black superior officers—three captains, six sergeants; we have maybe 35 percent black police officers. Other departments have been moving along in that direction. We have a bondsman that's black; we have a city controller that's black; we have a black that's head of the welfare department. They have good representation." Yet in the same city, after recounting the same positions held by blacks, a black official concluded, "But other than that you have nothing else. So I couldn't go overboard, no. I can't agree that blacks have adequate representation."

Adequate representation is in part an attitude. It is not solely determined by the number, quality, or background of officials. The term is shaped as well by one's sense of security, experiences with the political system, personal successes and failures. The question of adequate representation reams the core of perceptual differences between black and white officials. Their views become conveniences, justifications for what they wish. The belief by most whites that blacks are adequately represented is self-serving. It is for many an expression of insensitivity, inability to empathize. In Elizabeth and Passaic, two municipalities with no blacks serving in elective office in 1972, over half of the white citizens believed black interests were adequately represented, as did eleven of seventeen officials.

For many, therefore, it is easier to mislabel reality than to confront one's prejudices. Self-serving distortions cloak irrational bias. How else can one interpret these comments from white officials in communities with no blacks on the governing body? "I would strongly agree that their interests are being represented. Contrary to the doctrine that has been expressed many times by the blacks that a white man cannot think for a black, I believe that their interests are indeed being serviced." Said another: "I agree. They've been satisfied as far as I can see. They've been taken care of. I don't think they have any reason to think they're not being treated properly." A third councilman protested that if black interests were not adequately represented it was "because we have a goodly number of militants [among the citizenry], but they are not the constructive type that are willing to take part in levels of government."

Virtue is no more inherent in black elected officials than white. But their feelings of inadequate representation approximate reality more frequently than white views to the contrary. Nevertheless, distortions of reality can be as self-serving for blacks as whites. Thus a black official in East Orange, a municipality with equitable proportions of blacks at all levels of government, refused to grant that black interests were adequately represented. "I don't agree at all. It's meaningless. Sure we have a black mayor, five black councilmen—with no power. If they cater to the business interests, they can't represent the total community; that's what goes on here. Black people don't have any power because black people don't have any money. I don't care if he's mayor or congressman; he's powerless if he doesn't have any money."

Thus, it serves black advantage to equate representation of interest with numbers of officials—as long as the number of black officials is low. But as more blacks attain office, the tendency to look beyond numbers increases. Whites now minimize the importance of exact proportions because it is to their advantage to do so. Accordingly, blacks will dis-

count the importance of proportions as their numbers become equitable, that is, as equivalent proportions are
reached between black officials and blacks in the population.

This is not to deny the importance, ethically, morally, and
practically of fair proportions of blacks in government. But
in politics, in human affairs, the backwash of "solved" problems contains new ones.

Community Race Relations

In rounding out the inquiry into attitudes, respondents
were asked about overall relations in their cities between
blacks and whites. Officials tended to think relations were
better than did the rank and file, whites better than blacks.
Table VI-6 reveals that 61 percent of the white officials

TABLE VI-6: RESPONSES OF ELECTED OFFICIALS AND CITIZENS
TO THE QUESTION: WHICH OF THE FOLLOWING WORDS BEST
DESCRIBES RELATIONS IN YOUR CITY BETWEEN BLACKS AND
WHITES GENERALLY?

| | Elected Officials | | Citizens | |
| | Whites | Blacks | Whites | Blacks |
	%	%	%	%
Excellent	9	0	3	2
Good	52	36	23	16
Fair	34	52	47	57
Poor	3	13	23	20
Don't know, no opinion, etc.	1	0	5	4
Total	99 (96)	101 (31)	101 (411)	99 (140)

believed relations between the races were good or excellent, compared to 36 percent of the black. But only 26 percent of the white citizenry viewed relations favorably, and
the figure shrank to 18 percent among blacks. Thus elected
officials were considerably more sanguine than their
constituents.

Favorable responses among white officials tended to be personalized. They focused on their own experiences rather than those of the overall community. "Relations are excellent as far as I am concerned; I get along real nice with them." Or: "I think it depends on where you live and what the experience is. I live here in the ghetto and I know the people, and they seem to be cooperative. I don't see it as a bad relationship at all." Whites who viewed black-white relations as fair or poor, on the other hand, responded as observers rather than participants. They referred little to personal experience, but evaluated their municipality in overview. Thus: "I think there's racism on both sides, and I don't see things getting any better. I see more racism among the younger people than I see with the older ones." From another: "I see the communities [black and white] as separate, and I think that's not good. They don't pray together; they don't drink together; they don't socialize. It seems like they go their separate ways." A third white councilman labeled middle-class relations good, but overall relations fair because "black middle-class interests coincide more with white middle-class interests than with the interests of the ghetto black community." These views were in the minority, however. Most white officials viewed relations favorably.

But despite the question's unequivocal inquiry into overall community relations, several whites supported their favorable responses exclusively by personal experience. They seemed to say that since their own relations with blacks were good or excellent, so were everyone else's. This could arise for several reasons. First, the line between what is true and what one wants to be true is elusive. If officials want to believe relations between the races are good, they might ignore evidence to the contrary and cite selectively from their own experience. Second, as with other questions of attitude, the quality of "excellent" or "poor" is subjective. Some will think race relations excellent as long as there are no riots; others poor until residential patterns are indistin-

guishable by race. Finally, in their roles as government
leaders, white officials would wish to picture community
relations as favorably as possible. They might see themselves discredited for community disharmony, praised for
good relations. Said a white mayor, "Since my administration they [blacks] no longer feel there is any discrimination.
They feel there are people to talk to, people who are sympathetic with the problems they have had." His immodesty
pales, however, before a councilman's from another municipality: "I would say [city] is one of the most congenial cities
in the world—never mind the United States—the world."

Nevertheless, whatever the reasons (and probably all
enter the equation), white officials leaned toward favorable
views of black-white relations in their cities. The tendency
was reversed, however, among black officials; but even the
one-third who viewed relations as good, unlike their white
counterparts, demurred from personalizing. Few generalized from their own experiences. Rather, they thought relations "good" in comparison to other municipalities. "We
have a better relationship here than other communities."
Or: "I would say generally it's been good with the exception
of these occasional disruptions. But when I look at this town
and other towns, this is a good town."

The responses from black officials, especially those who
considered race relations fair or poor, were, like their responses to inquiries about black interest and representation
in government, more thoughtful and more analytical than
those from whites. Typically they were sensitive to the com-
plexity of the question:

We have a very subtle relationship. On the outside
anyone would say we have an excellent relationship—
black policemen, firemen, school principals. But in
fact we have two communities. There is very little
social intercourse. At five o'clock the whites go their
way and the blacks go theirs. It's all very superficial.
            ·   ·   ·

No matter what you do, there's nothing you can do to
change the attitudes of people who hate one another.
There are blacks who hate whites and there are whites
who hate blacks. You can try to get them together, and
if you are successful, fine. But changing attitudes of
people is the most difficult problem we have.

. . .

In light of the problems between blacks and whites
throughout the history of our country, we can't expect
much. The relationship has been so different in terms
of cultural background, economic status, political
achievement. All of the things affecting human
behavior have been so greatly different between
whites and blacks in this country, that the mere fact
that there is peaceful coexistence between the groups
is an acceptable relationship.

An encouraging aspect of the inquiry into black-white
relations is the leap in favorable responses from officials
and citizens in the four communities with the most equitable black representation (Hackensack, East Orange, Englewood, and Teaneck). Fourteen of the nineteen white
officials thought relations good or excellent in their
municipalities, as did eight of the eleven black. The number
of citizen respondents from the four municipalities (thirteen blacks and fifty-one whites) was too few to be more
than suggestive. But almost half of the respondents of each
race gave favorable interpretations to the question, well beyond the proportions in the overall survey. While conclusions can only be presumptive, the tendency is noteworthy.
Whether cause or effect, favorable attitudes toward race
relations appear positively related to fairness in proportions
of elected blacks.

In sum, whites—officials and citizenry—far more than
blacks believe blacks should be content with existing governmental arrangements, that things are "not bad." They
believe, more frequently than do blacks, that black elected

officials place the interests of blacks ahead of those of their city. They believe black interests are adequately represented in government, even where no elected blacks hold office. White officials and citizens perceive race relations in their cities more favorably than do their black counterparts. And, while most whites think it important that blacks hold elective office, their conviction is lukewarm compared to that of their black counterparts.

The data suggest, therefore, that whites tolerate if not embrace black political aspirations; that racial antagonism among whites, often disquieting, nevertheless yields to a sense of political justice. But black electoral success has emerged principally from black political consciousness. Though often abetted by whites, black political achievements are a product of black recognition of their political due.

VII

Issues and Actions

Public officials ultimately express their powers through prescribed, formal procedure—a judge's decision, an executive's order, a legislator's vote. The formal act may generate momentous change, yet disclose little of the background that molded the decision. External events as well as the values and social environment of a legislator may be climaxed in his vote.

In earlier chapters we examined background features—the paths to office of elected officials and their philosophies and perceptions, particularly as they relate to black affairs. Now, however, we observe the translation of philosophy and perception into action and behavior. In this chapter we examine the importance of issues as defined by black and white officials. We find that the supreme requirement of maintaining civil peace is joined by all officials. Finally, voting records of councilmen (and mayors empowered to vote on their councils) are analyzed by race.

Issues

James Q. Wilson differentiates between "welfare" and "status" goals among black leaders. Welfare ends, he says, "are those which look to the tangible improvement of the community or some individuals in it through the provision of better services, living conditions, or positions." He cites as examples better education, housing, and health care for blacks, as well as increased political representation.[1] Status ends, in contrast, "seek the integration of the Negro into all phases of community on the principle of equality—all Negroes will be granted the opportunity to obtain the services, positions, or material benefits of the community on the basis of principles other than race. Such principles include the ability to pay and personal achievement or qualification." Examples include school integration, equal treatment of blacks in allocation of public offices and honors, and establishing the principle of open occupancy in housing markets.[2] In his Chicago study, Wilson found that moderate black leaders tended to seek welfare ends, militant leaders status ends. Though disproportionately concerned with race, militants shared "the values of the white liberal or radical."[3] Moderates, on the other hand, tended "to share the political value system of the white conservative, again with race displaced to a higher—but not always the highest —point."[4]

Local officials in New Jersey, however, black and white, appear to be wedded to welfare as distinct from status concerns. Officials were asked: "What are the major issues, in your judgment, that your city faces?" No number or hierarchy was solicited. Table VII-1 reveals minimal concern with status ends gauged either by the number of status issues cited or the percentage of officials who mentioned them. Of the twenty issues mentioned by white officials, only four could be construed as status related: the need to bring people together, school integration (by busing), lack of confidence in present administration or displeasure with the city's image, and alienation of youth. Among the eighteen cited by black officials, three were status oriented: school integration (by busing), the need to bring people together, and the need for equal opportunity in general.

[1] James Q. Wilson, *Negro Politics* (New York: The Free Press, 1965), p. 185; see also Everett Carll Ladd, Jr., *Negro Political Leadership in the South* (Ithaca, N. Y.: Cornell University Press, 1966), p. 155.

[2] Wilson, *Negro Politics*, p. 185.

[3] *Ibid.*, p. 217.   [4] *Ibid.*, p. 233.

TABLE VII-1: RESPONSES BY ELECTED OFFICIALS TO THE
QUESTION: WHAT ARE THE MAJOR ISSUES, IN YOUR JUDGMENT,
THAT YOUR CITY FACES?

Whites		*Blacks*	
	Percentage Who		*Percentage Who*
Issues	*Mentioned*	*Issues*	*Mentioned*
Tax/money	65	Housing	65
Housing	33	Education/schools	45
Crime/safety	30	Tax/money	32
Education/schools	28	General services (garbage, roads, sewers, etc.)	29
Rebuild city/urban renewal	16	Narcotics	23
Retain and attract business/industry	15	Unemployment	20
Narcotics	14	Crime/safety	19
General services (garbage, roads, sewers, etc.)	14	Lack of police protection	10
Keep middle-class in city	8	Parks/recreation	10
Bring people together	8	Welfare burden	7
		Need better police-community relations	7
Unemployment	7	Need to change form of government or party in control	7
Parks/recreation	7	School integration (by busing)	7
Overall planning and development	6	Rebuild city/urban renewal	3
Welfare burden	6	Keep middle-class in city	3
School integration (by busing)	6		
Need to change form of government or party in control	3	Bring people together	3
Lack of police protection	2	Equal opportunity (in general)	3
Lack of confidence in city's administration/ image	2	Need more blacks in city's government	3
Need better police-community relations	1		
Alienation of youth	1		

The welfare orientation of black officials, most of them liberal (see Chapter V), appears to contradict Wilson's thesis that black liberal leaders are status oriented. In fairness to Wilson, however, it must be noted that he wrote of Chicago's black leadership in general during the late fifties, not only of elected officials. Evidently the assumption of power and responsibility leads black politicians as well as white to focus on "bread-and-butter" goals.

But while members of both races emphasized welfare ends, the issues they named reflected differences by race. Two-thirds of the white elected officials mentioned tax or money problems as major issues, but only one-third of the blacks. Conversely, while two-thirds of the black officials cited housing, one-third of the whites did.

Although no hierarchy was sought, most officials emphasized one issue or another. Among whites this usually meant taxes or money. Said one white mayor: "The overriding issue is financial. Not that money buys happiness, but to go with the trite old saying, I'd rather have the chance to be miserable and a little less strapped than not. The property tax situation, given our community with the poor and the aged, is oppressive." Another mayor spoke similarly: "I would say that the first issue is the incredibly high, confiscatory level of local property taxes. It's a cycle—an exodus of people who can't afford to pay it, and a severe economic handicap to those who remain." And a third: "Money is always the number one priority. Greater increase in demand for services from the tax paying public—but while they're making the demand they're looking for tax relief."

The predominant view among white officials suggested that money would take care of all difficulties, that other problems hardly needed mention. Despite encouragement during interviews to mention "other major issues," the gap between money/taxes and other issues was enormous. Money was mentioned by white officials twice as often as housing, crime and safety, or education.

In contrast, most black officials were concerned with housing, and almost half with education. Except for taxes and money, the six issues most frequently named by blacks were of less concern to whites. In addition to housing and education, more black officials than white cited general services (garbage, roads, sewers, etc.), narcotics, and unemployment among "the major issues that your city faces." Thus reliance on money/tax relief as a solution to other problems was not nearly as common among blacks as among whites. Indeed blacks frequently reversed the whites' conception of problem and solution. Said one: "The three top issues very definitely are lack of decent housing, education, and police protection. If we could correct these three ills, we can overcome financial problems; we can fight them off and pay through the nose and work two jobs, and anything else." Cause and effect exchanged positions by race. Not all black officials held that financial problems would evaporate as other problems were solved, but the emphasis most gave to other issues implied that blacks were less concerned with revenue sources, more with spending priorities. Black officials often ignored money or tax problems while insisting "the major issues are those that we call the quality of life issues—education, housing, health, employment." Or: "The major one is housing. With proper housing I think we can clean up the crime." "Of course, the major issue—there's no question about it—is the quality of education in our schools."

Though we have characterized responses by race, it is important to recognize that we speak of the typical, not the total. Thirty-five percent of the white officials did *not* cite taxes or money as a major issue, and others were equivocal about their primacy. Some cited the importance of financial relief, but felt "crime might be on top of the list; if you did away with crime you can live with the other things." Or: "I think the biggest problem is simply the ability of people to get along with each other." From a third: "The number one priority of this administration is to enhance the educational system, and then there is the infuriating problem with housing." Tax/money issues therefore, important to most whites, were not their exclusive concern.

Moreover, while taxonomy is useful, the distinction between welfare ends and status ends is not always clear. Better education, for example, a welfare goal, relates inextricably to equal opportunity, a status goal. A black politician may say that quality of education is the most important issue in his community. Yet with this he says tacitly that better education is a path to equal opportunity. A poorly educated person has less opportunity—less control over his own life—than one better educated. The blurring of welfare and status ends is revealed in the comments of a black councilman:

Major issues here, as in any city, and they always will be until a lot more is done, are fair housing, adequate or really more than adequate economic opportunity, and better schools. Now a lot of people seem to think everybody desires integration. Maybe they do; maybe they don't. But I do know that many black people buy homes in black communities because the home happens to be in good condition. I'd do the same thing. I would have bought a home in a white community if I had seen one that I wanted, but I saw one I wanted already in a black community, and I bought it from another black family. . . .
The only thing that I can see that most people want that I talk to is a chance to make it without someone putting unnecessary obstacles in their paths. If he has an opportunity to get a job, promotions, increases in salary, he doesn't care whether he's working in a black community or a white community. If his youngster can read on grade level and think for himself, he's not concerned whether it's a black or a white school. If he has worked all year he wants to be able to take a vacation and take his family with him. You see, just

because a person happens to be of a different faith or
different color doesn't mean that he doesn't have the
same desires that other people have. And this is the
thrust of the whole fight, if you want to call it a fight.

Welfare and status ends, therefore, are not categorical
absolutes; they label tendencies. While black officials listed
welfare issues as major, their responses revealed broader
underpinnings. Welfare achievements are concrete, measurable, but perceived also as spawning status ends, fluid
and elusive. Though black officials are concerned with
equal opportunity and ending racism, these ends are seen
as inevitable outgrowths of the fulfillment of day-to-day
needs.

The National Advisory Commission on Civil Disorders inquired into grievances of black citizens following the 1967
riots. While intensity varied, issues cited by black citizens
in the Commission's report paralleled those by black officials in this study. Housing, education, general services,
unemployment were emphasized in the report, as they were
by the officials five years later.[5] One may regret that the
same issues remained preeminent, yet feel encouraged that
local officials—particularly blacks—are attuned to the
grievances of the citizenry.

The two issues most commonly mentioned by blacks in
this study, housing and education, will be examined in
Chapter IX. But what can be said of these two holds for
others. Black officials have attempted to transform concern
into action, though with mixed results. Black interests, like
other interests, face systemic obstacles: conflicting aims
among local officials, lack of power to implement policies
independently of higher authority, inadequate commitment
to correct urban problems on the part of federal and state
governments.

Whatever the obstacles, however, local officials are com-

---

[5] *Report of the National Advisory Commission on Civil Disorders*
(New York: Bantam Books, 1968), pp. 143-44.

mitted to working within the political system. They despair of violence, and would hold with the National Advisory Commission that "preserving civil peace is the first responsibility of government. Unless the rule of law prevails, our society will lack not only order but also the environment essential to social and economic progress."[6] And as most officials recognize, they themselves may be central to the preservation of civil peace.

Civil Disorder

In the mid and late sixties violence wrenched American cities. Paradoxically, black rioting followed a decade of unparalleled government commitment toward equal rights. For the first time in the nation's history the three branches of the federal government simultaneously moved against racial discrimination. Racism was attacked in Supreme Court decisions, by the executive and the Congress. Institutional segregation in the South receded before federal pressure, while programs to help the poor, the deprived, the city dweller (terms often synonymous with black), poured out of federal offices. Why, then, the riots?

Government commissions and critics examined the question. Conclusions ranged from castigation of the entire political-economic system to local idiosyncrasies. Parenti and Katznelson blamed the "system of power, privilege, and profit" that makes people poor and leads them to riot,[7] while the McCone Commission blamed the Los Angeles riots on the heavy influx and unrealistic hopes of black migrants, suggesting that "the generosity of the California welfare program" contributed to the influx.[8] But the most

[6] *Ibid.*, pp. 17-18.

[7] The quotation is cited and supported by Ira Katznelson in "Power in the Reformulation of Race Research," *Race, Change, and Urban Society*, Peter Orleans and William Russell Ellis, Jr., eds. (Beverly Hills, Calif.: Sage Publications, 1971), p. 57.

[8] Cited in Raymond J. Murphy and James W. Watson, "The Structure of Discontent: Relationship between Social Structure, Grievance,

comprehensive, the most celebrated report was that of the National Advisory Commission on Civil Disorders. In the wake of the urban disorders in 1967, the Commission confronted the nation with its history of racism, offering neither patronizing excuses about migration nor ideological critiques that obscured the immediate challenge. "Discrimination and segregation have long permeated much of American life; they now threaten the future of every American," said the *National Report*. "What white Americans have never fully understood—but what the Negro can never forget—is that white society is deeply implicated in the ghetto. White institutions created it, white institutions maintain it, and white society condones it." With respect to the riots, "the most fundamental [ingredient] is the racial attitude and behavior of white Americans toward black Americans. . . . White racism is essentially responsible for the explosive mixture which has accumulated in our cities since the end of World War II."[9] Referring to the effectiveness of government action, the National Commission found that conditions for blacks remained unsatisfactory, that blacks were still "severely disadvantaged, especially as compared with whites; that local government is often unresponsive to this fact; that federal programs have not yet reached a significantly large proportion of those in need; and that the result is a reservoir of unredressed grievances and frustration in the ghetto."[10]

The Commission devoted hundreds of pages to recommendations. The overarching effort, however, was toward integration, toward "a single society, in which every citizen will be free to live and work according to his capabilities and desires, not his color."[11] Programs would be directed to "the only possible choice for America, . . . policy which

and Riot Support," *The Los Angeles Riots*, Nathan Cohen, ed. (New York: Praeger Publishers, Inc., 1970), p. 145.

[9] *Report of the National Advisory Commission* (henceforth referred to as the *National Report*), pp. 1, 2, 203.

[10] *Ibid.*, p. 136.   [11] *Ibid.*, p. 23.

combines ghetto enrichment with programs designed to encourage integration of substantial numbers of Negroes into the society outside the ghetto."[12]

The relationship of the *National Report* to this study is fundamentally twofold. First, New Jersey urban areas provided a disproportionate base for the *National Report*. The first chapter reviews "Profiles of Disorder," and, remarkably, over half of the chapter describes New Jersey municipalities. Four of the eight chapter sections are about Newark, northern New Jersey, Plainfield, and New Brunswick. (The other four are about Tampa, Cincinnati, Atlanta, and Detroit.) Moreover, the *National Report* cites fourteen New Jersey municipalities as comprising the largest "cluster" of cities throughout the country to suffer disorder.[13] Ironically, a 1968 report by the New Jersey Commission on Civil Disorder is less comprehensive about New Jersey than the *National Report*. The State Commission concentrated on Newark with brief references to Plainfield and Englewood. But its theme paralleled the National Commission's, that the disorders were "a manifestation of a deep failing in our society," and that "the central issue [is] to make equality real for the black man."[14] It recognized, furthermore, that racial difficulties in the cities and suburbs of New Jersey reflected those across the country, that "the problems we looked into are national in origin and scope."[15] Thus the national and state reports rely heavily on New Jersey conditions for generalizations about the nation. The New Jersey setting in the reports, as in this study, serves substantially to characterize urban America.

Second, both reports noted the dearth of local black officials. New Jersey cities were named in the *National Report* and included in palliative suggestions: "The number of Negro officials in elected and appointed positions in the riot

---

[12] *Ibid.*, p. 22.   [13] *Ibid.*, p. 114.

[14] Governor's Select Commission on Civil Disorder, State of New Jersey, *Report for Action* (Trenton, N. J., 1968), pp. x, xi.

[15] *Ibid.*, p. v.

cities is minimal in proportion to the Negro population. The alienation of the Negro from the political process has been exacerbated by his racial and economic isolation."[16] The New Jersey report pointedly urged the election of blacks: "To help relieve the feeling of Negro powerlessness, both political parties should support the emergence of more Negro candidates and should encourage active participation of Negroes of all economic levels in the political process."[17] Of course a sense of political powerlessness was only one of the catalysts prompting disorders. But the dramatic increase in the number of black officials since 1967 provides the basis of our study and, at this point, of inquiry into views of civil disorder.

A measure of the dissipation of racial violence since publication of the national and New Jersey reports was the infrequent reference to civil disorder as a major issue by officials interviewed in 1972. Welfare issues (as defined by James Q. Wilson) predominated. While satisfaction of welfare needs presumably lessens the likelihood of rioting, the tie was rarely mentioned. Fear of riots had receded, and officials appeared to weigh community needs in their own right rather than as social fire extinguishers.

When asked whether racial differences had prompted serious civil disorder in their city in recent years, however, officials responded unevenly. Their answers again recall the importance of individual perception, for in only five of the sixteen municipalities did elected officials unanimously agree whether or not their city had endured serious disorder (Table VII-2). Officials in New Brunswick, Plainfield, and Trenton agreed they had, and in Hackensack and Teaneck that they had not. Of course a problem turns on the word "serious." The National Commission ranked the 1967 disorders in three categories based on the amount of violence, the number of participants, and the level of law enforcement response. Disorders were classified as major,

16 *National Report*, pp. 69, 287.
17 *Report for Action*, p. 162.

TABLE VII-2: Responses of Elected Officials to the Question: Have Racial Differences Been Responsible for Serious Civil Disorder in Your City at Any Time in the Past Five or Six Years or So?

	White Officials			Black Officials		
	Yes	No	Don't Know	Yes	No	Don't Know
Atlantic City	1	3			2	
Camden	5	1		1	1	
East Orange		5		1	6	
Elizabeth	2	8				
Englewood	3	1		2		
Hackensack		4			1	
Jersey City	6	3		1		
Montclair	3	1		1		
Newark	5	1		3	1	
New Brunswick	5			1		
Orange	1	3			1	
Passaic	6	1				
Paterson	8	1	1	2	1	
Plainfield	5			4		
Teaneck		6			1	
Trenton	7			1		

serious, or minor, though the report recognized that interpretations "vary widely."[18] Thus, while no classification stands immutable, eleven of the sixteen municipalities in this study were cited in the report as having had disorders in 1967.[19] Subsequent disorders in three others left only Hackensack and Teaneck virtually trouble-free into the early seventies. Indeed only in these two communities did elected officials agree without dissent that their city had suffered no serious disorder. Since "serious" is a subjective

[18] *National Report*, pp. 112-113.
[19] *Ibid.*, pp. 158-59. Newark and Plainfield were listed as having had "major" disorders, Montclair and Paterson "serious," and East Orange, Elizabeth, Englewood, Jersey City, New Brunswick, Orange, and Passaic "minor," all in 1967.

calculation, however, challenging any official's response becomes tenuous. Of greater moment is the rationale of those who believed their city had no serious disorder; and of those who said there had been disorder but that the potential had diminished. What, in a word, reduced the likelihood of disorder?

Four reasons emerged from the interviews. The first, high police capability, was mentioned by a few white officials. "We haven't had too much friction. The police officers know the trouble areas, and they seek information from troublemakers before they can start something." Another emphasized lessons learned by police from previous incidents: "We never had them [disorders] before, and once you have them the police know how to handle them and who the ring leaders are. Also we get good cooperation from the state police, and it looks like the trouble-makers are scared of them. They mean business—they really did a wonderful job the few times they came up." A mayor recounted that "six years ago we had a one-night situation that was quickly crushed by force combined with negotiations with black leaders. From that time on we have had no serious racial disturbances. The number one reason was that the violence aspect was crushed immediately."

A second reason, cited by whites and blacks, but also infrequently, was that the likelihood of riots had diminished because blacks recognized they were self-destructive. Thus a white official said: "One of the reasons there's no trouble is really they're not doing anything more than burning themselves out—they're only hurting themselves." A black official who felt frustrations had not diminished nevertheless believed that "blacks have become more sophisticated about rioting than they were. I don't think they'll run out now in front of national guardsmen and state troopers with their hostility."

A third observation related to socioeconomic levels. One white official who judged his city free of disorder echoed a black from another city. The white: "I don't know wheth-

er you can say we've been lucky, but I think it's more than
that. I think our black population in [city] is stable. I would
say the majority of them are homeowners, and they have a
big stake in this community." The black: "The citizens of
[city] are probably a little better educated than some other
communities, and their economic bracket is probably higher. But my contention is the main reason that you haven't
seen a great many disorders is that most of the folks are
homeowners. They are not just tenants of someone else.
People don't destroy their own property."

Finally, most officials, black and white, emphasized the
importance of responsive and sympathetic government. The
potential for violence had decreased or was never realized,
they believed, because of heightened government concern.
Few spoke with the arrogance of Newark's former mayor,
Hugh Addonizio, who after the 1967 riots said, "I don't care
if a Negro sat here as mayor, he couldn't do anything more
for the Negro than I've done."[20] Most were circumspect,
though blacks tended to stress the contribution of black
elected officials. The first three of the following responses
were, typically, from white officials, the last four from black:

I think the potential for serious incidents is much less
now. The people in general and governments from the
federal and state on down are more aware of why
these disturbances came about and are trying to solve
some of the difficulties. There are many programs and
projects that deal with the underprivileged and poor,
whether it be housing, jobs, or education.
         .   .   .
The potential is there, but there's less likelihood of its
being triggered. I think there is a lessening nationally
of interest on the part of the black community to
take that route. . . . The city administration has with
federal help under the emergency employment act
afforded employment opportunities to a number of

20 Quoted in *Report for Action*, p. 2.

minority group members. I have appointed two black
members to department directorships and blacks as
health, education and welfare director and model
cities director. I put the first Puerto Rican on the
school board and added a black to the school
board. . . . Any mayor who says you can't have racial
trouble today is completely unrealistic. But I think the
tone one sets, the programs one tries to inaugurate
have a lot to do with attitudes—which of course are
basic with any trouble.

. . .

I don't know. I think that every disturbance becomes
racially categorized almost immediately to the point,
you know, if two kids have a fight in high school and
they're both white or they're both black that's not
newsworthy. But if one happens to be white and one
black, that's front page news. . . . Every disturbance
or upset is generally a little more complicated than
just a white versus black situation. I would say that
in terms of representation, participation, and the
"establishment," the situation is better. But in terms
of housing, unemployment and education, we still
have some rather serious problems that have not
been totally overcome.

. . .

From the standpoint of hostility and frustration the
potential is still there. If you look at it from the
standpoint of response, blacks are less likely to riot.
I think now they'd be more subtle in their approach to
the system. Hopefully the impact of black elected
officials and appointed officials would have some
mitigating effect.

. . .

I think the best way to eliminate the threat is greater
communication between the city administration and
the people. And there definitely is a great amount of
attention being given to this. We have a community-

police human relations unit, and they're in touch with
the community. For years we didn't have a civil rights
commission, but we have one now, and people have
some redress there. And now we have what you might
call mini-city halls—an action bureau that comes into
the community. . . . I think if you can get team work
as far as leadership, people like myself, with the
NAACP and with the Urban League, and the clergy
and other community leaders, you know, who are not
necessarily elected to office—this is the way I think
we can head these things off.

    . . .

The city of [city] has been extremely lucky. I would
like to think, although it would be very presumptuous
—well actually it happened to be me that went into
office, but any black person who went into office might
have helped the situation. I think the work I did that
the newspapers and the general public is not aware
of—going around to the various militant groups at
night, working and talking and trying to get them to
participate, not desecrate, to tell their governing body
what they think, how they feel—I think that had
something to do with it. I think a lot of other people
that I talked to, mostly blacks who were thinking
along the same lines, had something to do with it. I
think that white people in the community that were
willing to sit down and talk and were sincere—though
you've got a lot of fakers—had something to do
with it.

    . . .

One of the primary reasons I feel we haven't had
racial disorders is simply because the people in [city]
know their representatives. And when they feel that
something is not going as it should, they're on the
phone, they're at your house, in your office, at city
council meetings saying, "Look, this is not what we'd
like to see. If you can't do better or bring about a

change, the next election is right around the corner."
So things take place. Now when we had the riots in
Newark in sixty-seven there were several rumors that
it was supposed to break out here. But from the time
it started until everything had cooled down, I was out
on the streets talking to all of our constituents on the
city borderline. And thank goodness I knew most of
them personally and they knew me personally. And
when some of the more-or-less inflammatory people
came here, our people didn't respond because they
knew they had elected officials who were there to
make sure things were in top order.

While government officials may have exaggerated their
own influence in reducing disturbances, three develop-
ments in the past half-dozen years are irrefutable. First,
serious disorder has been reduced. Second, federal and
state aid to cities has been increased in directions urged by
the *National Report* (though some has been curtailed since
1973) . Third, the increase of elected and appointed black officials has been the most visible and dramatic change recom-
mended by the National or New Jersey Commissions on
Civil Disorder. While black officials are not alone responsible for the recession of violence, they deserve substantial
credit. Not only has their presence been symbolically important; but most have responded skillfully to the demands
both of the black community and their entire city.

Nowhere is this skillful response better gleaned than
from the proceedings of local councils. They reflect one of
the most important contributions of black elected officials:
sensitization translated into programs. For, despite the belief expressed in interviews by many white officials that
blacks care only about black interests, this perception does
not describe week-to-week conduct. Neither white antagonism nor black parochialism is usually discernible from
local officials' behavior; quite the contrary.

Council Proceedings

In their comprehensive study of city councils, Heinz Eulau
and Kenneth Prewitt recognize the incomparable significance of the voting stage of the legislative process. Voting,
as the authors say, is the "definitive and final" act of each
legislator. It is of a different order from other legislative
activity. Voting is "the point of no return . . . when each individual participant commits himself and through his action
commits the council."[21] But while recognizing the importance of voting analysis to determine bloc patterns and de-
cisional structure, Eulau and Prewitt faced a dilemma. Roll
calls at council meetings in their San Francisco area study
were not recorded by name. Thus roll calls could not be
employed to analyze voting patterns. The authors had to
resort to a less desirable alternative—asking councilmen
sociometric questions about their own and others' voting
behavior.[22]

Fortunately, the minutes of municipal meetings in this
study do contain roll call votes. Irrespective of governmental form or party arrangements, roll calls are recorded by
name. Tabulation becomes difficult in some instances because of the recording format used by the local clerk, but in
all cases it is possible.

I examined the minutes of the fourteen governing bodies
on which blacks served in 1972. The proceedings of each
council or commission were reviewed for 1972, or for 1971
in three cases where black tenure was interrupted (Atlantic
City, Montclair, Plainfield). Except for motions to adjourn
and to accept minutes of previous meetings, every vote was
tabulated. The votes, whether on motions, resolutions, bills,
or ordinances, were examined by race. Table VII-3 reveals

[21] Heinz Eulau and Kenneth Prewitt, *Labyrinths of Democracy:
Adaptations, Linkages, Representation, and Policies in Urban Politics*
(New York: The Bobbs-Merrill Co., 1973), p. 189.
[22] *Ibid.*, pp. 172-73.

TABLE VII-3 Votes Cast by Councilmen, Commissioners, or Aldermen during One Calendar Year, by Race[a]

	% Unanimous Votes		% Voting Divisions by Race (all blacks vs. all whites)		% Voting Minority All Black (though some blacks in majority)		% Voting Minority All White (though some whites in majority)		% Voting Minority Mixed—(black and white)		Total Number Votes
Atlantic City	99.9	(980)					0.1	(1)			(981)
Camden[b]	99.3	(415)			0.2	(1)	0.5	(2)			(418)
East Orange	82.6	(651)			4.1	(31)	9.0	(71)	4.4	(35)	(788)
Englewood	87.1	(575)	0.3	(2)			12.6	(83)			(660)
Hackensack	99.5	(385)					0.5	(2)			(387)
Jersey City	97.7	(1165)					2.3	(27)			(1192)
Montclair	98.9	(267)					1.1	(3)			(270)
Newark	82.0	(1880)	3.0	(69)[c]	10.6	(242)	2.7	(62)	1.7	(39)	(2292)
New Brunswick	100.0	(517)									(517)
Orange	92.0	(619)	0.9	(6)			4.8	(32)	2.4	(16)	(673)
Paterson	92.0	(112)			0.8	(1)	7.4	(9)	0.8	(1)	(123)
Plainfield	91.2	(402)	0.2	(1)	3.6	(16)	4.1	(18)	0.9	(4)	(441)
Teaneck	87.9	(478)	0.4	(2)			11.4	(62)	0.4	(2)	(544)
Trenton	99.4	(1568)	0.1	(2)			0.3	(4)	0.2	(3)	(1577)

[a] Tabulations were for 1972, except for Atlantic City, Montclair, and Plainfield, which were for 1971. Motions to adjourn or approve minutes of previous meetings were not counted. Abstentions were counted as dissents.

[b] The minutes of Camden's council meetings were tabulated only for six months, January through June, 1972.

[c] Included are thirty-six votes cast by Councilman Dennis Westbrooks alone when the other two black councilmen were absent.

the striking pattern of unanimity on all the councils.[23] The data tend to support Eulau's and Prewitt's conclusions that large councils are more likely to exhibit conflict than small.[24] The mean number of councilmen on the seven legis-

[23] Reference to "councils" will here include elected commissions and aldermen. "Dissent" implies dissent from the voting majority, not necessarily opposition to an issue.

[24] Eulau and Prewitt, *Labyrinths of Democracy*, pp. 98-101, 187-88.

lative bodies least often unanimous is 7.7. The mean on the seven councils most often unanimous is 6.3. But more impressive than this tendency is the overall frequency of unanimity on all councils, and to this we shall return in a moment.

Equally striking, however, is the infrequency with which blacks and whites separate into voting blocs, that is, when all blacks in attendance vote one way, all whites the other. A "bloc" vote here includes the dissent or abstention of a single black official, if he were the only black in attendance. Thus, in Newark on thirty-six occasions when Councilman Dennis Westbrooks was the lone dissenting or abstaining member the two other black councilmen, Sharpe James and Earl Harris, were not present.[25] Since on other occasions James and Harris voted independently of Westbrooks (and each other), the 3 percent frequency of Newark's "race" voting is, if anything, overstated. Nowhere else, including municipalities with only one black councilman, did racial divisions account for more than one percent of all votes. In East Orange, where blacks held five of ten council seats, not one issue cleanly divided blacks from whites.

There were tendencies toward bloc voting, however, some with racial implications but most not. In Newark, 11 percent of the votes found at least one black dissenting or abstaining apart from whites while the other black(s) voted with the white majority. This was true especially for Westbrooks, who dissented or abstained more than any other Newark councilman. On the other hand, in East Orange and Englewood, one or two whites dissented or abstained far more frequently than their fellow councilmen. In East Orange, Nancy Schron, the single Republican on the council, alone or with Francis Craig, a conservative Democrat, accounted for thirty-seven of the seventy-one "all-white" dissents. "All-black" dissents in East Orange totaled thirty-one. In Englewood, Jerry Hersch alone or with the council's

[25] Minutes of Newark city council meetings, June 28 and September 6, 1972.

other Republican, Judith Fernandez (or her successor later in 1972) accounted for seventy-eight of the eighty-three "all-white" dissents or abstentions. Vincente Tibbs, the only black on the Englewood council, however, was the lone dissenter only one time, the lone abstainer one other. Party and ideology unquestionably superseded race in voting divisions on these councils.

Nevertheless, the overriding feature remains the frequency of unanimity in all councils. But while the voting patterns imply minimal discord, this must be amplified. Three reasons contribute to frequent, in some councils undeviating, unanimity. First, most votes are about non-controversial issues. Second, councilmen, like most humans, prefer to cooperate than to stimulate controversy; it is easier to comply than dissent. Third, councilmen trade votes, supporting some issues unenthusiastically in exchange for support of their own causes.

The largest number of issues that councilmen decide are routine, administrative, and non-controversial. Motions to accept reports from other agencies, to refund tax overpayments, to authorize contracts, to discharge liens and settle claims, to grant raffle licenses, to renew liquor licenses, and to regulate parking and traffic are adopted perfunctorily. Occasionally a question is raised, a dissent expressed, but usually the stacatto of "ayes" is interrupted only by statement of the next motion. Whether attended personally or examined by minutes, meetings characteristically are a theater of boring procedural repetition. Not every portion of every meeting can be so described: Newark meetings, as we shall see in the next chapter, are highly charged. But most issues brought to vote are rudimentarily administrative and non-political.

Nevertheless, social, economic, and political interests do manifest themselves in city councils. After twenty issues are perfunctorily decided, a twenty-first may reveal community cleavages. Issues involving substantial financial outlays, changing physical or social configurations within a city often generate controversy. Thus, the wisdom of hiring more police, the creation of a redevelopment agency, construction of multi-family housing or shopping malls, or support of model cities' projects were argued in the communities, sometimes in their councils. Often, however, councilmen presented a united front amidst a community maelstrom. As a primary or peer group, the council promotes agreement among members. People are influenced by peer groups, and some are susceptible to reversing their views of reality.[26] But whatever the extent, the desire to conform helped sustain unanimity in city councils; this was obviously so in councils with records of absolute unanimity. The pressure on councilmen to conform is illustrated in an exchange involving Dennis Westbrooks and Newark's council president, Louis Turco.

In the summer of 1972, Turco introduced a resolution appropriating $159,255.60 in Board of Education funds to provide for a swimming program, the money having been previously authorized by the Board of School Estimate. Councilmen Sharpe James and Earl Harris and a white councilman Ralph A. Villani were absent. Westbrooks, whose record of dissent and imperviousness to council pressure was greater than any other's in this study, stated his opposition. He felt the project should not be the Board of Education's "main priority for the summer," and said he was informed "the Recreation Department can perform the same tasks at a savings of approximately $50,000.00 to the City."[27]

Since six councilmen were present and six votes were required to pass the authorization, if Westbrooks demurred, the resolution would fail. While the official minutes indicate

[26] The influence of primary groups "in defining 'social reality'" is discussed in Herbert McClosky and Harold E. Dahlgren, "Primary Group Influence on Party Loyalty," *American Political Science Review*, 53, no. 3 (September 1959), 757-59. Eulau and Prewitt, *Labyrinths of Democracy*, also note that "social pressures for conformity" in small groups will influence councilmen "to get along" (p. 109).
[27] Minutes of Newark city council meeting, June 28, 1972.

more pressure on Westbrooks than excerpted here, the following provides the flavor:

President Turco urged the Council to provide the six
votes necessary for the passage of this resolution
because the children need the swimming program. He
called attention [to the fact that] the Board of
Education does not meet until the latter part of July,
by the time the matter gets back to the Council it will
be August, and by the time the money is appropriated,
proper facilities established and proper personnel
hired, it will be Labor Day. President Turco asked the
Council not to sacrifice their principles but to consider
these children are not going to get to swim this
summer if the Council does not vote for this
resolution. Councilman James cast an affirmative vote
before the Board of School Estimate and he assumed
Councilman James would cast an affirmative vote if he
were here tonight.

President Turco stated it has been indicated a more
effective program can be initiated next year at
perhaps less cost. He asked in view of the practicality
of the situation that the Council go along with this
request made to supply these funds to the Board of
School Estimate so that the program could get off the
ground.

Councilman Westbrooks reiterated if the full Council
was present this evening he would be spared this
debate. He does not enjoy being in this position
because he would cast a dissenting vote and he does
not feel he should have to support it because the other
Councilmen are not present this evening. He
suggested the Council call an emergency meeting
when the other Councilmen return.

President Turco pleaded with Councilman
Westbrooks to vote in the affirmative on this
resolution to get these pools open.

The motion to adopt the resolution failed of adoption
by the following votes:
Yes: Councilmen Bontempo, Bottone, Giuliano,
        Megaro, President Turco.
No: Councilman Westbrooks.[28]

Thus, it is clear that Westbrooks was uncomfortable, even
though he would not yield. He sought desperately to avoid
the onus, even suggesting another emergency council meeting where he knew he would lose. A less adamant figure
probably would have changed his vote; but the effects of
council pressure even on one so independent were unmistakable.

Finally, the mutual support among councilmen is most
pertinent to the influence of black elected officials on
whites, and ultimately to programs and policies. Council
proceedings superficially reveal that blacks assume the role
of administrator and politician like "any other" elected official. In most municipalities they, like whites, perfunctorily
support issues, most of which have no racial implications.
But they get something in exchange. In city after city the
black elected official not only proposes motions, resolutions,
and ordinances of consequence to blacks, but his proposals
in turn are supported by his entire council. Thus in Trenton
W. Oliver Leggett, Jr., was the single dissenter only twice
throughout 1972. But he scattered across the calendar a
series of resolutions largely relating to blacks, and he was
invariably backed by a unanimous council: the execution
of a contract with the federal government on "open space
funds" for a park in a black area; a grant request to the Department of Health, Education, and Welfare for a lead-
poisoning control program; the participation of Trenton's

28 *Ibid.*

Department of Public Safety in a state program "to upgrade the educational level of personnel within the Police Division"; an ordinance to promote a city rodent and insect control project; an application to the United States Department of Labor for grant-in-aid for the city's Manpower Coordinator Program; authorization for a grant-in-aid program from the New Jersey State Department of Health for sickle cell anemia testing; provision of city funds for "summer special food services programs"; the extension of model cities programs; the expansion of the Community Relations Unit of the Trenton Police Division.[29]

In Orange, Benjamin F. Jones proposed with the commission's backing resolutions toward establishing a manpower planning system; programs for relocation assistance; "Emergency Appropriations of $25,000.00 for Relief of the Poor"; an ordinance to regulate, control, and stabilize rents and create a rent control board, aimed at "slum lords."[30] In Jersey City, William J. Thornton, supported unanimously by the council, moved resolutions on urban renewal; on promoting a public service careers program to "train and provide career mobility for model neighborhood residents in public service careers"; to rebudget and recycle existing city demonstration programs; for a program of "Vest Pocket Parks under the Model Cities Comprehensive Recreation Program."[31] In Hackensack, Howard Gregory proposed with unanimous backing that the city apply for a federal grant for land development, emphatically conforming to "the Civil Rights Act of 1964, and the regulations of the Department of Housing and Urban Development [providing] that no person shall be discriminated against because of race, color, or national origin in the use of the land ac-

[29] Minutes of Trenton city council meetings, February 3, March 16, April 6, June 15, August 29, 1972.
[30] Minutes of Orange board of commissioners meetings, April 4, June 6, July 6, 1972.
[31] Minutes of Jersey City city council meetings, February 1, March 7, June 6, July 6, 1972.

COLLEGE OF THE SEQUOIAS
LIBRARY

quired and/or developed."[32] In Plainfield, Richard L. Rountree entered almost all resolutions dealing with model cities projects, and another black councilman, Merton J. Gilliam, drew unanimous support for creation of a model neighborhood multi-service center, a public dental health program, and a playground project in a black section.[33]

The most penetrating motion pertaining to black interests was introduced by Councilman Vincente K. Tibbs in Englewood. It was approved without dissent. Is it conceivable that this could have been proposed, let alone adopted unanimously, without the energetic influence of a black on the governing body? The motion declared that all bidders for city contracts

propose programs of affirmative action for the employment and employment training of minority group members, and more particularly for black and Spanish-speaking persons with respect to the performance of the contract which proposed programs shall, if the bid is accepted and the contract awarded to the bidder, become a matter of contractual obligation between the City and the bidder. Said program of affirmation shall state specifically the number of persons expected to be employed by the general contractor for the completion of the contract, the number of minority group members whom he intends to employ, the precise manner in which he intends to recruit, select and employ said minority group employees, efforts which will be made by him to employ minority group subcontractors or to require subcontractors to employ as a condition of the subcontract a specified number or percentage of minority group employees.[34]

[32] Minutes of Hackensack city council meeting, March 6, 1972.
[33] Minutes of Plainfield city council meetings throughout 1970 and 1971 in general, and March 5, 1971, in particular.
[34] Minutes of Englewood city council meeting, September 19, 1972.

COLLEGE OF THE SEQUOIAS
LIBRARY

Not every proposal of interest to blacks received their council's support. Benjamin Jones's proposed ordinance for a civilian police review board in Orange was defeated four to one.[35] Richard Rountree and Merton Gilliam, two blacks on the Plainfield council, were the only opponents of a zoning ordinance permitting one-family rather than multi-family housing in a section of the city.[36] As will be discussed later, several issues supported by blacks were resisted by Newark's council majority. But in most municipalities, most of the time, issues of black concern proposed by black councilmen drew unanimous backing from white fellow councilmen.

In sum, the behavior of blacks in office and their priority of issues remain consistent with their political and social philosophies. They recognize their responsibility as elected officials to the entire city, and they act on this recognition. But they are spokesmen for black interests as well. Their emphasis on housing and education compared to white officials' on money and tax relief is a reflection of the needs of the black and white constituencies. Fewer blacks than whites earn enough to worry about tax relief; more blacks than whites suffer from inadequate housing and education.

But officials of both races recognize and act on the spectrum of issues. As democratic politics demands, they accommodate and compromise. They hold to the need for civil peace, and to the belief that the political system can be responsive; and indeed, black officials have effectively promoted programs. Unsolicited, whites rarely initiated action in the interest of blacks. But with blacks among them, white officials are more exposed, more sensitive, and more responsive to the needs of the black community.

[35] Minutes of Orange board of commissioners meeting, January 18, 1972.

[36] Minutes of Plainfield city council meetings, January 18 and February 1, 1972.

VIII

City and Suburb

Except for discussion of electoral determinants (Chapter IV), little has been made of differences between municipalities. Elected officials have been characterized by race irrespective of community disparities. But issues vary from community to community, and officials' responses in one city are not always comparable with those of another. Some communities, however, are more alike, and in this chapter we contrast two categories: city and suburb. The categories, based on population, largely correlate with socioeconomic status, which is higher in the suburbs (see Chapter IV). Moreover, the suburban communities in this study contain substantial black populations. Blacks who seek to rise in status or escape the larger city will likely seek one of these "zones of emergence."[1] The ten suburban communities whose populations are less than one hundred thousand comprise one category, the six "big cities" with populations over one hundred thousand the other.

The six cities share problems that plague urban areas across the country—inadequate housing and education, high welfare and crime rates, limited financial resources. But while the suburban communities also face such difficulties, they are less severe, more tractable. Moreover, the impact of elected blacks on their community's preeminent

---

[1] The term provides the title for a study about Plainfield, New Jersey. George S. Sternlieb and W. Patrick Beaton, *The Zone of Emergence* (New Brunswick, N. J.: Transaction Books, 1972).

issues appears greater in the suburbs than in the big cities. Except for Newark, black influence on the outstanding issues in the cities has been marginal, in the suburbs substantial. This is caused less by qualitative differences among officials than the nature of the issues—their susceptibility to black influence and the responsiveness of the local community to black leadership.

Cities

New Jersey's six largest cities have much in common beside geographic proximity. All have long been industrial centers, Newark, Jersey City, Camden, and Elizabeth being ports. All are old, Paterson founded ,in 1791, the others settled in the seventeenth century. In recent years their social and physical fabrics have deteriorated rapidly. Crime has increased. Housing is deficient. Family income has decreased relative to the state median. (By 1970 only Elizabeth's median family income remained higher than the state's.) Businesses have closed. Middle-class residents have moved. Between 1960 and 1970 minority populations (mostly poor and unskilled) increased while overall populations decreased or remained constant.

Political conditions seemed little better. In the early seventies elected officials in four of the cities had been indicted (Jersey City, Newark, Elizabeth, Camden). The proportion of elected blacks was much lower than that of the black population in each; Elizabeth has yet to elect a black. Nevertheless, there were threads of hope. Federal and state programs, though insufficient, remained focused on the cities. Reform administrations were elected in Jersey City and Newark; Paterson's archaic form of government was about to be changed; and, of concern to this study, most locally elected black officials displayed responsible leadership.

While the cities faced a gamut of problems, one issue or another might flare, dominating local attention. Long-standing issues in Camden, Jersey City, Paterson, and Newark surfaced in the early seventies. In each, black officials participated responsibly, though without particular distinction. We shall summarize the principal issues in the first three cities, stressing the roles of their black elected officials. Then Newark, where black officials are central to policymaking, will be discussed more fully in the perspective of racial polarization.

Camden: Urban Renewal

On August 19, 1970, a coalition of citizens' groups filed a suit in federal court to halt publicly financed construction in Camden. The coalition of civil rights, religious, and community organizations objected to the lack of low-income housing and relocation plans for displaced families. A confrontation with city officials ensued, blocking urban renewal for two years. Elijah Perry, Camden's first black councilman, played an ambiguous but ultimately helpful role in reaching a settlement.

With other elected officials, Perry, now president of the city council, criticized the coalition. Paradoxically, three years earlier he had fathered the idea of a "local coalition" of government agencies, civil rights, business and industrial groups to press for jobs and housing.[2] Business organizations and government agencies (except for the federally funded regional legal services) did not participate; but the coalition otherwise represented a broad section of the community. When the suit was begun in 1970, Perry chastised the coalition for not leaving "the job of rebuilding Camden to its elected leaders, who are certainly more qualified to get the job done."[3]

Neither the coalition nor city officials budged for more than a year, but in early 1972 conciliatory efforts were increased. In May, Joseph P. Keene, a black, was appointed chairman of the housing authority, replacing a man who

[2] *Courier-Post* (Camden), August 25, 1967.
[3] *Ibid.*, August 22, 1970.

had held the position for twenty-five years. Perry welcomed the appointment, saying he and Keene might break the impasse with the coalition. He cited their race as giving them "better rapport," and, in a turnabout, said that he and Keene essentially "sympathized with their [the coalition's] views."[4]

Angelo J. Errichetti, however, the city public works director and Democratic party chairman, assumed the initiative in private negotiations. He drew Perry's backing while some officials like Mayor Joseph M. Nardi, Jr., remained obdurate. Nardi opposed additional public housing, claiming the city needed a middle-income tax base.[5] But a compromise yielding benefits to low-income residents was hammered out.[6] Construction resumed on June 20, 1972, and the coalition's lawsuit was dismissed several months later.

While Errichetti, a white man, was the linchpin of the negotiations, Perry contributed. His earlier moves toward conciliation lent support to Errichetti's efforts. Mayor Nardi remained sullen after the agreement, according to a reporter, but Perry and Errichetti were elated—"they couldn't have smiled harder if they tried."[7]

Jersey City: Reform

For sixty years Jersey City had been dominated by a corrupt political machine. Mayors Frank Hague, John V. Kenny, and Thomas J. Whelan successively controlled local politics without opposition. But in 1971 Mayor Whelan and others in his administration were convicted of extortion. The local Democratic machine was injured, and reform opportunities seemed ripe. Paul T. Jordan, a thirty-one year

---

[4] *Ibid.*, May 6, 1972.   [5] *Ibid.*, June 30, 1972.

[6] Twenty to 30 percent of 1,500 units to be constructed would be for low-income families. The agreement further guaranteed 20 percent minority employment on all construction; and recreational facilities, commercial establishments, and a day care center were added to plans for one of the high rise locations. See *ibid.*, June 30, 1972.

[7] Mark S. Klein, *ibid.*, July 1, 1972.

old public health physician, was supported by a "community action council" pledged to revitalize the city and end corruption. He was elected in November to complete Whelan's term from a field of fifteen candidates—including one belatedly named by the Democratic organization.

Though Jordan had broad community support, only two of Jersey City's councilmen endorsed him, a third running for mayor himself; most supported the organization candidate. One of the two, William J. Thornton, was the only black on the council. While Thornton had an independent following in his ward, supporting a reform candidate in a machine-dominated city carried risks. But Thornton's political prescience as well as social instincts drew him behind Jordan six weeks before the election. Jordan, he declared, could "fuse the many various forces of this city, regardless of color or party affiliation, into a viable, homogeneous working unit with one goal in mind—the revitalization of our city." Thornton continued: "I have every confidence and assurance that Dr. Jordan possesses the wisdom, the vision and the compassion to address himself to the needs of this community and city that have historically cried out for service and priority—be it crime, narcotics, housing, welfare, taxes or general services."[8]

Thornton's admiration was reciprocated. "His reputation and intimate contact with the progressive sentiment of the community," said Jordan, "extend far beyond the confines of his ward. I gladly extend my hand to Bill Thornton and I'm grateful for his confidence."[9]

When the mayor and council ran for full terms in May 1973, Jordan's reform image remained untarnished. State and federal aid to the city had increased, and the pledge to eliminate corruption was being fulfilled. Moreover, Jordan now had a firmer political base, and, with seven of the nine council candidates he endorsed, was elected to a full four-

[8] *The Jersey Journal* (Jersey City), September 16, 1971, p. 1.
[9] *Ibid.*

year term. One of the successful councilmen Jordan backed was William Thornton who, as before, campaigned for reform government and the new mayor. But while Thornton's support was welcomed by Jordan, it was not crucial to his election. A worthy gesture toward reform, Thornton's support nevertheless hardly affected the results.

Paterson: Form of Government

In the previous chapter, Table VII-3 indicated that Paterson is New Jersey's third largest city, yet its legislative body held fewer votes than any other city's. A peculiar decision by the state legislature in 1907 empowered the mayor of Paterson to appoint members to the boards of finance, public works, and fire and police commissions without consent of the elected aldermen. The boards and commissioners became semi-autonomous, and the aldermen were left with little power beyond issuing licenses and enacting antinuisance ordinances.

In July 1972, however, Superior Court Judge John F. Crane upheld a suit brought by the board of aldermen and others challenging the constitutionality of Paterson's form of government. The decision was later upheld by the state Supreme Court. Crane ruled that power must revert to the elected aldermen on January 1, 1973, unless the voters decided by referendum to consider another form.

The board of aldermen could have enacted an ordinance to hold a referendum on charter study, thereby avoiding the need for a public petition to place the question on the ballot. But the proposal was rejected by the aldermen, six to four. The two black aldermen, Odis B. Cobb and Junius Sturdifen, voted with the majority, holding that the board should be given its "rightful authority and responsibility," that a charter revision was unnecessary.[10] Others argued that the citizenry ought to have a fresh opportunity to re-

10 *The Record* (Hackensack), July 25, 1972, p. A-10.

view alternatives. Petitioners obtained the required signatures, however, and a charter commission was elected in November.

The role of the black aldermen was undistinguished. But they were part of the board that unanimously initiated the challenge. While they acted out of self-interest, they nevertheless must be credited with helping to crack an archaic, undemocratic imposition on the citizens of Paterson.

Thus, while the behavior of black elected officials in Camden, Jersey City, and Paterson in their cities' principal issues was respectable, their impact was marginal. We turn now, however, to Newark, where black officials are central to forming public policies.

Newark

Newark, settled in 1666 by Puritan pioneers, was incorporated in 1836. Shortly after incorporation, the first of Newark's large waves of immigrants, the Irish, came to work in industries and on the docks and canals.[11] While blacks had resided in Newark since slave days, by the twentieth century they were but one of several ethnic minorities that comprised most of Newark's population. A 1911 survey showed 11,000 Negroes plus 224,000 "foreigners"—those of foreign parents—in a population of 350,000. The breakdown by nationalities was:

Italians	50,000	Slavs	20,000
Jews	50,000	Others	34,000
Germans	40,000	Negroes	11,000[12]
Irish	30,000		

A surge in black immigration from the South during World War I raised the black population to about 30,000.

[11] Governor's Select Commission on Civil Disorder, State of New Jersey, *Report for Action* (Trenton, N. J., 1968), p. 3.
[12] *Ibid.*, p. 4.

In 1940 blacks comprised 11 percent of Newark's 430,000 residents. By 1950 the black population of 74,965 was 17 percent of the city's total. Newark's leadership had long reflected its ethnic diversity: mayors had been of Irish, Jewish, and Italian background. But not until 1953 when Irvine Turner became councilman from the Central ward was a black elected to office. In 1966, while Kenneth Gibson ran third in a field of six for mayor, Calvin West became councilman-at-large, the first black elected city-wide. Four years later, Newark's black population (though not voters) comprised a majority, 54 percent in a shrunken city population of 380,000. Blacks and Americans of Italian background now dominated local politics.

When Gibson ran successfully for mayor in 1970, three blacks were elected to the city council, all with the endorsement of a black and Puerto Rican political convention. Earl Harris was elected councilman-at-large, Sharpe James and Dennis A. Westbrooks from the South and Central wards. The election at the same time of six Italian-Americans— Michael A. Bontempo, Anthony J. Giuliano, Ralph A. Villani as councilmen-at-large, and Michael P. Bottone, Frank G. Megaro, Louis M. Turco from the West, North, and East wards—symbolized Newark's ethnic cleavage.

The city was a trough of urban despair, labeled by reporters a "crucible of the urban crisis," "the epitome of the urban crisis," "America's Bangladesh."[13] George Sternlieb, a specialist on urban affairs, called Newark "the most accelerated case of the death of the old central city as we know it."[14] Even other big-city mayors attending a national conference joined in special sympathy for Newark, "the composite of all the problems in urban America."[15]

One-fourth of Newark's residents were receiving public assistance. The nation's unemployment rate was 5 percent,

[13] See editorial in *The New York Times*, August 30, 1972, p. 36; Sharon Rosenhause in *The Record* (Hackensack), March 16, 1972, p. A-1; William V. Shannon, *The New York Times*, June 25, 1972, p. 15-E.

[14] *The New York Times*, August 15, 1971, p. 63.

[15] *The Star-Ledger* (Newark), March 24, 1972.

Newark's 14. Rates of infant mortality, new cases of
tuberculosis and venereal disease were higher than in any
other American city. Newark's 1972 property tax of $9.63
for every hundred dollars of assessed valuation was one of
the state's highest.[16]

Public agencies and private groups were not oblivious to
the situation, however. Particularly after Gibson became
mayor, and in part because of his energetic efforts to inform, Newark's plight became well-known. Indeed a sign
or two permitted cautious optimism for the long term. The
opening of Newark's new international airport in 1973 provided jobs and reinforced the city's importance as a transportation hub. A $2.5 billion twenty-year project to build
an elevated city over more than three hundred acres was
introduced soon after.[17] Even short-term indicators occasionally countered the avalanche of unpleasant trends. The
city's crime rate decreased in 1972 by 10 percent, compared
to a 3 percent decrease throughout the country. The property tax rate for 1973-74 was slightly reduced with the help
of revenue-sharing and continued state aid.[18]

But the Newark in the minds of most people was the
Newark of despair, a city of social and political deterioration. Many assumed erroneously, for example, that "voting
on the city council usually breaks down along racial lines,
with the six white councilmen voting against the three
blacks."[19] Cynicism was common: "They even voted that
way [black versus white] on approving a hot-dog stand
ordinance."[20] But while grounds for pessimism are real,

[16] The facts were reported in *The Record* (Hackensack), March 16,
1972, p. A-1, and April 23, 1973, p. A-23; *The New York Times*, June
25, 1972, p. 15-E, and January 28, 1973, p. 61. In early 1975 the nation's unemployment rate reached 9 percent, and Newark's about 25
percent.
[17] *The Record* (Hackensack), August 12, 1973, p. A-7.
[18] *The New York Times*, March 30, 1973, p. 43, and July 8, 1973, p.
34.
[19] Quoted in *The Record* (Hackensack), April 5, 1973, p. A-13.
[20] *Ibid.*

they should not be exaggerated. In fact, as noted earlier, in 1972 all three black councilmen voted separately from the whites less than 2 percent of the time.

This misperception of black-white voting is lamentable, for it unjustly reinforces the belief that blacks and whites in Newark are hopelessly divided. Community and council divisions are substantial without false embellishment. Actually the behavior of Newark's mayor and council, confronted by political necessity, is often conciliatory.

Newark does not face an occasional, prominent issue as do other municipalities; rather, four or five "crises" continually fulminate. They revolve about one constant, race. In 1972 and 1973 several issues surfaced about which blacks and whites polarized. In the course of a council meeting on March 21, 1973, for example, six issues erupted separating whites from blacks.[21]

Two of these, as divisive as any, will be reviewed here: the appointment of Edward L. Kerr as Newark's first black police director, and efforts to construct Kawaida Towers, a black-sponsored housing project in a predominantly white area. They will be discussed in the perspective of the city council's actions. Both issues appeared clear-cut, black versus white in the community, six to three on the council. Yet each revealed more accommodation and compromise on the part of councilmen than is generally recognized.

A BLACK POLICE DIRECTOR

On November 30, 1972, John L. Redden announced that he would resign as police director on January 1 because of heightened racial polarization over the Kawaida

[21] They included refusal of several blacks in the audience to stand for the pledge to the flag; black opposition to construction of the New Jersey College of Medicine and Dentistry until more housing is provided; black opposition to a guidance counselor at Vailsburg High School; effort to recall the three white councilmen-at-large; white opposition to appointment of a black police director; white opposition to construction of Kawaida Towers.

Towers housing project, which is discussed in the following section. Redden, a white, had been named by Mayor Gibson two years earlier and held confidence among both races. A week after the announcement, Dennis Westbrooks, Central ward councilman, urged the appointment of a black police director "who we know will be able to cope with the demands of black people for justice and more effective police protection for all the people in the city of Newark."[22] Gibson rebuked Westbrooks and insisted "I will not deal with the color of the police director, no matter who thinks they are in a position to make demands on the office of mayor."[23]

Two days later, however, Gibson nominated Edward L. Kerr, a black police lieutenant. Gibson maintained he had not "bowed to pressure," that "the decision was made on ability and ability alone."[24] Kerr, who had been on the force for fourteen years, would have to be confirmed by the city council. Council President Louis M. Turco unenthusiastically announced he would interview Kerr. Like other councilmen, he emphasized that "very many qualified white deputy chiefs and inspectors have been passed over by Mr. Gibson today."[25] The nominee would need five votes for confirmation.

On December 20 the council rejected Kerr's appointment. Five of the six whites—Ralph A. Villani was absent—voted against and the three blacks for the appointment. As reported in the press, when the vote was announced the predominantly black audience jumped up chanting "recall, recall, get rid of the racists."[26] Councilmen traded charges of racism. Black members denounced their white colleagues for "always oppressing black people"; whites insisted they

22 *The New York Times*, December 8, 1972, p. 49.
23 *Ibid.*
24 *The Record* (Hackensack), December 10, 1972, p. A-7.
25 *The New York Times*, December 10, 1972, p. 1. Similar remarks were attributed to Councilman Frank Megaro; see *ibid.*, December 11, 1972, p. 43.
26 *Ibid.*, December 22, 1972, p. 35.

had voted on merit, that the black councilmen "never voted for a white man."[27] Emotion generated hyperbole.

After the meeting, Gibson designated Kerr acting director, a post he could hold for ninety days without council approval. Three months later Gibson again urged the council to confirm. He contended that "a fair evaluation of Director Kerr's performance to date would produce a unanimous vote from the council to confirm his appointment."[28] The mayor said that as acting director Kerr had "demonstrated his superior professional administrative ability under extremely difficult conditions." He further appealed to the council to keep issues "from degenerating into black-white situations."[29] At the meeting on March 21, however, Kerr's appointment was again rejected, only the three blacks voting in favor. (Turco, Bottone, and Megaro voted against; the other three whites were absent.)

But by this time some of the white councilmen had softened their views. Those present voted to renew Kerr's term as acting director for ninety days. Turco said that Newark was too polarized to appoint any new police director at the moment. Nevertheless, "I think the best thing to do is to appoint the lieutenant to another temporary position. . . . I'd probably vote for him as permanent director when he comes up for vote next time."[30]

In May, Ralph Villani resigned from the council because of illness, and his wife, Marie L. Villani, was unanimously chosen to succeed him. On June 6, when Kerr's nomination was again considered, Mrs. Villani and Michael Bontempo joined the three blacks to vote for his appointment. The remaining four councilmen abstained. Kerr's appointment appeared settled. Following the vote, however, Dennis Westbrooks assailed the abstaining members, accusing them of reneging on a deal. "If I knew this would happen, I would

27 *Ibid.*; also minutes of the Newark city council meeting, December 20, 1972.
28 *The New York Times*, March 12, 1973, p. 35.
29 *Ibid.*
30 *The Record* (Hackensack), March 22, 1973, p. A-23.

not have supported Mrs. Villani," Westbrooks shouted.[31] He insisted that Turco told him "in order to get Kerr, we've got to get Mrs. Villani in." Turco heatedly replied, "That's a lie . . . that's a lie."[32]

When Westbrooks questioned whether Ralph Villani was really "on his death bed," Mrs. Villani, "visibly shaken" according to a newspaper account, rose, stated "I change my vote," and walked out of the meeting.[33] Shouted exchanges continued among the councilmen as Turco announced that Kerr's appointment would again be reconsidered.

A week later, the council again divided by race on Kerr as the six whites abstained. Earl Harris appealed to the white members to use "good sound judgment" and vote for Kerr, that he had "proved he's capable and has performed well."[34] Mrs. Villani agreed that "common sense" should be used, and she "had done this initially last Wednesday." But, she added, "charges of deals and other alleged commitments cause me to consider this matter further."[35] Westbrooks was silent throughout.

Finally, on July 11, the city council confirmed Kerr's appointment, five in favor, three abstentions. Bontempo and Mrs. Villani joined the three blacks; Giuliano, who was absent, said he would have voted to confirm. Bontempo revealed that "pressure has been put on me" not to support Kerr, but "I am not worried about the political tragedy some predict." Bontempo said Kerr had "proven himself, and I'm voting for what is good for the people and citizens of Newark."[36] Mrs. Villani also stressed that Kerr merited the promotion. Facing Westbrooks she concluded: "As you said, I should not vote for Kerr on your actions. If I did, Director Kerr would not be confirmed today."[37] Thus six

31 *The Star-Ledger* (Newark), June 7, 1973, p. 24.
32 *Ibid.*   33 *Ibid.*
34 *Ibid.*, June 13, 1973, p. 6.
35 *Ibid.*
36 *Ibid.*, July 12, 1973, p. 11; *The New York Times*, July 12, 1973, p. 43.
37 *The Star-Ledger* (Newark), July 12, 1973, p. 11.

months of racial division over the police directorship, what Westbrooks called "racism and deceit" (though of course he was referring only to the white councilmen), ended in accommodation.

Perhaps no "deal" was made as blatantly as Westbrooks alleged, but an understanding of some sort was certainly entered. Oherwise, all three blacks would hardly have supported the wife of a councilman whom blacks were seeking to recall for his "racist" views. In exchange, the white councilmen probably agreed to see Kerr appointed, though not necessarily unanimously; while Westbrooks sought enthusiastic unanimity. But, despite a flurry of confusion, the outcome was a political "trade-off," a blurring of racial division. Bontempo resisted constituency pressures and supported Kerr; Westbrooks checked his constituency's anger (and his own) after Kerr's initial approval was reversed.

Ironically Westbrooks, Kerr's most vocal admirer on the council before confirmation, later became critical. In December 1972 he enthusiastically supported Kerr, for his "experience with him has been truly positive."[38] In July 1973, however, shortly after Kerr's approval, Westbrooks characterized him as part of an "elite 'Negro' bourgeoisie."[39] The turnabout paralleled Imamu Amiri Baraka's. The black nationalist leader, also an earlier supporter, denounced Kerr after confirmation as "ignorant and reactionary . . . frightened that white folks will disapprove of him."[40] At the same time, Anthony Imperiale, Newark's best-known white militant, declared his dissatisfaction. He urged Kerr to resign because he was "not qualified."[41] Meanwhile, Kerr announced his own views on extremism, perhaps with Baraka and Imperiale in mind: "When you speak of law and order, you have to speak also of justice and equality. . . . If you use them together, then the police will have no problem. But the people who preach hate will have problems."[42]

[38] Minutes of the Newark city council meeting, December 20, 1972.
[39] *The New York Times*, July 25, 1973, p. 47.
[40] *Ibid.*   [41] *Ibid.*   [42] *Ibid.*

KAWAIDA TOWERS

By the end of 1972, racial polarization and Kawaida Towers were synonymous terms in Newark. Whites and blacks split over the construction of a housing project sponsored by members of the Temple of Kawaida, a pan-African organization. The high-rise project, barely begun, is in Newark's predominantly white North ward. The issue not only pitted the races, but was accentuated by the reputations of opposing leaders. Imamu Amiri Baraka formed and led the Temple of Kawaida, and though a Kawaida Towers Corporation was created to sponsor the project, the black nationalist remained the project's major protagonist.

Opposition to the project was led by State Assemblyman (and former Newark councilman) Anthony Imperiale. Imperiale headed the militant North Ward Citizens Committee, formed after the 1967 riots as a white "self-defense" group. The two men symbolized racial extremes.

Baraka said he had sought in vain to sponsor housing on urban renewal land but was unable to gain approval from the predominantly white Newark Housing Authority.[43] With the support of Mayor Gibson, the city council on September 15, 1971, adopted a resolution providing for tax abatement for the planned Kawaida project. The city would accept 15 percent of the rents in lieu of taxes.

At a meeting in March 1972 attended by Baraka in Mayor Gibson's office, officials of the state Housing Finance Agency approved an application for a $6.4 million mortgage to run forty-eight years. Two months later the 1.5 acre site in the North ward was purchased for $225,000, and excavation began in September. On October 12, after the foundation had been laid, a formal ground-breaking ceremony was held.

Criticism of the project by local residents, particularly by leaders of the Italian community, erupted after the ceremony. On November 9 a group of demonstrators blocked

43 *Ibid.*, December 5, 1972, p. 51.

workers from the construction site. Thus began a series of confrontations involving workers, citizens, police, the courts, and city and state officials; and the resolution of the problem into 1975 was still uncertain.

Opponents of the sixteen-story, 210-unit apartment building objected to its size and its potential impact on already crowded schools, and expressed fear that the neighborhood would become a slum. But a reporter observed: "The racial issue has become predominant principally because of its discussion at several meetings called by Mr. Imperiale. Speakers such as Deputy Police Chief Dominick Spina have charged that Mr. Baraka espouses 'an alien philosophy' and have compared his writings with those of Adolph Hitler."[44]

Following the first demonstration led by Imperiale in November, black and white antagonism remained high. The cleavage was reflected by a six to three split on the council in favor of rescinding the previous year's resolution to grant tax abatement. The city's corporation attorney advised that the reversal was illegal, a view subsequently upheld by the courts. But the council continued to reflect the city's brittle racial composition. Construction was halted by pickets and by pending court decisions.

The Kawaida Towers issue is certainly not an exemplary statement of public accommodation or black-white comity. But even on this, the most divisive of racial issues, elected officials belied the rigid polarization often ascribed to them. In the first place, Frank Megaro, councilman from the North ward (and also a state assemblyman), led the recision effort in the council. But he was the man who originally introduced the tax abatement resolution in 1971. The issue had appeared three times on the council's agenda before it was finally voted on. But on September 15 the council voted for the resolution eight to zero (Councilman Bontempo was absent). A "mix-and-match" system had been devised to insure black participation along with the expertise of white architects, builders, and planners. Every white was matched

44 Joseph F. Sullivan in *ibid.*, p. 5.

with a black in the same field who would assist and learn.[45]
Moreover, the corporation title originally presented to the
city council included the name "Kawaida," an unmistakable
reference to the pan-African organization; and Imamu
Baraka had been visible throughout the planning and preparation of the project.

Yet only after the ground-breaking ceremony in October
1972 did Megaro and other white councilmen reconsider
their approval, claiming they had not known of the involvement of Baraka or his organization. What the councilmen
knew or did not know has been argued about since. But
Megaro's response appeared to be principally a function of
community resentment and Imperiale's assumption of leadership. Megaro saw his political future as dependent on
whether he could help kill the project.[46] Labeled a moderate by an observer, he was "trying to stop the project,
sensing that the militant stance of Mr. Imperiale has
vaulted him into the role of the ward's leading political figure."[47] Baraka understood the white councilmen's actions
as a response to "community pressure," and believed they
knew what they voted for from the beginning.[48]

Megaro and the other white councilmen can be criticized
for not standing up to community pressure. But community
resentment fanned by Anthony Imperiale would probably
have smothered their opposition anyway. It is no defense
of character to say that the white officials chose the ex-
pedient alternative; but neither does this make them racists.
Indeed, if Baraka was correct and the councilmen knew
what they voted for in 1971, their support of the Kawaida
project was a bold statement against racism—though unsus-
tained in the swamp of community antagonism.

Another smudge on the picture of a neat black-white split
arose from disagreements between Mayor Gibson and the

[45] *The New York Times*, November 13, 1972, p. 41.
[46] *Ibid.*, December 1, 1972, p. 43.
[47] *Ibid.*, December 3, 1972, p. 23.
[48] *Ibid.*

black councilmen. While all were supported by the black
and Puerto Rican political convention in their 1970 campaigns, issues sporadically separated Gibson from the council as a whole and from black councilmen individually.
Kawaida wedged such division. Gibson never wavered in
support of the project: "The sponsors of the project have
fulfilled every legal requirement and I am still firmly resolved that Kawaida Towers should be built."[49] But by
March 1973, as pickets and court hearings frustrated construction efforts, Baraka and his followers voiced impa-
tience with the mayor for not putting "pressure on the court
to move the pickets and demonstrators away from the
site."[50]

Baraka's criticism swelled in the following months. By
August he was calling Gibson a "puppet" of the business
community: "It is a Charlie McCarthy-Edgar Bergen relationship with the Negro's mouth flapping but white racist
words coming out."[51]

Meanwhile, Baraka's harsh stance had been joined by
Councilman Westbrooks who accused the mayor of "forget-
ting about the communities and the masses of blacks that
put [him] where [he is]."[52] Gibson reacted caustically, saying that Westbrooks, who led a march on city hall to protest
inadequate garbage collection, did so simply to "increase
[his] political base."[53] Division among the black officials
had moved from Kawaida to garbage. Westbrooks later
called on the mayor to resign.[54]

Kawaida and its offshoots became instruments for political leverage. Imperiale, Megaro, Gibson, Westbrooks, and
Baraka were thinking of the mayor-council elections in
1974. Demagogy and racism would enter into electoral tac-
tics, but they were not points of division between all blacks
and whites. Some politicians of both races practice dema-

49 *Ibid.*, March 7, 1973, p. 47.   50 *Ibid.*
51 *Ibid.*, August 18, 1973, p. 1.   52 *Ibid.*, July 25, 1973, p. 47.
53 *Ibid.*, August 17, 1973, p. 35.
54 *The Record* (Hackensack), August 20, 1973, p. A-7.

gogy; others demur. While racial division among Newark's elected officials might sharpen under community pressures, officials of both races also demonstrated willingness to lead beyond racial division.

Such leadership is of course more easily exercised in non-polarized communities. Thus in the suburbs, where race relations are less abrasive, relations among elected officials are more harmonious as well.

Suburbs

The ten New Jersey suburbs in this study are more diverse than the six big cities. Though they are not as large, Passaic and Atlantic City share urban and racial problems as severe as those of the inner cities. But most suburbs do not. East Orange, Englewood, Hackensack, Montclair, New Brunswick, Orange, Plainfield, and Teaneck retain a substantial middle class. Moreover, their residents are more optimistic about the future of their communities than the urban residents.

Social and economic trends of the inner suburbs generate concern but not the despair of the cities. As discussed earlier, blacks in suburban communities are more likely to be equitably represented in government. Further, black elected officials appear more influential in the resolution of their municipalities' principal issues than black officials in the larger cities.

After prominent issues and the roles played by black elected officials in Montclair and Teaneck have been summarized, East Orange will be examined more fully. Newark and the other big cities are commonly seen as racially polarized, East Orange and the other suburbs as harmonious. Both characterizations are imperfect. But if East Orange and other integrated suburbs are only the shadows of an ideal, they offer hope. In quest of interracial harmony their black elected officials, and frequently their white, have taken leadership.

Montclair: School Bonds

Montclair's most durable issue has involved its schools. For ten years disagreement over educational philosophy, expenditures, and race sustained a thicket of educational controversy. Voters rejected bond proposals for a junior high school plan in 1964 and a middle school plan in 1966. High costs and the desire to retain neighborhood schools were cited. But the reason least mentioned publicly, yet most controversial, was race. While some schools were racially mixed, several were substantially imbalanced. The plans would have reduced the imbalance.[55]

By 1970, the physical deterioration of two schools as well as social pressures to integrate forced residents to another confrontation. Under directive from the state education commissioner to correct racial imbalance, the Montclair board of education introduced a new middle school plan.

Matthew G. Carter, mayor since 1968 (and the first black to lead any major New Jersey municipality), supported the proposed $9.86 million school bond issue. The money was to provide for physical improvements of the two elementary schools, facilitating their conversion to accommodate all fifth through eighth grade students. Carter introduced the bond ordinance to the five-member town commission in June 1970, and the following month was pivotal in a three to two vote for passage. Now the issue would be placed before the voters in November.

During the campaign Mayor Carter led a steering committee of Citizens for the Bond Issue. The organization was supported by diverse local interests—the Clergy Club, Policemen's Benevolent Association, Chamber of Commerce, Board of Realtors, League of Women Voters, PTAs.

Carter emphasized the need for "improved school facilities," shunning arguments about race or busing. He reminded listeners that "in 1968 when I took the oath of office as mayor, I said that the two most important problems fac-

[55] *Montclair Times*, March 3, 1966, and November 5, 1970.

ing Montclair were housing and our public schools. I said that both of these issues must be resolved if Montclair were to keep pace with today's world and continue as a community with a fine reputation. As 1970 begins drawing itself into a new year, we can see forward motion with regard to housing under our urban renewal plans. I am hopeful that on November 3 we can see the same kind of future for our schools."[56]

The two commissioners who opposed the bond issue spoke exclusively about cost. But other citizens, less discreet, hinted that the plan would generate "massive cross-busing," which was untrue according to supporters of the plan.[57] The principal opposing organization, Citizens to Defeat the Bond Issue, issued statements catering to racial fear. "Social conditions at the [integrated] high school are shocking," said its spokesmen. "Boys and girls are being mistreated every day. . . . Most of the high school students are living in a state of fear and tension."[58]

In November 1970 the voters defeated the school bond, the third such rejection in seven years. How much fear and unreason contributed to the defeat was uncertain. Carter could only say: "Despite the bond issue defeat we must look forward to do what we can."[59] The board of education later suggested alternatives to comply with the state directive to achieve racial balance. But since no bond issues were proposed, the mayor and commissioners were not directly involved. Though Carter had been instrumental in getting the issue before the public, the matter was still unresolved when he left office in May 1972.

Teaneck: Blockbusting

Teaneck has been portrayed as a community idyllic for its black-white relations. A town-wide vote in 1965 supporting school integration through a middle school plan

---

56 *Ibid.*, October 29, 1970.   57 *Ibid.*
58 *Ibid.*, October 22, 1970, p. 4.   59 *Ibid.*

prompted a book titled *Triumph in a White Suburb*.[60]
Though the integration decision encouraged exaggerated
descriptions of Teaneck's social responsiveness, it was more
advanced than that of other communities.

In the early sixties, 8 percent of the township's population
of 42,000 was black. Racial imbalance in the schools was a
reflection of residential patterns: blacks were confined to
one section. Thus, housing issues were entangled in the
school controversy. Blockbusting by real estate agents contributed to "ghettoization."[61] But Teaneck's blacks and
whites were largely well educated, professional, middle
class. As Teaneck was the first predominantly white community to vote for integration, so, consistently, did the
township council in 1966 become the first in New Jersey to
legislate against blockbusting.

A leading advocate of the anti-blockbusting ordinance
was the head of the Fair Housing Committee, a black lawyer named Isaac G. McNatt, who later in 1966 was elected
to the Teaneck council. The ordinance instructed the real
estate agents to notify the municipal clerk where they intended to canvass, that is, to inquire of homeowners if their
houses were for sale. The township's community relations
advisory board would then canvass the neighborhoods tell-
ing homeowners that if they mailed a form to the board the
agents could not visit them.

By the early seventies, with a black population grown
to 15 percent, Teaneck's race relations remained relatively harmonious. Nevertheless, at the end of 1972 simmer-
ing dissatisfaction with weaknesses in the blockbusting
ordinance surfaced. For two years charges of blockbusting
had been brought to the council with increasing frequency.[62] Homeowners were receiving anonymous calls

[60] Reginald G. Damerell, *Triumph in a White Suburb* (New
York: William Morrow and Co., 1968).
[61] Blockbusting is the effort of real estate agents to frighten people
into selling their homes at lower prices by suggesting that the neighborhood's racial, religious, or ethnic character is changing.
[62] *The Record* (Hackensack), November 13, 1972, p. B-2.

asking if they wished to sell. Members of the community relations advisory board discovered rising numbers of realtors canvassing in Teaneck. "The realtors are putting scares into the residents," said one member. "They are saying black people are moving in. The people are afraid if they wait too long they'll lose money."[63]

A committee of local attorneys called Teaneck Together urged a two-year moratorium on canvassing by real estate agents.[64] Meanwhile McNatt, now deputy mayor but still the only black on the council, had proposed an amendment to the 1966 ordinance. Real estate agents would be permitted to canvass no more than ten houses every thirty days, and notice of intention to canvass would be extended beyond the existing ten-day requirement.[65] McNatt, upset, insisted "we have to tighten the present law, otherwise the real estate people will make a mockery of it."[66]

In April the council backed McNatt's amendment. But the following month McNatt introduced stronger restrictions, again supported unanimously by the council. An agent would have to obtain written permission from a homeowner before he could canvass. Moreover, an agent's interest could be expressed only by mail, not by hand delivery.[67]

The restrictions were a compromise between doing nothing and suspending canvassing altogether. Councilman Francis E. Hall supported McNatt's amendment in preference to a complete moratorium because "there are only a few agencies which give us problems. And we need the cooperation of the rest."[68] Real estate spokesmen, however, unhappy with the restrictions, vowed to see them eased.[69]

McNatt's amendment sought a balance of interests, though not at the expense of fundamental aims. As in other

---

[63] *Ibid.*, p. B-1.   [64] *Ibid.*, April 5, 1973, p. A-16.
[65] *Ibid.*, March 13, 1973, p. A-16.   [66] *Ibid.*
[67] *Ibid.*, April 4, 1973, p. C-1, and May 16, 1973.
[68] *Ibid.*, April 5, 1973, p. C-32.   [69] *Ibid.*, June 8, 1973.

municipalities, a black elected official introduced legislation of particular concern to blacks. Short of the demands of some, beyond those of others, McNatt's proposals nevertheless drew general community support, unanimous council support, and sustained the loyalty of black residents.

East Orange

East Orange is categorized as a suburb despite several urban characteristics. Its substantial population (77,000), business community, and high-rise apartment houses are city attributes. But compared to New Jersey's largest municipalities, especially its neighbor Newark, East Orange's suburban qualities are prominent. It has no slums, its black and white residents are distributed throughout town, and the population is essentially middle class. Further, it typifies New Jersey's "zones of emergence" like Plainfield, New Brunswick, Montclair, Teaneck, suburban communities to which blacks have migrated to escape the sorrows of the inner city.

East Orange's black population mushroomed to 53 per cent in 1970, double that of a decade earlier. While many suburbs reveal a greater propensity than cities to elect blacks in proportion to their black populations, East Orange is politically the most precocious. A majority of its elected officials since 1969 have been black, the mayor and five of ten councilmen. Their actions refute those who anticipate that black political control would lead either to nirvana or abomination. It has meant neither. Black concerns are heeded; so are those of whites. East Orange's black elected officials govern with sensitivity to the interests of blacks as well as to those of the entire community. Moreover, neither black nor white officials operate as immutable racial blocs— in reality or in popular perception.

Between 1971 and 1973 two issues successively dominated local attention. The actions of East Orange council-

men revealed little of the racial division or tension familiar
to Newark. Through mid-1972 the council and the community debated the wisdom of constructing a new middle
school for all seventh and eighth grade students. After the
issue was resolved, attention fastened on questions about
tax abatement for proposed high-rise housing projects. Both
issues stimulated town-wide division, yet elected officials
never divided by race.

MIDDLE SCHOOL

In 1967 the East Orange board of education and school
administration proposed plans for an educational plaza, a
single complex of buildings for all students in the system.
The plan's educational and financial soundness were debated during the years following. By 1970 the plan was
pared to create only a new middle school accommodating
1,800 students, about 20 percent of the public school enrollment. The city council officially entered the matter in January 1971 when it passed on first reading an ordinance au-
thorizing $10.3 million in school construction bonds.

Passage was recorded as unanimous, though two white
council members, Vincent Smith and Nancy J. Schron, abstained (council rules hold that in such votes abstentions
are counted with the majority). They expressed dissatisfaction with the limited information available about the ordinance's effect on taxes as well as the plan's educational
validity.[70] Their skepticism was shared by two black councilmen, Alfred E. Brown and Thomas H. Cooke, Jr., who
announced their inclination to vote against it. They joined
the majority for the moment, however, but declared they
would oppose the ordinance at its second reading unless
their doubts were resolved.[71] Other members also supported
the ordinance with reservations. But final passage came the
following month with only Nancy Schron opposed and Vin-

[70] *East Orange Record*, January 21, 1971, pp. 1, 7.
[71] *Ibid.*

cent Smith abstaining. Brown and William C. Holt (another black member) announced they had engaged in probing inquiries and were now satisfied. The uncertainties of other members appeared resolved as well.[72]

Nevertheless, cost and design continued to be debated. The board of education proposed a redesigned structure reducing the cost by $900,000. In September the council voted for an ordinance conforming to the board's new proposal, authorizing a bond issue of $9.4 million, and rescinding the old authorization. Only Schron voted no.

In January 1972 the state Department of Education approved the plan, and building bids were solicited. The land area had been razed, and years of controversy appeared to be ending. But in March, Mayor William S. Hart, Sr., who had been a supporter of the new building, suddenly announced opposition. He urged the board of education to consider an existing office building and forget the proposed new construction. The alternative would be cheaper, he said; and in a stunning reversal of his earlier position Hart announced disagreement with the philosophy behind the proposed school; "there's just too great a change," he said.[73]

Objections to the mayor's proposal came quickly as groups led by the League of Women Voters sponsored a petition drive to save the original project. The president of the board of education, Winfred S. Gideon, said the board would study the mayor's proposal but "the board is unanimously in favor of building the middle school as it has been planned."[74] Representatives of the state Department of Education were invited to evaluate the office building, and reported it would need massive restoration to meet educational standards. By the end of March, Hart retreated: "To renovate the office building would take more time and considerably more money than I had anticipated. It would be just as well to proceed with a brand new building, and I

[72] Ibid., February 12, 1971.   [73] Ibid., March 16, 1972, p. 1.
[74] Ibid., March 23, 1972, p. 1.

support the board's position 100 percent."[75] Again the issue
appeared settled.

Yet a month later a new obstacle emerged at a city council meeting. A proposed appropriation of $200,000 for train-
ing minority residents for employment in the school's
construction was defeated. The appropriation, to be added
to the $9.4 million bond issue, was supported by the four
blacks in attendance, Alfred E. Brown, William C. Holt,
William S. Thomas, and Earl Williams (Harold J. Smith
was absent), plus one white, L. Harold Karns. But six votes
were necessary for passage, and the other four white members, Francis T. Craig, Robert M. Moran, Nancy J. Schron,
and Ben Sweetwood, opposed.

The "affirmative action" proposal was racially sensitive.
Until then the middle school, East Orange's most persistent,
prominent issue during the previous five years, had carried
little racial inference. Blacks and whites, residents and
councilmen positioned themselves on either side, many reversing themselves over the years. Now, however, a program clearly intended to help blacks was thwarted. White
council members who opposed insisted that their reasons
were financial. Said Moran: "The taxpayers of this city are
in revolt and I in conscience can't vote yes for this expenditure." Or Craig: "I'm not against the idea of an affirmative
action program. I'm against the expenditure. The burden
on our taxpayers is getting heavier and heavier."[76] Blacks
responded more in sadness than anger. Holt, hopeful that
the matter would be reconsidered, could "not conceive how
people can rationalize opposing spending $200,000 to train
people. If they objected to the concept of the program, I
might concede the benefit of the doubt." Brown said it was
"a sad commentary when we [even] have to pass a resolution to insure equal opportunity employment. It's incum-

[75] *The Star-Ledger* (Newark), March 30, 1972.
[76] *East Orange Record*, April 27, 1972, p. 1.

bent on the council to provide this opportunity for the residents."[77]

The following month Harold Smith joined the original five supporters for an amendment now expanded to $450,000 to provide for a building modification as well as the affirmative action program. On June 26 a required two-thirds council majority gave final approval to the ordinance. Still objecting to costs, Councilmen Craig, Moran, and Schron voted no; but with Sweetwood absent the remaining six members carried the issue.[78] Ground-breaking took place that week, construction began without incident, and the middle school finally ceased being the community focus. By the end of 1974, construction was virtually complete and the facility in use.

Except for the affirmative action proposal, the middle school issue was free of racial division. Blacks and whites argued both sides of the issue. Even the amendment to provide money to train minority workers did not cleanly divide the council by race. Though Karns was the only white member to vote consistently with the blacks, the other whites' concern about finances must be understood in the context of a municipality with one of the highest tax rates in the state. Moreover, disagreements among council members bore none of the acrimony, none of the racial charges exchanged by Newark councilmen.

THE HOUSING PROJECTS

In March 1972 the East Orange city council passed resolutions pertaining to tax abatement for three proposed low- and moderate-income housing projects. The projects would be built by private corporations and financed by the New Jersey Housing Finance Agency. The votes were unanimous and generated little public discussion. But by the fall councilmen, builders, attorneys, and citizens were arguing over the meaning of the resolutions as well as the wisdom

77 *Ibid.*   78 *Ibid.*, June 29, 1972, p. 1.

of the projects. The housing projects replaced the middle school as the town's principal issue.

At a council meeting in October, contradictory legal opinions were expressed. Some insisted that the original resolutions bound the council to grant tax abatement, others that a commitment would require another vote.[79] The argument raged into November when three councilmen, Schron, Craig, and Moran, sought unsuccessfully to rescind the original resolutions. The city attorney, Julius Fielo, held that a second resolution would have to be passed before tax abatement was granted. But the three challenged this view, basing their challenge on legal interpretations from others.[80]

The argument over the validity of the resolutions became confused with the merits of the projects. Though seven councilmen, including the five blacks, refused to rescind the original resolutions, several qualified their positions. Alfred E. Brown held that "if tax abatement has been issued, we the Council as well as the public have been greatly misled." He implied he might reverse his position if this proved true.[81] A request was made of the state attorney general for clarification.

Nevertheless, citizens and council members continued to polarize, those in favor insisting that the municipality needed more housing, that despite tax abatement the properties would bring money to the city (a percentage of rents in lieu of property taxes). Opponents argued there were too many apartment buildings in the proposed neighborhoods, that population concentration, crime rates, and school overcrowding would worsen. Moreover, they continued, tax abatement for some was unfair while others had to pay a full share.[82] City council chairman Harold Smith, however, doubted that new housing would be built without tax relief. He said East Orange "cannot afford not to have tax abate-

[79] *Ibid.*, October 26, 1972, p. 1.
[80] *Ibid.*, November 16, 1972, p. 1.
[81] *Ibid.*, October 26, 1972, p. 1.
[82] *Ibid.*, November 16, 1972, p. 1.

ments. We must provide adequate housing for our citizens and we need more ratables in the city."[83]

Pressure to air the issue increased and a public hearing was announced for December 13. Before the meeting council members, black and white, admitted to confusion and uncertainty.[84] The local newspaper, sensing a climax, called the tax abatement issue "perhaps the most crucial one that Councilmen will be asked to vote on this year."[85]

The public hearing was attended by six hundred residents, freely cheering and booing. The hearing provided no new information, but the councilmen's positions hardened. Schron, Craig, and Moran adamantly opposed abatement, while the others supported it. By early 1973 the issue appeared settled in favor of the projects; but by then federal mortgage money had become so scarce that construction was postponed indefinitely.

Land for the intended projects was in largely white neighborhoods, and the year's debates were sometimes tinged with racial innuendo. Mayor Hart, who favored the housing, traded charges with Chester K. Ligham, the Republican municipal chairman. Ligham denied an inference by Hart that some of the opposition might be racially motivated. He attacked with invective: "The mayor seems to encourage the present mass exodus of white and black homeowners from East Orange so that East Orange and Newark can become a power base for him and Baraka's black nationalism philosophy and politics."[86] Hart accused Ligham of "starting his mayoral campaign already. . . . The whole thing is emotional and very racial." He continued, however, "I don't play on racism because it simply is not an issue here in East Orange. I have never used the racial issue in a political campaign."[87]

[83] *Ibid.*, p. 16.

[84] See comments by Councilmen Thomas, Moran, and Schron in *ibid.*, December 7, 1972, pp. 1, 5.

[85] *East Orange Record*, December 7, 1972, editorial, p. 4.

[86] *Ibid.*, December 14, 1972, p. 1.

[87] *Ibid.*, pp. 1, 16.

While Hart underestimated the element of racism in East Orange, it was not preeminent among the city's major issues. At the public hearing on the housing projects, blacks and whites took positions on both sides. While the council division ultimately found all blacks in favor, they were firmly allied with two whites. Moreover, though some black councilmen may have committed themselves before the public hearing, at least two, Brown and Thomas, were skeptical until the hearing.

Although the East Orange housing projects bore similarities to Newark's Kawaida Towers, the contrast in community and council response was striking. In Newark questions about the merits of the project shrank before questions about race, in East Orange the reverse.

Optimism-Pessimism

Views by urban and suburban residents about the future of their communities conform to expectations. Responses to the question "How do you feel about the future of your city in the next several years—does it look good or bad?" are tabulated in Table VIII-1: A. The figures are delineated by race under three categories: Newark, the other five big cities, and the suburbs (the ten municipalities with populations under 100,000). Responses of Newark's residents and those of the other big cities are almost identical. But sharp contrasts occur between cities and suburbs. Between 60 and 70 percent of the big cities' residents, black and white, are pessimistic about their municipality's future, but less than half the suburbanites are. The tendency of suburban residents to be more optimistic holds for both races, though especially for blacks. This is contrary to the urban pattern, in which blacks are less optimistic about their city's future than whites. Optimism among blacks in the suburbs and pessimism in the cities, in both cases more exaggerated than whites', accords with "zone-of-emergence" expectations. Those still in the big cities despair most about their city's

TABLE VIII-1: Responses to the Question: How Do You Feel about the Future of Your City in the Next Several Years—Does It Look Good or Bad?

	Newark %	Other Big Cities %	Suburbs[a] %
A: Residents			
Whites			
Optimistic	33	30	46
Pessimistic	63	60	49
Don't know, no opinion, etc.	5	10	5
Total	101 (86)	100 (200)	100 (125)
Blacks			
Optimistic	22	20	53
Pessimistic	69	70	39
Don't know, no opinion, etc.	9	10	8
Total	100 (64)	100 (40)	100 (36)
B: Officials			
Whites			
Optimistic	67	81	75
Pessimistic	17	19	21
Don't know, no opinion, etc.	17	0	4
Total	101 (6)	100 (42)	100 (48)
Blacks			
Optimistic	100	100	90
Pessimistic	0	0	5
Don't know, no opinion, etc.	0	0	5
Total	100 (4)	100 (7)	100 (20)

[a] The big cities are those with populations over 100,000, the suburbs the rest.

future. But those who "rose" to the suburbs anticipated a good future for themselves and, implicitly, for the community to which they moved, this being their reason for moving.

When elected officials were asked about their city's future, optimism abounded in every category (Table VIII-1: B). A few officials admitted they felt obliged as municipal leaders to be optimistic. Yet in discussing reasons most appeared sincere. Statements by a few of the white pessimists were bleak: "Of course a miracle can happen, but I see the cities, particularly in the Northeast, as becoming reservations for blacks. The planning and the way we're going leaves no alternative but for whites to keep fleeing the cities, the same for moderate-income blacks. I think this city is going to be a black welfare reservation."

Most white officials, however, were optimistic. Those in larger municipalities tended to emphasize their city's functional uniqueness—geographic, industrial, governmental (state or county capital). Said one: "I don't think a city like Newark could completely go down the drain because of the facilities at its disposal. You've got one of the greatest seaports, the biggest airport—it's the hub of finance and banking throughout the state." From another: "I am most optimistic about the future of Elizabeth. It is an ideal location; it has all the facilities necessary for success. It has water facilities being developed by the Port of New York Authority, a good system of highways, good schools. I'm certain the future is good." From a third: "I'm optimistic about this city for two reasons. We have several thousand acres of undeveloped land around our water front which is a resource that other cities don't have. Secondly, our geography— we're right across the river from the financial capital of the world and we can do things here that maybe others could not."

White officials in the suburbs were far more "people-oriented" in describing their optimism or pessimism. Their community's social composition, rather than its location or industry, was the principal determinant. A pessimist worried that "a lot of white families are moving out and are being replaced by blacks, and I just feel they don't have the same feeling of responsibility to the community that the whites have had over the years." But an optimist said: "We have such a diverse population that it's fascinating. If you give a party and invite fifty people, you'll have fifty different interests and enthusiasms. If this kind of mixture can continue, this is going to be a fantastic place to live." Optimism by white suburban officials was usually qualified, however. Typically:

> I suppose I would say that I am optimistic, but with
> reservations. This is a changing town. We have an
> annual population turnover of roughly 10 percent.
> While houses are selling well, we are now getting
> buyers of a different group than have lived here in the
> past . . . and it may be we have less grounds for
> optimism than I basically feel.
>   • • •
> I think you can see around our city a gradual
> improvement in relations with various citizens. I think
> we're winning the battle on crime and the drug
> problem. . . , beginning to see the other person's side
> and not be adamant in our own opinions.
>   • • •
> I think it would be a shame if we can't solve our
> problems and learn to all live together. We have a
> good mixture here of working and living together. If
> we can't do it in Plainfield, you certainly are not going
> to do it in the big cities like Jersey City, Newark,
> Camden. If they go down the drain, what do you have
> left?

Black officials, virtually all optimistic, also tended to divide by municipal categories. Like whites, some in large cities reiterated confidence in local facilities: "We're in the center of a megalopolis from Boston on down. We have a tremendous waterway, railroads. We have everything here to make a city grow, and we're making it grow." Others held ill-defined convictions that the nation would not let big-city conditions worsen: "I'm optimistic because I'm optimistic about the future of this country. I view the cities much like I view the vital organs of the body. The state and nation cannot survive unless the heart and lungs all function. If Newark, which I consider the heart of New Jersey, doesn't survive, neither does New Jersey. If New Jersey doesn't survive, neither does the country. I have to be optimistic—if we can go to the moon and bring back rocks to study, we can certainly deal with the problems of Newark."

In the suburbs black officials, like white, based their optimism on social composition. But their optimism was less diluted:

I'm optimistic. I must say that the town is undergoing change, social change. But I would say a good change has been taking place in people, and you know we can make all kinds of material accomplishments and progress, but unless you have change in people's minds and attitudes, you're not getting anywhere. And I've seen that happen—people are changing for the better. I think I've made a contribution to that.

. . .

We haven't had problems as have other cities of our size and lesser sizes in terms of the black-white situation. Of course we have our problems, but we do have a dialogue with the white community—and I think this is one of the reasons. This is one of the reasons we haven't had too many problems, and why I'm optimistic. As long as there is communication, there is opportunity to advance.

. . .

I am optimistic. Some of the white people I talk with purposely selected [city] for their home because they

want their children to have an integrated kind of life.
. . . Also I am optimistic because the mayor and
governing body last year chose to have citizens
participate even before the budget was presented to
the council. Citizens had three weeks to interview
department heads, to make suggestions. And in many
instances their suggestions were taken. . . . I think that
when you get to a place where the governing bodies
are willing to listen to citizens, that's important, and
I'm not pessimistic at all.

    • • •

I'm first of all very optimistic because of the type of
people we have in [city]. It's a very active community
and the people are happy. I won't say there's a
closeness in a sense like going next door to borrow a
cup of sugar. But just about everyone in this
community is aware of what the problems are and
what is happening. There's no hostility shown, but the
people are not afraid to speak their minds. As they
come out to meetings, talk about the problems, they
become more and more involved. And that kind of
involvement is the thing that will end up making the
government work.

    Thus, while officials of both races in all municipalities are
optimistic, their suburban constituents are less so, and city
dwellers least of all. It is sobering that pessimism among
residents of integrated suburbs is substantial, in the case of
whites slightly exceeding optimism. The inner suburbs contend with racial antagonism, increased crime, shrinking
white middle-class population, and disproportionate black
enrollment in the public schools. In a word, problems familiar to the inner city have crept into the inner suburb.
    Yet while trends foster unease, they have not bred the
pessimism that permeates Newark and other large cities.
Blacks who come to the suburbs want better lives than they
had in the cities. They move among whites who are more

likely to be tolerant. White "hard-core" racists fled when
the black influx began; black racists don't come in the first
place. For a period the best of both predominates. But
while the inner city rightfully commands national attention,
the inner suburb wrongfully is forgotten. And this is a little-
noted misfortune. For as a councilman asked, if East
Orange, Plainfield, Montclair, Englewood, Teaneck cannot
remain models of black-white amicability, what can?

Even if attitudes within a community are positive, this
does not insure continued integration.[88] New white families
as well as black must fill vacancies in normal turnover. But
as Anthony Downs points out, whites who otherwise wish
to live in an integrated neighborhood are reluctant to move
to an area they think will become "heavily dominated" by
blacks.[89] Yet if residential opportunities for blacks are limited to a few suburbs, pressure on these communities becomes enormous. However positive the attitudes of residents, or enlightened their political leaders, community
efforts to maintain racial balance remain threatened.

The increase of blacks between 1960 and 1970 in the
municipalities of this study varied considerably. East
Orange's black proportion rose from 25 to 53 percent,
Montclair's only from 24 to 27 percent. A sense of stability,
of continued biracial community, is obviously greater in
Montclair than in East Orange. Yet even in Montclair per-
manence is uncertain. For in Montclair, as in Englewood
or Teaneck, despite their relative biracial stability, the
white proportion has gradually become smaller.

These communities are fragile crucibles of human relations; if they crumble, the loss will be greater than the municipalities'. Confidence that multi-racial communities can
thrive in this country would shrivel. Yet inordinate pressure
on cities and inner suburbs continues, and local govern-

[88] Harvey Luskin Molotch, *Managed Integration* (Berkeley, Calif.:
University of California Press, 1972), esp. chap. 10.

[89] Anthony Downs, *Urban Problems and Prospects* (Chicago: Markham Publishing Co., 1970), p. 36.

ments cannot alone stem the deterioration. Only institutional changes that equitably distribute burdens and benefits throughout the population can bring long-term relief.

Proposals to maintain balance have included creating resources attractive to whites (like a college or research park), government subsidies to biracial communities, or residential quotas.[90] But the simplest and fairest, the most democratic approach is to ensure that no municipality exempts itself from sharing responsibilities with its suburban neighbors. Dispersing responsibility among many communities relieves pressure on the few; and to this we turn in the next chapter.

Whether integration can work is not in question. Several communities in this study demonstrate that it can. But how long racial balance can be sustained may depend more on regional or state mandates than local attitudes.

[90] *Ibid.*, p. 37; Molotch, *Managed Integration*, p. 207; Herbert J. Gans, "The White Exodus to Suburbia Steps Up," in Thomas R. Dye and Brett W. Hawkins, eds., *Politics in the Metropolis*, 2nd ed. (Columbus, Ohio: Charles E. Merrill Publishing Co., 1971), p. 159.

Busing and Zoning

The backgrounds, perceptions, and behavior of elected officials have been traced, but a comment about the future
remains to be made. This chapter is organized around my
own inclination, one that is shared by virtually all the officials interviewed (though one expressly did not)—that we
should move toward an integrated society. It rests in the
belief that a nation of "two societies, one black, one white—
separate and unequal" suffers a moral blight; that separation fosters fear and bigotry, integration trust and social
enrichment.[1]

Two determinants of the social composition of a community, housing and education, are largely controlled by municipalities. Mayors and councilmen share powers in these
areas with other local officials—those on boards of education and zoning and planning commissions. But beyond authority to legislate, elected officials exert moral, social, and
political influence on a community. When they take a position, especially on controversial issues, they set not only
policy, but a tone, an atmosphere that can be critical to community sentiment. In studies of two communities facing
school integration, for example, differences in successes
were laid to the difference in local leadership. In Teaneck,
New Jersey, decisive support by a board of education and
city officials was central to gathering community support

[1] The quotation is from the *Report of the National Advisory
Commission on Civil Disorders* (New York: Bantam Books, 1968), p. 1.

for town-wide integration.² But in Richmond, California, early indecision by the school board "encouraged the opposition and facilitated its mobilization. By the time they did take the step, it was too late." Opponents of integration were elected to the board and the plan rescinded.³

Critical questions about education and housing emerge in debates over busing and zoning. As determinants of school and residential patterns, busing and zoning aroused little controversy for decades. Recently, however, they have become foci of arguments and distortions. Not only are they fundamental to retarding or promoting social integration, but they are also issues over which local officials wield more power than those at any other level of government. The views of local officials, accordingly, are of paramount importance.

Busing

In the early seventies busing as a means of desegregating schools became a national issue. The issue evolved in three stages. The first began after the 1954 *Brown* v. *Board of Education of Topeka* decision by the Supreme Court that "separate educational facilities [for black and white students] are inherently unequal." Local resistance left segregation patterns relatively unchanged until the mid-sixties. Then a spate of court orders invalidating segregation laws rapidly altered southern patterns, and by 1970 only 14 percent of black students in eleven southern states attended all-black schools.⁴

Racial isolation in the northern and western states continued, however. But court authority to order busing in cities outside the South was confirmed by a 1971 Supreme

² Reginald G. Damerell, *Triumph in a White Suburb* (New York: William Morrow and Co., 1968), pp. 348-51.

³ Lillian B. Rubin, *Busing and Backlash* (Berkeley, Calif.: University of California Press, 1972), p. 203.

⁴ *Education for a Nation* (Washington, D.C.: Congressional Quarterly, Inc., 1972), p. 33.

Court decision that "desegregation plans cannot be limited to the walk-in school."[5]

Communities began to comply with court orders, but at the end of 1971 the Nixon administration postured against "forced busing."[6] Thus the administration and the courts began to contradict each other. Federal court decisions provided for busing to achieve racial balance, in two cases—in Richmond, Virginia, and Detroit—across city and suburban lines. In May 1973, however, the Richmond plan was effectively invalidated by the Supreme Court. The vote was four to four (Justice Lewis F. Powell, Jr., disqualified himself), and the decision by the fourth circuit court of appeals to overrule the federal court was thereby upheld. But because of the tie, precedent was not established. The Detroit plan, on the other hand, was upheld by the sixth circuit court of appeals, but in July 1974 the Supreme Court held five to four that the lower courts had erred.

Chief Justice Warren E. Burger wrote for the majority that the suburban districts had not themselves discriminated and their borders with Detroit should not have to be crossed. He affirmed that racial segregation in schools should be eliminated, but that Detroit would have to solve its problems within its borders.[7] Detroit's student population, however, was 70 percent black, and the decision seemed incongruous with the majority's reaffirmed dedication to integration. Opinions of the four dissenting justices were bitter. William O. Douglas argued that the ruling would create black schools that were not only separate but inferior.[8] Thurgood Marshall, who before his appointment to the Court had argued the 1954 *Brown* case for the NAACP Legal Defense and Educational Fund, said the

[5] *Swann* v. *Charlotte-Mecklenburg Board of Education*, quoted in *Education for a Nation*, p. 32.

[6] The political effect was noted in Chapter I. Nixon's opposition to busing for integration was joined by his successor, Gerald R. Ford, in the early months of his administration.

[7] *The New York Times*, July 26, 1974, pp. 1, 17.

[8] *Ibid.*

majority ignored "the neutral principles of law," and catered to "a perceived public mood."[9]

Nathaniel R. Jones, general counsel for the NAACP, remained optimistic though he was disappointed. The Court, he emphasized, ruled for the first time that district boundaries *can* be crossed, that is, when practices of one district produce segregation in another. Further, the decision affirmed standards by which discrimination could be gauged. These included actions by local boards and administrators involving optional attendance zones, school construction in areas of racial concentration (white or black), and school transportation policies. Jones said the NAACP would return to the courts, and he believed the four dissenting opinions in the Detroit case were "so powerful that they inevitably will be vindicated."[10]

Meanwhile, for a decade New Jersey actively confronted the problems of racial segregation. The New Jersey Supreme Court in 1965 ruled that the state Commissioner of Education must enforce a requirement of the state constitution outlawing segregation by race in the public schools. In *Booker* v. *Plainfield* the Court said:

> In a society such as ours, it is not enough that the
> three R's are being taught properly, for there are
> other vital considerations. The children must learn to
> respect and live with one another in multi-racial and
> multi-cultural communities, and the earlier they do so
> the better. It is during their formative school years
> that firm foundations may be laid for good citizenship
> and broad participation in the mainstream of affairs.
> Recognizing this, leading educators stress the
> democratic and educational advantages of
> heterogeneous student populations, particularly

9 *Ibid.*

10 Interview, August 9, 1974. For a more comprehensive analysis of the prospects for school desegregation see Gary Orfield, "Federal Policy, Local Power, and Metropolitan Segregation," *Political Science Quarterly*, 89, no. 4 (Winter 1974-75), 777-802.

when they are composed of a racial minority whose
separation generates feelings of inferiority. . . .

When the sufficiency of the local choice is brought
before him [the state Commissioner of Education],
he must affirmatively determine whether reasonably
feasible steps toward desegregation are being taken in
proper fulfillment of state policy; if not, he may
remand the matter to the local board for further
action or may prescribe a plan of his own.[11]

In 1969 the state Board of Education directed the commissioner to determine which school districts contained racially imbalanced schools, and to "undertake such steps as
he shall deem necessary to correct such conditions."[12] The
commissioner identified eighty-eight such districts, direct-
ing them to submit plans to eliminate the imbalance. Guidelines for correction included altering school attendance
zones, pairing of schools, grade level reorganization, and
voluntary exchange between districts. He determined that
busing in almost all the communities would be minimal or
unnecessary.[13]

Recognizing that some districts contained substantial majorities of black students, the state Supreme Court informed
the commissioner in 1971 of his right to regionalize to maintain racial balance. In *Jenkins* v. *Morris Township*, the
court found that the commissioner held "many broad super-
visory powers designed to enable him, with the approval of

[11] *Booker* v. *the Board of Education of Plainfield*, 48 N.J. 161 (1965).
Article I, paragraph 5, of the New Jersey Constitution says: "No person shall be . . . segregated . . . in the public schools, because of
religious principles, race, color, ancestry or national origin."

[12] State of New Jersey, Department of Education, *Resolution by
the State Board of Education* (Trenton, November 5, 1969).

[13] State of New Jersey, Department of Education, *School Desegregation in New Jersey*, prepared by Commissioner of Education Carl L.
Marburger and his Special Assistant, Clyde E. Leib, mimeo., March
1971, p. 5.

the state Board of Education, to take necessary and appropriate steps for fulfillment of the state's educational and desegregation policies in the public schools." Among his powers was the right to "direct a merger on his own as he finds such course ultimately necessary for fulfillment of the state's educational and desegregation policies."[14] Subsequently the commissioner ordered a merger of Morristown and Morris Township schools, and received petitions from two other districts, New Brunswick seeking regionalization with North Brunswick, Plainfield with North Plainfield.

Thus by 1972 court rulings, policies of the state Board of Education, and actions of the state commissioner appeared to have firmly committed New Jersey to desegregation. Indeed in December 1972 the state board reported that half of the eighty-eight racially imbalanced school districts identified in 1969 had implemented acceptable desegregation plans; the remainder were in the process.[15]

But November 1972 marked a setback. The state senate rejected Governor William Cahill's renomination of Carl L. Marburger to a second five-year term as Commissioner of Education. The commissioner's position on desegregation was central to his defeat. After his appointment in 1967 he promised "to move on the nagging problem of racial imbalance and segregation in our public schools."[16] But his subsequent actions were carried out strictly under court or state Board of Education directives. Before the senate vote, the vice-president of the state board deplored reports about Marburger that tended to "distort and confuse"—to attribute to him statements never made, actions never taken.[17]

After the senate's nineteen to nineteen vote denying Mar-

14 *Jenkins et al.* v. *Township of Morris School District et al.*, 58 N. J. 1 (1971).
15 State of New Jersey, Department of Education, *Statement of the State Board of Education* (Trenton, December 6, 1972).
16 *The Record* (Hackensack), November 15, 1972, p. A-18.
17 Letter from Katharine L. Auchincloss to *ibid.*, November 16, 1972, p. A-23.

burger's reappointment, the president of the state Board of
Education, Calvin J. Hurd, issued a statement for the board,
denouncing "the reasons expressed by some legislators who
were opposed to him." They "falsely attributed" to the commissioner responsibility for actions to achieve balance "directed by the State Board [and] ordered by the Supreme
Court of New Jersey," and contrary to fact said he endorsed
"large-scale busing."[18]

Marburger left office in March 1973 with several decisions on regionalization pending. New Jersey's commitment
to racially balanced schools became uncertain, enmeshed
in the national confusion.

As detailed by the United States Commission on Civil
Rights, the gap between fact and myth about school busing
is enormous.[19] The principal distortions in New Jersey and
the nation are about neighborhood schools, cost, safety, and
popular opposition.

NEIGHBORHOOD SCHOOLS

By 1919 tax revenues were used in all states to trans-
port children to schools. Fifty years later 43 percent of the
nation's public school students were being bused.[20] Thus
school busing has been long-standing and uncontentious. In
New Jersey over a third of 1.5 million public school stu-

[18] State of New Jersey, Department of Education, State Board of
Education, *Statement by Calvin J. Hurd, President of the State Board
of Education, Affirmed by the State Board of Education* (Trenton,
December 6, 1972).

[19] See esp. The United States Commission on Civil Rights, *Your
Child and Busing* (Washington, D.C.: Clearinghouse Publication No.
36, May 1972). Other Commission publications with reference to
busing include *Understanding School Desegregation* (Washington, D.C.:
Clearinghouse Publication No. 28, 1971); *School Desegregation in
Ten Communities, a Report of the United States Commission on
Civil Rights*, June 1973; *Public Knowledge and Busing Opposition:
an Interpretation of a New National Survey* (Washington, D.C.:
Office of Information and Publications, The United States Commission on Civil Rights, March 11, 1973).

[20] *Education for a Nation*, p. 32.

dents were bused during 1972. Moreover, in the nation as a whole less than 3 percent of school busing was for desegregation, in New Jersey less than one percent.[21] Passion for "neighborhood schools" is only as new as busing for desegregation. Public school transportation is traditional in New Jersey as in the nation.

COST

The cost of busing has remained between 3 and 4 percent of total educational expenditures for forty years across the nation.[22] In New Jersey the pupil transportation system costs more than $72 million a year. The cost to the state of busing for desegregation is about $260,000, to the municipalities somewhat more. But as a report from the state commissioner's office indicates: "In many instances, school districts had previously been busing students as part of the normal administrative process. As students were assigned to different schools, they continued to be transported by bus. Thus, there is no way of ascertaining whether such busing would not have been necessary under prior circumstances."[23] Nevertheless, the cost of busing relative to total educational expenses has remained about the same. Busing for desegregation has had little impact.

SAFETY

According to the Metropolitan Applied Research Center, "transportation by school bus is the safest means of transportation in the nation."[24] The National Safety Council reports that accident rates for students walking to school are more than three times that for students riding a bus.[25]

[21] Statement by Calvin J. Hurd, president of the state Board of Education, in *The New York Times*, March 5, 1973, p. 33.

[22] *Education for a Nation*, p. 32.

[23] *School Desegregation in New Jersey*, pp. 8-9.

[24] "Fact Book on Pupil Transportation," MARC Document no. 2, reprinted in *School Board Notes*, New Jersey, August 31, 1972.

[25] *Your Child and Busing*, p. 13; *The Facts about Busing* (Washington, D.C.: The National Urban League, 1972), p. 4.

POPULAR OPPOSITION

Paradoxically, studies show people supporting integration, yet opposing busing. Opposition to busing, however, is often grounded in myth, and surveys have generally not inquired about attitudes in depth. The United States Commission on Civil Rights, dismayed by "contradictions in the existing data and the defects of the previous questions," engaged in the most comprehensive survey analysis yet undertaken. The results of 2,006 interviews conducted in November and December 1972 by the Opinion Research Corporation are reported in *Public Knowledge and Busing Opposition.*[26] Only 22 percent of the respondents opposed integration as a national objective, but 70 percent opposed busing.[27] Yet in-depth questioning revealed that "busing opposition turned out to be less overwhelming and less implacable than earlier polls had reported. More than a fifth of those generally opposed to busing, for example, support changing the routes of existing school buses to increase integration." Moreover, "when those who were opposed to busing were asked a further question—whether they would support busing as a 'last resort' if 'other ways of overcoming unlawful segregation could not be found or didn't work'— an additional 7 percent were ready to support busing. *Thus, when one asks about a limited scale of busing where there was no other alternative to segregated education, the public is supportive by a narrow margin.*"[28]

The national survey, according to the Commission, produced "three basic findings": "The public seriously misunderstands the facts of the busing controversy; those who best understand the facts are more supportive of busing and much more opposed to Congressional action or a Constitutional amendment to forbid court-ordered busing; most

[26] *Public Knowledge and Busing Opposition: an Interpretation of a New National Survey.*
[27] *Ibid.,* p. 2.
[28] *Ibid.,* p. 13 (italics in original).

people expressing an opinion are willing to support strictly limited busing when there is no other way to desegregate the schools."[29]

Attitudes toward busing in New Jersey

Residents in the sixteen New Jersey communities in this study were asked if they thought busing of children a proper means to integrate schools. Responses, like those in the national survey to a similar question, were negative. Presumably, New Jersey respondents parallel the nation's in agreeing that busing becomes acceptable when alternative means to desegregate are absent. Moreover, our data reveal that white residents in communities that have experienced busing for desegregation are more receptive to busing than whites in communities that have not.[30]

Table IX-1 shows that about a quarter of black and white respondents in municipalities that bus think busing proper (though the sample of blacks is very small). Whites in non-busing municipalities support busing the least, their black counterparts the most. Doubtless the high proportion of black support in non-busing communities relates to the fact that New Jersey's six largest cities are among the eleven non-busing municipalities. Blacks in these cities are less well off socioeconomically, attend overwhelmingly black

29 *Ibid.*, p. 3.

30 Many citizens in busing communities reported satisfaction with desegregation arrangements in their own communities, yet opposed busing as a general proposition. The United States Civil Rights Commission Report on *School Desegregation in Ten Communities*, p. 10, concluded that: "Most parents interviewed by Commission staff are satisfied with desegregation as it affects their own children. The bus ride that their children take causes them no concern and they approve of the educational program offered since desegregation. Yet many of these same people, on local and State referenda concerning busing for school desegregation, vote overwhelmingly in the negative. So powerful is the rhetoric concerning busing that it has blinded them to the reality of their own experience."

TABLE IX-1: Residents' Views on whether "Busing of Children Is a Proper Means to Integrate Schools"—by Municipalities with Busing for Desegregation and Those without[a]

| | Busing Municipalities | | Non-busing Municipalities | |
| | Whites | Blacks | Whites | Blacks |
	%	%	%	%
Strongly agree	5	6	3	4
Agree	22	18	16	41
Disagree	27	53	50	40
Strongly disagree	36	23	24	7
Don't know, no opinion, etc.	9	0	8	9
Total	99 (55)	100 (17)	101 (356)	101 (123)

[a] Busing municipalities included Englewood, Montclair, New Brunswick, Plainfield, and Teaneck. All had instituted desegregation plans involving busing, though in most cases minimally.

schools, and believe a racially balanced system would provide them with better education.[31] Impressive, however, is the tendency of whites who have experienced busing to be somewhat more supportive than whites who have not.

One of the conclusions in a Civil Rights Commission analysis of *School Desegregation in Ten Communities* was "the way in which school officials, civic leaders, and the news media respond . . . can serve either to preserve an atmosphere of calm or heighten tensions."[32] Thus, while local boards of education and school administrators set desegregation policies, mayors, councilmen, and commissioners contribute to community receptivity—they are "opinion-leaders." Table IX-2 indicates substantial support of busing

[31] They are correct. Black academic performance in desegregated schools improves; white performance improves or remains the same. Critical literature is summarized in *Public Knowledge and Busing Opposition*, Appendix 5, pp. 8-9.
[32] *School Desegregation in Ten Communities*, p. 9.

TABLE IX-2: OFFICIALS' VIEWS ON WHETHER "BUSING OF
CHILDREN IS A PROPER MEANS TO INTEGRATE SCHOOLS"—BY
MUNICIPALITIES WITH BUSING FOR DESEGREGATION AND THOSE
WITHOUT

	Busing Municipalities		Non-busing Municipalities	
	Whites	Blacks	Whites	Blacks
	%	%	%	%
Strongly agree	0	0	3	14
Agree	63	100	10	50
Disagree	13	0	37	23
Strongly disagree	17	0	37	14
Don't know, no opinion, etc.	8	0	13	0
Total	101 (24)	100 (9)	100 (72)	101 (22)

by elected officials in busing municipalities. Sixty-three percent of the white and all the black officials think busing
proper. But in communities without busing for desegregation, only 13 percent of white and 64 percent of black
officials think it appropriate. Thus, in each racial category,
elected officials in communities with busing are more supportive than in communities without, paralleling the tendency among white residents.

White officials in non-busing communities repeatedly
cited "harmful" though factually erroneous consequences
of busing. According to one: "This is the way kids get
killed, and since busing has happened there have been
quite a few fatalities." From another: "I read something in
the paper about a government survey where it's not working out. It's not giving children from the ghetto quality education." Or: "I don't think we have to go for that—it seems
like a very expensive method of accomplishing that goal
[i.e., desegregated schools]." "I believe it's not good for either
student. You take a child from the squalor of the city, bring

him to the green fields, and return him at three o'clock.
You've done nothing for that child. Quite the contrary, I
think you've hurt him more."

These officials rarely recognized the inconsistency between their rejection of busing for integration, and their
acceptance of it on a large scale for other reasons—parochial schooling, community tradition, to ease overcrowding. When confronted with the contradiction, officials often
jettisoned their "facts," but remained adamant about
"forced busing." Thus:

> I don't think you should have busing. I think
> children should go to neighborhood schools. I think
> it's an inconvenience for the child whether he's black,
> white, or whatever. I wouldn't want my child to be
> bused to another neighborhood. I have it right now.
> I have a girl going to high school and she gets up at
> six o'clock in the morning to take two buses. It's an
> inconvenience, but it's by my own choosing, but I
> don't think a child should be forced into it.

Contradictions so permeate this response as to make it
ludicrous; but the message is typical. Attitudes are not easily
changed, whatever the facts.

White officials in communities that bused for racial balance (in most cases modestly), were more supportive of the
policy and knowledgeable about the facts. Enthusiasm was
rare, however. Most viewed busing as undesirable but necessary. Responses characteristically were hedged: "It's
about the only way you're going to get any racial balance."
"In certain cases busing may be an appropriate means,
though in my judgment the really appropriate way to integrate schools is to have adequate housing for all segments
of the population in all parts of town." "Busing has to be a
short term palliative to integrate schools, but it's about the
worst way to solve the problem. You need integrated hous-

ing patterns and economic patterns, and that will solve the problem of integrated education."

Thus white officials in busing communities tentatively supported busing. But white opponents in these communities were also more tentative than opponents in non-busing municipalities. Where busing programs had been undertaken, opposition appeared less obdurate, more uncertain. From one opponent: "I don't believe in busing little kids around, but I think on a high school level it's all right. I believe in the regional high school not for pure integration purposes, but just because the costs are lower, and this way at least you do achieve integration even though it's not forced." From another: "I'm not objecting [to busing for integration] in the higher grades—fifth, sixth, seventh, and into high school. They've done it in town and it's worked fairly well. But I am objecting to busing little kids, unless they can prove to me it's better for education. My wife has been a teacher for forty years, and she said the educators aren't sure that just because a black sits next to a white he'll learn better."

Black officials who supported busing, whether from busing communites or not, responded alike. But they showed little more enthusiasm than white supporters. Busing was, according to one, "a kind of thing that we must do temporarily, but it's not a long-range goal. But certainly for the time being, until we can implement better zoning laws and housing patterns, it's a solution on a temporary basis." From a second: "I agree to some extent that busing is [an appropriate] means of integration. I'm not in love with the method, but I'm convinced of the ultimate goals—I believe in integration. I wish we had another means of doing it, but I don't know of any other way." A third: "I would like to see another method, but we don't have an alternative to busing at this point. Nobody has come forth with anything better to maintain . . . equal education in the schools than mixing the races."

Blacks far more than whites, however, recognized the double standard. Black supporters of busing as well as black opponents commented virtually in unison that busing was a "completely false issue," that "people have been going to school on buses for as long as we've had buses in this country. The only reason that busing is an issue is because of racism." Other typical responses held: "For many years they've been busing and busing in the suburban communities where they've had regional schools. This has been true of the South too, where they've always bused. They've bused black kids right past white schools; but now that it's a turnabout, people are saying it's wrong." Or: "I think busing is an alternative to integrate the schools, and I don't know why people raise such hell about it. In the South where I come from, busing has always been part of the school system—never had any ill effects on education, not ever."

But despite cynicism about the motives of whites who are opposed to busing, most black officials held firmly that busing was necessary at least in the short run. A black mayor, earlier involved in his community's desegregation efforts, summed up the mood:

Busing has become necessary because of de facto
segregation. It exists in the North where whites have
moved out and continued to run. But the schools have
been left, and in many instances they've become
altogether black, or predominantly black. I think our
children *must* have the exposure to the various
cultural patterns that exist within ethnic groups. And
we get this only by busing. And if it's the only way we
can do it, then we have to do it by busing. If we had a
normal community pattern where people were mature
enough to develop on the basis of fair play and not
exclude minority groups from various areas, then I'd
see no need for this. We could then develop the kind

of spacial composition where people would not feel
that their children would be short-changed.

Thus, as most officials recognized, busing was an imperfect solution. Effective school integration and social integration in general are ultimately related to housing patterns.
In their authority to zone, to delineate these patterns, local
officials confront the fused issue of race and housing.

Zoning

Local zoning, land-use regulation, has been widespread for
less than fifty years. The primary objective of zoning ordinances in the twenties was the same as today, "insulation of
the single-family detached dwelling."[33] A decision by the
United States Supreme Court in 1926 upheld zoning as a
barrier to public nuisance. "A nuisance," said the court,
"may be merely a right thing in the wrong place, like a pig
in the parlor instead of the barnyard." In a single-family
zone, "apartment houses, which in a different environment
would be not only entirely unobjectionable but highly desirable, come very near to being nuisances."[34]

Exclusion of blacks was not the principal thrust behind
zoning. Until civil rights laws and court decisions in the
sixties, legalisms were unnecessary; sellers could legally
refuse to sell and real estate agents to show homes to blacks.
But as suburban zoning practices excluded people of
modest income, blacks were affected, along with the young,
the old, the unskilled, and other minorities. By 1970, however, the American Civil Liberties Union, the National
Committee against Discrimination in Housing, and the Suburban Action Institute were attacking exclusionary zoning
in the suburbs as a key obstacle to housing for blacks.[35]

[33] Richard F. Babcock, *The Zoning Game* (Madison, Wis.: The
University of Wisconsin Press, 1969), p. 3.
[34] *Village of Euclid* v. *Ambler Realty Co.*, quoted in *ibid.*, p. 4.
[35] The American Civil Liberties Union originated the only suit
joined by the federal government against a suburb's use of zoning

Zoning as it affects blacks and the suburbs faces three contradictions. First, industry is locating increasingly in the suburbs, and blue-collar jobs multiply. But the cost of houses continues to rise, and moderate-income workers must commute from central cities, which are often in a state of deterioration. Second, single-family dwellings are viewed as an attribute of the suburbs, multi-family units a nuisance. But insofar as this thinking promotes affluent white insularity, the ideal of a racially mixed society is thwarted. Third, there is conflict between home rule and higher authority. Local zoning control has offered little to low-income families, let alone to the ideal of an integrated society. Thus, if integration is to be encouraged, a municipality must be made accountable to a county, regional, or state authority for its residential patterns. A planning and zoning authority beyond the municipalities must have power to distribute moderate- and low-income housing evenly and fairly.

As in other states, the New Jersey Constitution grants to its legislature authority to enact "general laws" under which municipalities may adopt zoning ordinances (Article IV, section 6, paragraph 2). But the zoning statute grants the 567 municipalities virtual independence. The governing body of each municipality, according to statute, "may by ordinance . . . regulate and restrict the height, number of stories, and sizes of buildings, and other structures, the percentage of lot that may be occupied, the sizes of yards, courts, and other open spaces, the density of population, and the location and use and extent of use of buildings and structures and land for trade, industry, residence, or other purposes."[36]

---

to exclude federally subsidized low-income housing, in Black Jack, Missouri. See *The New York Times*, October 1, 1972, p. 58, and April 1, 1973, p. 70. Almost all exclusionary zoning suits in New Jersey since 1970 have been brought by the National Committee against Discrimination in Housing, the New Jersey Civil Liberties Union, or the Suburban Action Institute.

[36] *New Jersey Statutes*, Title 40:55-3.

After decades without serious challenge, however, municipal autonomy was successfully protested in 1971. A superior court judge invalidated a Madison Township ordinance that required one- and two-acre lots for single-family dwellings and that prohibited multiple-family housing. Judge David D. Furman held that: "In pursuing the valid zoning purpose of a balanced community, a municipality must not ignore housing needs, that is, its fair proportion of the obligation to meet the housing needs of its own population and of the region. . . . Large areas of vacant and developable land should not be zoned as Madison Township has into such minimum lot sizes and with such other restrictions that regional as well as local housing needs are shunted aside."[37]

Shortly after, another superior court judge invalidated Mount Laurel Township's zoning ordinance. Going beyond the Madison Township decision, Judge Edward V. Martino ordered Mount Laurel to produce plans for enabling development of low- and moderate-priced housing.[38] The cases were appealed, and in March 1975 the New Jersey Supreme Court upheld the Mount Laurel decision. The court concluded that "every such municipality must, by its land-use regulations, presumptively make realistically possible an appropriate variety in choice of housing." Further, a municipality "cannot foreclose the opportunity of the classes of people mentioned for low- and moderate-income housing, and its regulations must affirmatively afford that opportunity, at least to the extent of the municipality's fair share of the present and prospective regional needs."[39]

[37] Quoted in League of Women Voters, *Where Can I Live in Bergen County?* (Closter, New Jersey, January 1972), p. 10.

[38] *The Record* (Hackensack), July 3, 1973, p. A-2.

[39] *The New York Times*, March 25, 1975, p. 27. Other New Jersey municipalities against whom suits have been brought include East Brunswick, Franklin Lakes, Hasbrouck Heights, Holmdel, Livingston, Mahwah, Ramsey, Saddle River, Upper Saddle River, Washington Township, Wayne, and the Townships of Bedminster, East Windsor, Freehold, Harding, Randolph, and Weymouth. In July 1974 the National Committee against Discrimination in Housing and the New

Meanwhile, in October 1973 Superior Court Judge George B. Gelman, surpassing previous court involvement, threatened to rezone Washington Township for multi-family housing if the township did not alter its own plans. Though granting that zoning was a legislative responsibility, he cited the court's obligation when the legislature or municipality "fail to exercise [their] duties." He recalled precedents upheld by the United States Supreme Court in school desegregation and legislative reapportionment cases.[40] The case awaits review on appeal.

Thus, although the issue of zoning is in flux, the pressure against restrictive zoning is mounting. Whether by judicial order or state legislation, local zoning autonomy is likely to be checked.

Views of Local Officials

The most improbable concession a politician can make is a concession of power, and that is what would be demanded of locally elected officials if they were to share their zoning power. Nevertheless, a substantial number in this study recognized the incongruity in present arrangements: 567 fiefdoms all acting with little regard for their neighbors. Table IX-3 indicates that 41 percent of the white officials and 65 percent of the black do not believe that local governments should remain the final authority in determination of zoning patterns. Concern with the inequitable distribution of low-income housing is central to their response, especially among blacks. Fifty-eight percent of the white officials and 96 percent of the black oppose local zoning laws that exclude low-income housing (Table IX-4).

Jersey Civil Liberties Union announced suit against twenty-three municipalities in Middlesex County, the first regional challenge to exclusionary zoning. See *The Record* (Hackensack), July 24, 1974, pp. C-1, C-9.

[40] *Ibid.*, October 7, 1973, p. A-4.

TABLE IX-3: Officials' Views on whether "Local Government Should Remain the Final Authority in Determination of Zoning Patterns"

	Whites %	Blacks %
Strongly agree	31	10
Agree	24	23
Disagree	31	42
Strongly disagree	10	23
Don't know, no opinion, etc.	3	3
Total	99 (96)	101 (31)

TABLE IX-4: Officials' Views on "Local Zoning Laws that Exclude Low-Income Housing"

	Whites %	Blacks %
Against them (absolutely)	25	77
Against them (with qualification)	33	19
For them (with qualification)	26	3
For them (absolutely)	8	0
Don't know, no opinion, etc.	7	0
Total	99 (96)	99 (31)

Of course, it is inconsistent to oppose exclusionary zoning and regional control at the same time. Officials of both races were troubled by the conflict. Said a white: "I have great difficulty right there. I would like to think that people should elect their local officials to truly represent them, and my exercise of judgment on many matters [unfortunately] has been preempted by the state. At the same time, each community can and should make provisions for a mixed segment of society. I suppose I really want the better half of both worlds." A black: "You're charged with the responsibility of running your own community, and if you don't have the final say then there is something wrong there. But

it's kind of difficult in answering this because I know that
if local communities control their zoning it's possible for
them to legislate against low-income housing. So I guess I'm
stuck in-between."

Most, however, were consistent. Officials who favored
zoning laws that excluded low-income housing (34 percent
of the whites but virtually none of the blacks) tended to
favor local zoning autonomy. Those opposing such ordinances supported a higher final authority.

White supporters of exclusionary zoning spoke inferentially of a "natural" right to be exclusionary. Everybody,
according to the argument, has equal opportunity to work
hard, to make a lot of money, to live where he wishes, and
then to exclude others of lesser accomplishment. Thus, from
two white officials:

> I think the municipalities that are governed in such
> a way that they will have say five-acre or ten-acre
> zoning—I don't see anything wrong with it. No one is
> guaranteed the right to live in the finest area. I have
> never been guaranteed that, but I have the right to
> earn my way up there. And I think that is a good part
> of our government. . . . I think you have to have some
> incentive, because if everybody can go up to
> Livingston [an affluent suburb] and move into a
> house, it leaves a little to be desired. It leaves a lot to
> be desired in the way of having a drive within.
>
> · · ·
>
> I'm not a racist. I'm not a bigot. In my lifetime I've
> had some black partners. I was in business with a heck
> of a lot of black people and Spanish-speaking. I don't
> believe I have any prejudices because I can't afford
> it—I'm part of a minority group, Italian-American.
> But I say this—that we can't change all the principles
> of the country. If you are willing to work twenty-
> four hours a day to save money and make sacrifices,

and if you want to have a home on two acres, and this
is your dream, then you're entitled to it. I feel that if
a fellow wants to get into that community, let him
work as hard as the next guy, and then he can afford
it. Every man is entitled to the fruits of his own efforts.

On the other hand, several white officials opposed to exclusionary zoning and local autonomy were unequivocal,
a few moralistic: "I am totally opposed. I think that's the
illness of our society, exclusion of people by economics."
"Absolutely wrong—the parochial concept of home rule
should be absolutely dead." "When a municipality zones in
such a way that says we don't want any poor people, especially black people, I think that's not only unhealthy, it's
unconstitutional, and to begin with immoral." Most, however, were eclectic:

Perhaps a town should have the right to
exclusionary zoning, but there should be at least a lack
of any state benefits that accrue to that. If they are
going to have an industry as in Mahwah [Ford Motor
plant is in Mahwah], they're getting a fantastic ratable
and can keep most of their land green acres or vacant
because of it. Then you should have to house the
people who are employed there. . . . The local
government should have a great deal to say, but the
government of the state should set parameters.
        •   •   •
Whether excluding low-income housing is a good
thing or a bad thing may depend on what the need is
for that sort of housing in that locality. If you have
a case where a town is excluding low-income housing
by its zoning laws, but at the same time encouraging
plants and industry that require a lot of low-income
workers, it seems to me they are trying to do two
things at once that are mutually contradictory. I think

the question cannot be answered in the abstract.
You've got to look at the individual case and each
situation.

Some whites said their views changed with experience. In
all cases, however, the change was away from local autonomy, toward regional control. One said he "did always approve of the home rule concept, but with the influx of low-
income people to the center cities, it's gotten to the point
where we can't afford that. So at this point I would recom-
mend a county-wide or regional planning and zoning
board." Another echoed: "I'm inclined to say I agree that
the local government should have the final say. But I've become more and more aware that a provincial attitude leads
to patterns of exclusion that are detrimental to the flow of
community relations. I'd have to say I've changed my mind
and don't think we ought to have exclusive control."

A few black officials reported mixed feelings. Thus: "I
can see the value of having local people make the final determination. However, putting in various types of housing
will not come about if you left it up to local officials in some
municipalities; and sometimes I think it is necessary for a
higher authority to make the decision." From another: "If
I speak as an official of [city], I would say I agree [with
local autonomy]. But now I got the flip-flops because I think
the only way you can straighten out some of those other
communities would be through the state legislature." A
third: "I don't think you can say yes or no on something like
this. You have to deal with specific instances. I believe that
local officials should have input, but where the zoning laws
are so restrictive, then I think a higher authority may be
needed."

Most blacks, however, were unambiguous. Black elected
officials not only tended to oppose exclusionary zoning more
than white, but they stressed morality and ethics. Although
white responses were not necessarily amoral, emphasis was
on their municipality's "unfair share of the burden," or that

"too much low-income housing in any city [will lead to] bankruptcy." Black officials, in contrast, spoke of the moral perverseness in exclusionary zoning. Common were statements like: "I think that the only way to get some semblance of people understanding other people is to have all types of people living in various neighborhoods. You don't want to concentrate people [of one ethnic or racial background]. You want to spread them out—to become a part of the community." A second: "I think the zoning laws are very, very wrong. They're unconstitutional and discriminatory. I'm a strong believer in home rule, but when people are being zoned out of certain areas because of someone's personal discriminatory habits, the state must certainly get involved." A third: "It's not only foolish but un-American. If you want to name what America is all about, it's about people of all different political persuasions, nationalities, everything—who practice living together. . . . I believe that people who live in a certain area should somewhat determine what the area should be, but if it's not consistent with the basic beliefs of the country, [a higher authority] should supersede." Another: "I think exclusionary laws are un-American. Those who support them have a false sense of superiority. But they must pay for the social ills that arise thereby—preventing the emergence of hidden talent and leadership stifled by their action." Finally: "I think a community does a disservice to the people when it keeps poor people out, because our society is not built this way. We need to see the poor as well as the middle income and rich. All are part of the society. All are contributing factors." The morality theme ran deeply among black officials.

Toward regionalization

Officials in this study were from interracial communities, some suffering from severe urban problems. Thus it is not surprising that many opposed exclusionary zoning, in the words of one official, as "a noose around [our city's] neck." Doubtless, officials of all-white municipalities see the problems differently—as custodians of white middle- and upper-class insularity. Morality aside, however, pressure against local autonomy continues to mount, born of advancing technology and increased demand for services. An official spoke to the question:

Local areas to a great extent are historic accidents, unrelated to geographic, economic, or demographic factors. I think we have to look at planning and development on a much broader basis than historic accidents that created lines on maps. Technology to some extent is forcing this. We see it already in waste disposal, sewage systems, water supply. . . . We will have to do something to peel away the layers of independent authorities and agencies, and to some extent the confines of historic boundaries on maps.

Home rule has been challenged on still another front. The New Jersey Supreme Court has mandated that the state legislature remove community disparities in financing education. About 70 percent of local school financing comes from local property taxes. Tenafly, a wealthy community, spends $2,100 annually per student, Camden $1,000. The court ordered the disparities ended by 1975, though it later granted an extension until October 1975. Here as with other impositions on local autonomy, higher authority enters when municipalities do not or cannot act in the general interest. For the general interest is that of the state and all its citizens, including those too shortsighted to recognize the dangers in maintaining exclusionary enclaves. The deterioration of cities and inner suburbs, their services, their people, harms everyone. Affluent, white suburban residents may pretend nearby problems are nonexistent, but the problems encroach; deterioration spreads unless it is checked.

Some fear that regionalization would dilute black political power, that in an enlarged electorate black electoral chances would diminish. But, as demonstrated in Chapter IV, blacks frequently achieve election in predominantly white constituencies. Moreover, experience with black electoral achievement in some metropolitan area governments has been favorable. Before the consolidation of Nashville, Tennessee, 10 percent of the city council but none of the county supervisors were black. After consolidation, however, blacks held 14 percent of the seats on the metropolitan council. In the metropolitan area government of Jacksonville, Florida, 32 percent of the city-county legislators were black, against 23 percent of the population.[41] Willis D. Hawley concludes that, far from having their influence diminished, "racial minorities, especially Blacks, are among those who can gain most from *appropriately designed* regional approaches to many problems of metropolitan areas."[42]

The increase of black elected officials is likely to continue, whatever the pace of regionalization. Governmental form seems secondary to emergent black political consciousness and white responsiveness to black political leadership. Local black officials, willing to yield power to regional authority, sense this. Almost all hold the election of blacks to be essential, yet on the issues of busing and zoning would yield

[41] Willis D. Hawley, *Blacks and Metropolitan Governance: The Stakes of Reform* (Berkeley, Calif.: Institute of Governmental Studies, University of California, 1972), pp. 24-25.

[42] *Ibid.*, p. 2 (italics in original). Reviews of the literature for and against regionalization as it affects blacks conclude: "a definitive answer . . . must await further analysis" (Tobe Johnson, *Metropolitan Government: A Black Analytical Perspective* [Washington, D.C.: Joint Center for Political Studies, 1972], p. 7). Or: "The incomplete and impressionistic evidence on the relation of metropolitan government to minorities makes the need for more study painfully obvious" (Dale Rogers Marshall, "Metropolitan Government: Views of Minorities," *Minority Perspectives*, Lowdon Wingo, ed. [Washington, D.C.: Resources for the Future, Inc., 1972], p. 30). They recognize inexorable trends toward regionalization, however, and that minority involvement in planning will maximize their interests in final arrangements.

to higher final authority. They anticipate undiminished black electoral influence at regional levels.

This chapter has demonstrated that experience with busing and zoning helps sensitize people to the needs of the deprived. Busing for desegregation was supported more often by people in busing communities; and their views tended to be structured by fact rather than myth. Similarly, many officials who expressed opposition to exclusionary zoning did so on experience gained during their tenure. They believed that a long-term solution to residential inequities would have to mean changes in present zoning arrangements. Municipalities could no longer be permitted to exclude people explicitly for economic or implicitly for racial reasons. Moreover, in New Jersey judicial and political momentum against local zoning autonomy has been increasing.

On the national level, busing describes the development of policy based largely on myth and fear, fanned by the chief executive, later reflecting "a perceived public mood" by a Supreme Court majority. (Four of the five-member majority in the Detroit case were, notably, the Nixon appointees.) But while busing for school integration has been set back, integration as process and goal has not suffered fatally. Integration ultimately will depend on residential patterns that foster interracial relationships. Busing, as recognized by officials, can be a palliative. In the long run, however, zoning will be a major determinant.

Conclusions

1973 and 1974 were extraordinary years. Richard M. Nixon began his second presidential term with one of the largest popular majorities in history, at the same time that American military forces were withdrawing from Vietnam. Popular optimism and confidence in the government abounded. But by the end of 1974 the President's closest aides, Vice President, and former cabinet members were convicted criminals. The President himself had resigned rather than face almost certain impeachment. In October 1973 the nation confronted the Soviet Union in a full military alert during the fourth Arab-Israeli war. Fuel shortages during the summer, intensified by an Arab oil embargo, escalated to an energy crisis in the winter. Secretary of State Henry A. Kissinger threatened retaliation against the Arabs. In 1974 inflation ran at the highest levels of a generation while recession deepened. By the end of the year economic conditions were more precarious than at any time since the Depression of the thirties. Polls revealed unparalleled distrust of the government.

Barely noticed, however, was the acceleration of a trend begun in 1967 when Carl B. Stokes of Cleveland became the first black to lead a major city. In 1973 more blacks became mayors of important cities than in all the preceding years. Voters of Los Angeles, the nation's third largest city, elected Thomas Bradley; Detroit, fifth largest, Coleman A. Young; Atlanta, twenty-seventh, Maynard H. Jackson. Blacks were elected mayor in Dayton, Grand Rapids, and Raleigh, and reelected in Chapel Hill and East Orange. In 1974, seventeen blacks were elected to the House of Representatives, more than ever before. Three blacks became state executives, including two lieutenant governors, bringing to seven the number of blacks chosen for political office by statewide electorates (in Massachusetts, Michigan, Pennsylvania, Colorado, Connecticut, and two in California). Threats of chaos, domestic and foreign, failed to impede this unprecedented leap to elected power by an ethnic minority.

This was also a time of debate about black economic and social progress. Observers who proved statistically that life for blacks had improved were contradicted by others who proved statistically that it had not. "While black-white differences have not disappeared, a convergence in economic position in the fifties and sixties suggests a virtual collapse in traditional discriminatory patterns in the labor market," said Richard B. Freeman, an economist.[1] Ben J. Wattenberg and Richard M. Scammon pondered figures "proving" that the liberal policies of the past forty years had been successful—that, for example, "a special Census report in 1944 showed black family income at 47 percent of white earnings. Today black family income is 63 percent of white income."[2]

Sanguine arguments were attacked on the grounds that they were based on selective interpretations and convenient definitions. They disregarded the fact that black families tended to be larger than white, that while the proportional gap in family income narrowed the absolute gap increased from $2,500 in 1947 to $4,000 in 1971.[3] In response to the

[1] Quoted in *The New York Times*, July 2, 1973, p. 39.

[2] From a letter to *ibid.*, July 11, 1973, p. 40. The letter summarized the authors' argument developed in "Black Progress and Liberal Rhetoric," *Commentary*, 55, no. 4 (April 1973), 35-44. Some economic indicators between 1971 and 1973, however, revealed a possible reversal of the trend. See *The New York Times*, July 24, 1974, p. 10.

[3] Facts cited by Herrington J. Bryce and Herbert L. Calhoun in letters to *Commentary*, 56, no. 2 (August 1973), 4, 12.

Wattenberg-Scammon argument, Herrington J. Bryce of the Joint Center for Political Studies applauded the increase in black elected officials, yet recalled that blacks still comprised less than one percent of all elected officials. He concluded that there was "little reason for stretching or for hunting for isolated facts to defend the efforts of the 60s. We have tangible evidence that both races benefited. We also have tangible evidence that the task before us remains immense."[4] Immense it is, and the task will inevitably involve black elected officials.

The most compelling finding from thousands of hours of interviews and research for this study is that the election of blacks makes a difference. Black elected officials do not represent, as Hanes Walton suggests, simply "an illusion" of power.[5] On the evidence they make a difference in several ways.

First, they influence the formulation and implementation of policies. Blacks and whites on local governing bodies hardly ever form opposing voting blocs; bills beneficial to blacks introduced by black councilmen are commonly supported without dissent by white fellow officials (Chapter VII). Further, major municipal programs and issues are frequently influenced by black officials expressing black interests (Chapter VIII). Others have found "the evidence indicates that black officials can bring about real changes that improve the lives of their constituents in such important areas as jobs, housing, food, health care, day-care centers, education, and job training."[6]

Second, black elected officials influence the number of blacks appointed to government positions, and the levels of those appointments. Few black officials during the interviews failed to mention their efforts to obtain appointments of more blacks in their municipality's government. More-

[4] Bryce, *ibid.*, p. 8.
[5] Hanes Walton, Jr., *Black Politics* (Philadelphia: J. B. Lippincott Co., 1972), p. 196.
[6] Ronnie Moore and Marvin Rich, "When Blacks Take Office," *Progressive*, 36, no. 5 (May 1972), p. 31.

over, they regarded their efforts for the most part as successful. The debate on the nomination of a black to be police director in Newark, for example, turned largely on race. His appointment was indisputably attributable to the persistence of black officials (Chapter VIII).

Third, black elected officials sensitize their white associates not only by overt proposals but simply by their presence. Paradoxically and perversely, the tendency among whites to believe that black interests were well represented was greater in communities with no elected blacks than in those that had elected them. This was true for citizens and officials (Chapter VI). It appeared that white officials became more aware of black needs and concerns when blacks sat among them. Their presence was a constant reminder.

Fourth, elected blacks provide a link between government and the black citizenry in ways that whites cannot. Some recounted to me their experiences during civil disorders when they entered riot areas and negotiated with participants in a way that whites could not have done. Many meet regularly with black civic leaders, ministers, and youth groups to inform them of government activity, and in turn take their thinking back to government. For many in the black community trust was forged by an official's civil rights activities a decade or more earlier (Chapter III).

Fifth, they are role models for the black community, particularly for the young. Not only do most officials recognize this (Chapter III); but black citizens can identify black elected leaders more frequently than they can white, and believe it important that they hold office (Chapter VI).

Sixth, their positions reverse traditional images of white superiority. When a white police captain salutes a black mayor at a public function, the symbolism necessarily affects traditional attitudes among blacks and whites about "superiority." Black citizens' comments when Matthew Carter became Montclair's first black mayor implicitly recognized this (Chapter IV).

Seventh, as black elected officials serve, they establish a sense of legitimacy and normalcy about blacks holding office. Their service answers the skepticism about their ability expressed by some before blacks held office. They almost invariably draw increased white support in reelections. Thus their presence tends to internalize among whites and blacks a recognition that blacks govern no less fairly and wisely than whites. The more blacks are elected, the more acceptable the idea becomes. The pattern parallels that followed when blacks originally became national entertainment and sports figures—rejection, then grudging capitulation, finally matter-of-fact acceptance. (The pattern has been repeated in the breakdown of institutional segregation in the South and, as discussed, in desegregated schools across the country.)

Integration or Separation?

Separation appears unfeasible as an economic, political, or social tactic. Literal economic separation is in fact impossible. Economic interdependence weaves across geographic, class, and social divisions. Blacks, like any group in a technological society, could not survive on goods and services provided solely by its own members. Conversely, if blacks withdrew from farming, automobile manufacture, civil, military, or domestic services, the disruption to the nation's economic system would be substantial. True, blacks in particular are economically vulnerable. They are less wealthy, less skilled, less likely to be hired and more likely to be fired than whites. While their economic position may have improved in the past decade, they are still behind. But what does economic separation mean? If blacks were to buy food only from black merchants or cars only from black dealers, this would provide an illusion of independence. For unless all food and automobile production and associated industries were dominated by blacks, they would remain subject to white economic influence. This does not diminish the importance of expanding the role of blacks in the economy. But economic integration is unavoidable; to suggest otherwise is quixotic.

If political separatism means exclusive political control by and for blacks, political separation is also illusory. Even if local officials are black, whites at state and federal levels will influence policies affecting blacks. In Congress, in state capitals, in county seats, separation is impossible. If blacks choose not to enter political office, default, not separation, would be the apt description. But now, as more black elected and appointed officials assume office, they are inextricably involved not only with white fellow officials but with white constituents. From the vantage of political power, as demonstrated here, black officials can influence policies favorable to blacks. Thus, political integration is not only unavoidable but, in terms of black interests, useful.

Recognition of this by black officials appears to have muted the drive for independent black political movements.[7] In 1969 an exclusively black and Puerto Rican political convention in Newark endorsed Kenneth Gibson for mayor and three blacks for city council. All were elected. Four years later the mayor and two of the three councilmen snubbed the convention and were denied reendorsement. They were reelected, however, by larger margins than four years earlier. Only the incumbent endorsed by the convention was defeated. The trend away from independent black political movements was mirrored at the second National Black Political Convention in 1974: fewer than half the number of delegates and guests that had attended the first in 1972 attended this one. Moreover, unlike the first, as an

[7] The first National Black Political Convention held in 1972 called for "an independent Black political movement" because the major political parties "have betrayed us." *The National Black Political Agenda*, reviewed and ratified May 6, 1972, Greensboro, North Carolina, pp. 2-4.

observer noted, the 1974 convention had neither "flair" nor a large number of black elected officials.[8]

Only in the social sphere is separation possible—and common. Social relationships may be intimate or casual. But we mean relationships in hierarchically neutral environments like schools, neighborhoods, churches, and voluntary organizations, not those that imply rank, as between employer and employee. Of course even in integrated environments close relationships may not evolve. Black and white children may sit in the same classroom, yet have no other contact. But friendship and trust between blacks and whites can never develop if their lives are spent entirely apart. While it is not the sole criterion for interracial friendship, social integration is essential.

Carmichael and Hamilton reject not only integration but interracial coalitions, because blacks comprise a "politically and economically insecure group."[9] In consequence, blacks would be dominated by their white "associates." But if, as indicated, economic and political separation are illusory, then the ostensible benefits of social separation cannot be economic or political. We are left with what Drake called "psychological independence."[10]

Psychiatrists William H. Grier and Price M. Cobbs emphasize that "of the things that need knowing, none is more important than that all blacks are angry."[11] They dismiss integration as a "social perversion" because "it is the white man who determines which black man will be worthy of his company, since no black man can integrate any situation."[12]

[8] Paul Delaney in *The New York Times*, March 22, 1974, p. 28.

[9] Stokely Carmichael and Charles V. Hamilton, *Black Power: The Politics of Liberation in America* (New York: Vintage Books, 1967), p. 66.

[10] St. Clair Drake, "The Social and Economic Status of the Negro in the United States," in Edward S. Greenberg, Neal Milner, and David J. Olson, eds., *Black Politics* (New York: Holt, Rinehart and Winston, Inc., 1971), pp. 47-48.

[11] William H. Grier and Price M. Cobbs, *Black Rage* (New York: Bantam Books, Inc., 1969), p. 2.

[12] *Ibid.*, p. 166.

Historically this has been true, and on the surface remains so. Yet recent trends cannot be ignored. The communications media, government, universities, corporate enterprises, institutions that historically discriminated against blacks (and others) in the past decade have sought to enroll or employ them. Black newscasters, reporters, judges, professors, students, and executives now sit where none was permitted ten or fifteen years ago. Some of this is the result of tokenism, some of a sincere effort to rectify injustice. Few could be unimpressed, for example, by seeing 40 blacks among 180 Rutgers Law School graduates in 1974. Until 1971, classes rarely contained more than one or two. Similarly, black apprentices for unions in New Jersey nearly doubled between 1972 and 1974. Of 8,455 apprentices recorded by the United States Department of Labor in 1974, 955 were black. The figures for 1972 were 576 out of 7,373.[13] Moreover, such institutional change is consistent with the increasing acceptance of integration by whites in everyday activity—in schools, restaurants, hotels, parks, and neighborhoods.[14]

All this does not negate the proposition that integration is ultimately determined by whites. Blacks could not join institutional America if whites were unwilling. But the point is that whites are becoming more willing. Discrimination has lessened, and the biggest problem for most blacks has become the residue of history, the economic and political deprivation wrought by centuries of racism. Students of urban affairs recognize that "suburban exclusivity has, in recent years, been more economic than racial. Middle-income black families typically encounter far less antagonism than white welfare recipients searching for public

[13] Figures were obtained from the Bureau of Apprenticeship, U.S. Department of Labor, Newark, N.J. They represent a rise of black apprentices from 8 percent of the total in 1972 to over 11 percent in 1974.

[14] Andrew M. Greeley and Paul B. Sheatsley, "Attitudes toward Racial Integration," *Scientific American*, 225, no. 6 (December 1971), 13-19.

housing."[15] For blacks who have withstood, or can overcome, the legacy of deprivation, entry into the institutional mainstream has become increasingly possible.

Separation must ultimately be challenged on a comparative note. If every ethnic and religious group practiced social segregation would the groups—and the nation—be better for it? Hardly. Others have shown that blacks, unlike the early immigrant groups who overcame discriminatory obstacles, have been especially handicapped. Their color, their lack of a common culture or religion, the history of "legal" sanctions by government, the diminished need for low-skilled workers compared to the time when the immigrants sought jobs are obstacles never faced by the earlier newcomers.[16] But, as suggested in the introductory chapter, the immigrant experience has inferences for blacks today. The elimination of legal strictures, the softening of white obduracy, and an aroused black consciousness have enabled blacks to compete more fairly in the economic and political marketplace.

Black pride, culture, and traditions assuredly should be nurtured. To support integration is not to disregard the importance of group pride and solidarity. For, as discussed, racial integration is consonant with the pluralist interpretation of American politics. Blacks, like Irish, Jews, Italians— indeed unions, business, farm, and trade organizations— retain group interests. Each group has a unique history, bonded by pride, culture, or religion, perhaps by response to discrimination. But each contends in the political system for favorable policies and programs. Groups may coalesce

[15] Mary Costello, "Future of the City," *Editorial Research Reports on the Future of the City* (Washington, D.C.: Congressional Quarterly, Inc., January 1974), p. 6. For a statement that exaggerates the importance of class and the unimportance of race in describing black problems see Edward C. Banfield, *The Unheavenly City* (Boston: Little, Brown and Co., 1970), chap. 4.

[16] Charles E. Silberman, "The City and the Negro," in Edgar Litt, ed., *The New Politics of American Policy* (New York: Holt, Rinehart and Winston, Inc., 1969), pp. 213-17; Bayard Rustin, " 'Black Power' and Coalition Politics," *ibid.*, pp. 146-47.

with others; they may compromise and accommodate, bargain and complain. But, barring legal or unusual institutional stricture, the system can respond in favored directions, slowly and incompletely, but with the potential for more.

Integration—How Close Have We Come?

Integration, defined simply, is interaction between people without regard to race. But, paradoxically, race cannot be ignored if we are to approximate the ends of integration, to pursue and attain social, political, and economic benefits unrestricted by race.

Integration between blacks and whites here has connoted relationships like those of other social or ethnic groups—of Catholics, Protestants, and Jews, Italians and Poles, Irish and Germans. Not all groups are equally "integrated." Day-to-day contacts between members of some groups are largely limited to people within their own group. But limitations are by choice. During the past twenty-five years, ethnic or religious background has rarely been a stigma limiting social, political, or economic achievement for most. Only for groups "stigmatized by color," as Handlin puts it, have racist ideas affected the fluidity of the social order.[17]

As mentioned, a policy toward integration does not include the erasing of group identity or pride. Nor does it imply that every school, every neighborhood, be identically populated according to ethnic proportions. But it would mean an internalization of the idea, in Fred Powledge's words, that "a person's skin color is neither an asset nor a liability as far as his exercise of his Constitutional rights."[18]

[17] Oscar Handlin, "Historical Perspectives on the American Ethnic Group," in Harry A. Bailey, Jr., and Ellis Katz, eds., *Ethnic Group Politics* (Columbus, Ohio: Charles E. Merrill Publishing Co., 1969), p. 18.

[18] Fred Powledge, *Black Power, White Resistance* (New York: Clarion Book by Simon and Schuster, 1971), p. 265. Similarly, for

In 1965, Matthew Holden wrote of his commitment to integration, yet skepticism about its future.[19] He, like others, was troubled by the turmoil of the mid-sixties: civil rights activities and white "backlash" churning race relations into uncertainty. In assessing the possibilities for integration, Holden projected four steps necessary for its realization. His criteria provide a barometer to measure progress after ten years. They inform how much progress, or how little, we have made toward integration.

Holden's first and indispensable step requires a system of bargaining between authoritative spokesmen.[20] Government officials and spokesmen for blacks must know who they are, communicate, make claims, negotiate. They must recognize each other's legitimacy. Public officials, as Holden points out, have discretion about whom they grant audiences—with whom they bargain. Moreover, compared to labor or business, whose interests are usually definable and consistent, ethnic group interests are diffuse. Thus it may be difficult to pinpoint a "correct" spokesman for black interests.

But while black nationalists or separatists have had limited access to public officials, black integrationists have been accepted as authoritative spokesmen. As indicated, their authority has been rooted in approval by the black rank and file as well as acceptance by public officials.[21] Thus, as bargaining between black integrationists and public officials has become common, it has helped toward the achievement of an integrated society.

The second step requires "pragmatic accommodation by leaders on each side."[22] The bargaining product may be less

their description of the ideal "ethnic pattern" see Nathan Glazer and Daniel P. Moynihan, *Beyond the Melting Pot*, 2nd ed. (Cambridge, Mass.: M.I.T. Press, 1974), pp. xxii-xxiv.

[19] Matthew Holden, Jr., "The Crisis of the Republic: Reflections on Race and Politics," in Lenneal J. Henderson, Jr., ed., *Black Political Life in the United States* (San Francisco: Chandler Publishing Co., 1972), pp. 105-130.

[20] *Ibid.*, p. 119.   [21] See Chapter I, nn. 30 and 33.

[22] Holden, "Crisis of the Republic," p. 120.

than either side wished, but it is for the moment enough to
validate the process. "Leaders across the bargaining lines,"
says Holden, "must be able to take the position that there
is more to be gained than to be lost by continued bargaining."[23]

Measured against the past ten or fifteen years, the fulfillment of this criterion has been uneven. Separatists have
little faith in the bargaining-accommodation process. But
during the sixties, despite demonstrations and disorder,
simultaneous if less publicized activity in conventional politics increased—voting, lobbying, office-seeking, and "pragmatic accommodation." Through the early seventies, political activity and accommodation emerged as the principal
means whereby blacks sought and attained political influence.

The third step in the integration process requires "policies which will convey important benefits to the Negro population."[24] Essentially it calls for preferential treatment, or
in contemporary parlance, "affirmative action." Holden re-
minds us that preferential treatment is not new, that "all
agricultural policy is a policy of preferential support."[25] But
he need not have restricted his observation, for all policy
is preferential. Every law, every government decision
awards benefits or imposes liabilities—that is, shows preference. Tax preference for agriculture and oil are obvious
examples. But every variety of policy will benefit some and
cost others—veterans benefits, highway and school construction, health care, alignment of election districts, labor
laws, fluoridation of water.

Preferential policies, of course, are justified on the
grounds that they are beneficial to the general community.
Since every citizen needs farm products, transportation, and
fuel, policies that strengthen these sectors are ostensibly in
everybody's interest. But apart from the merits of the claims
they expose the fallacy that preferential policies for blacks
would depart from normal government function.

[23] *Ibid.*   [24] *Ibid.*, p. 121.   [25] *Ibid.*

Holden argues that the "main" reason blacks ought to receive preferential treatment is to narrow racial disparities, which are "a standing provocation to tension and strife, inconsistent with the public interest in domestic tranquility." He dismisses the "mystical doctrine of historical debt."[26] I suggested earlier that the social dividends of integration transcend the narrow (though important) question of civil order. But whatever the justification, 1964 heralded the beginning of a government confrontation with the most palpable legacy of discrimination—economic deprivation. The "war on poverty," preferential treatment for poor people (disproportionately black), began with the creation of the Office of Economic Opportunity (O.E.O.). It gave rise to manpower training, legal services, Headstart, health delivery, and other programs to help and involve the poor. The results have been mixed. In 1974 there were still poor people, and they were still disproportionately black. The future of the O.E.O. was uncertain, though Congress pointedly maintained most of the programs organized under it. But, as Roger Wilkins observed, while the "war" has not been won, "the poor are a little stronger, considerably more self-aware and somewhat more self-sufficient." Moreover, during these ten years "a foundation has been laid to await the next cycle of legislative creativity."[27]

Poverty was not the only target of government efforts against discrimination. Unions, business, educational institutions, state police, and national guard units were prodded —some by state governments—to increase their numbers of blacks. Again, while results were not always successful, there was progress.

Thus the first three requirements posed by Holden—bargaining, accommodation, preferential treatment—are under way. Though they were imperfectly instituted, in the perspective of a decade they have not been insignificant.

[26] *Ibid.*
[27] Roger Wilkins, "The War on Poverty: Ten Years Later," *The New York Times*, June 4, 1974, p. 37.

They have set in motion the final stage of the integration process suggested by Holden: development of values common to whites and blacks that would "govern the action which each takes toward the other in common-sense, everyday, garden-variety matters."[28] In other words, integration would mean casual acceptance with little regard to race. In fulfilling this final criterion, Holden envisions the need for private groups and interests to share concern with the government.

In 1965, Holden regretted that unions, corporations, financial institutions, and government agencies had "barely begun to notice the problem, let alone assume a role."[29] Ten years later, an amended statement might read that institutions and individuals do notice the problem, though too few have begun to "assume a role." But the past decade has demonstrated that policies toward integration and policies that benefit blacks can be mutually supportive.

The Future: Caution but Hope

In the introductory chapter we cautioned against facile generalizations made in the past—that black politicians are "like everyone else," that they are more "virtuous," that they are more "cautious." Although in this study we have generalized, sought typical attributes, we have carefully noted exceptions. Further, perception and behavior were examined separately, insofar as separation is possible. But while descriptions consequently become more complex, tendencies do become evident and generalizations appropriate.

Black elected officials, in self-perception and behavior, responded to the needs of the black citizenry as well as to those of their entire city. They acted in the interest of blacks; if they accommodated, they rarely sacrificed fundamental principles. Moreover, while they retained the loy-

[28] Holden, "Crisis of the Republic," pp. 121-22.
[29] *Ibid.*, p. 122.

alty of the black community, they gained increasing support from the white electorate. Their closest observers, white fellow officials, were curiously ambiguous about them, however. White elected officials divided over the belief that black officials placed the interests of blacks ahead of the city's. Yet, whether measured by votes in council meetings or by enunciated positions on their city's major issues, cooperation and accommodation were "interracial." The relationships between white and black officials, their behavior, their political techniques were devoid of racial implications in most communities most of the time.

In examining the three perspectives of this study—roads to power, perceptions, behavior—we find uneven comparisons between black and white officials. Their backgrounds and motivations for office were divergent. Their perceptions, though sometimes disparate, often overlapped. Their behavior in office, insofar as they accommodated and compromised, was rarely differentiable by race. Most important, however, is that while black officials accommodated they got something in return. White fellow officials responded to their values, their policy priorities, and the needs of the black community. The political techniques of blacks differed little from those of whites, but black officials continued to embrace the techniques precisely because they proved successful.

Whether black officials can continue to satisfy the black and white communities is uncertain. If the economic and social gaps between the races cease to converge, black citizens will spurn political leaders whatever their color. Black officials might be rejected more emphatically than white out of a sense of race betrayal. Second, the quality of the first wave of black elected officials may not persist among their successors. In occupational and educational backgrounds, and in commitment to humanitarian ideals, black officials have set uncommon standards; they have skillfully integrated idealism and pragmatism. This is not to overstate their "virtue"; one black, for instance, impressive during our interview, was subsequently convicted of criminal activity while in office. But unless later black politicians exhibit the commitment, social sensitivity, and political skill that characterize most of the present group, citizen support could wane.

Finally, if the interests of the two races come to be seen as inherently conflicting, incapable of harmony, the efforts of black officials, or white, become fruitless. But the continued election of blacks has until now mooted this assumption. Virtually all elected blacks stand on the proposition that neither race can achieve full social enrichment without the other, that morally and practically separate and unequal societies injure all society. In this they are supported by most of the black electorate and an increasing number of whites.

Black elected officials are not exclusively, in the words of Nathan Wright, Jr., "the present exemplars of humane values in our legislative halls." But they are, thus far, exemplars of hope to the entire electorate, black and white.

Appendix I

Elected Officials: Schematic Representation

The format of this study is schematically represented in Figure A-1. An elected official enters office with a set of values, philosophies, and myths determined by his background, personal experiences, political culture, and the laws and rules of his political system. While in office his behavior—policy pronouncements, relationship with fellow officials, voting patterns—is determined by his perceptions, as well as by external constraints like the structural authority granted his office and events and issues in his community. But the relationships are interdependent. His behavior in turn affects the external constraints; and his perceptions of the external constraints also influence his behavior, and ultimately the constraints themselves.

Figure A-1

Format for Study of Elected Officials

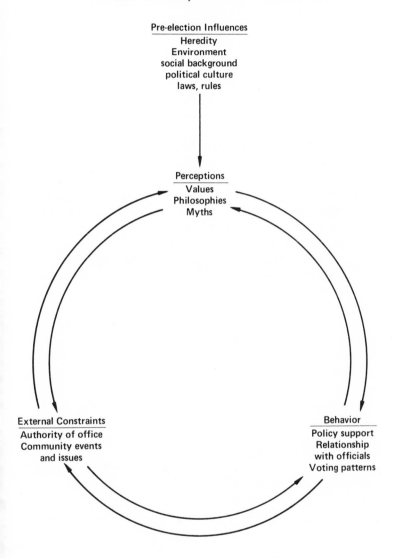

Pre-election Influences
Heredity
Environment
social background
political culture
laws, rules

Perceptions
Values
Philosophies
Myths

External Constraints
Authority of office
Community events
and issues

Behavior
Policy support
Relationship
with officials
Voting patterns

Appendix II

The Interviews

Elected Officials

In 1972, 135 people served as elected municipal officials in the sixteen cities of this study. Thirty-one were black. One who resigned at the end of 1971, though his term continued into 1972, was included to maximize the number of blacks interviewed. Another, an American Indian, was included, as explained in Chapter I, note 15. One hundred and twenty-seven officials were interviewed, including the thirty-one blacks. Most interviews ranged between thirty and sixty minutes; a few lasted several hours. Officials were promised they would not be quoted by name, and where feasible that their city identification would be deleted from their statements. All but six of the interviews were taped, though occasionally an official requested suspension for an off-the-record remark, despite assurances of confidentiality.

While a few officials initially might have felt inhibited by a recorder, as discussion continued they seemed to become oblivious to it. Moreover, taping permitted accurate reproduction and uninterrupted conversation. It proved far superior to note-taking or attempts at verbatim recall.

The question of inhibited responses is also raised by the fact that a white conducted all the interviews. In survey research blacks are commonly interviewed by blacks, whites by whites. But that pertains to interviews among the citizenry, not public officials. The approach here is justified on two counts. First, elected officials are public people. They have already spoken and leveled with citizens of both races, since the municipalities all have substantial black populations. Thus a black official's discussion with a white interviewer was not likely to be an unfamiliar, inhibiting experience. Black officials, in fact, appeared no less hesitant than white in responding critically to the most sensitive questions. Additionally, there is an advantage in one person's conducting all the interviews. Each interview involved open-ended discussion. Comments by officials would require decisions to pursue a subject or move to another, decisions more likely to be consistent when made by the same person. Moreover, possible psychological effects brought by a variety of personalities were obviated.

Citizens

The citizens survey was conducted by twenty interviewers. Since it was conducted by telephone, the race of the interviewer remained unidentified. Further, the structured, short-answer questionnaire for the citizenry discouraged extra comment. Thus interviewers did not have to guide inquiry beyond the prescribed format. The scope of the citizens survey was narrow. The views of citizens were compared with their elected officials on a limited number of issues. But the principal inquiry—on the importance of race as an electoral determinant—required few questions.

For in-depth interviewing, the telephone is less adequate than extended personal meetings. But given our limited aims and resources, the phone proved useful. Its advantages over a mailed questionnaire included greater likelihood of response and the opportunity for an interviewer to clarify meanings.

Respondents from each municipality were chosen in proportion to their municipality's percentage of the total population among the sixteen cities. They were determined by random intervals of page and column numbers in their city's telephone directory. The reliability of the technique was confirmed by members of the Gallup Poll organization and the Center for Urban Policy Research at Rutgers University. Unlisted numbers, however, are held disproportionately among households at economic extremes. Thus responses by the very wealthy and very poor were somewhat underrepresented. Random dialing was not used because prefixes for municipalities in the study also covered many that were not.

Of the 1,248 selected numbers, 551 yielded satisfactory interviews. The others included refusals, disconnected phones, no answers (after at least four calls), language difficulties, incomplete interviews, inappropriate respondents (principally because they were ineligible to vote). Table A-1 lists each municipality's population proportion among the sixteen. The figures for the number interviewed are equivalent to those based on the 1970 census. Table A-2 lists selective socioeconomic characteristics of the population sample.

The Questionnaires

Interviews were conducted with officials from January through August 1972; with citizens from October 1972 through January 1973. The questionnaire for officials sought short, scaled answers as well as extended comment; for citizens short answers only.

Questionnaire for Locally Elected Officials

1. What led you to seek public office in the first place?
2. Are your aims and expectations being fulfilled? Very much. Some. Not much. Not at all. Other. (Comment)
3. What philosophical or moral views about politics affect your decisions as an office-holder?
4. When your personal conviction differs from that of the people you represent, what position do you take?

TABLE A-1: Sixteen Cities: Population and Interview Proportions

	Population Proportion (1970 Census) %	Proportion of Completed Interviews %
Atlantic City	3.1	3.4
Camden	6.6	6.2
East Orange	4.9	4.9
Elizabeth	7.3	6.7
Englewood	1.6	1.5
Hackensack	2.3	2.2
Jersey City	16.8	15.8
Montclair	2.8	2.4
Newark	24.6	27.1
New Brunswick	2.7	3.1
Orange	2.1	2.0
Passaic	3.5	3.6
Paterson	9.3	8.0
Plainfield	3.0	3.1
Teaneck	2.7	3.1
Trenton	6.7	6.9
Total	100.0 (1,554,690)	100.0 (551)

Personal conviction always. Personal conviction usually or with qualification.
Usually go with the people. Always go with the people.
Other.
(Comment)

5. What is your position on local zoning laws that exclude low-income housing?
   Against them totally. Against them with qualification. For them with qualification. For them totally.
   Other.
   (Comment)

6. Some people say local government should remain the final authority in determination of zoning patterns. Do you:

TABLE A-2: Selective Socioeconomic Characteristics of the
Interview Sample (551)

Race	%
White	74.6
Black	25.4
Sex	
Male	43.4
Female	56.6
Age	
Under 30	19.8
30-39	16.5
40-49	18.0
50-59	17.4
60 plus	22.9
Refused response	5.4
Education	
Some high school (or less)	31.6
Completed high school	32.3
Some college (or more)	31.6
Refused response	5.5
Family income	
Under $5,000	21.4
$5,000-$10,000	30.9
$10,000-$15,000	20.0
Over $15,000	12.3
Refused response	15.4

Strongly agree that it should.   Agree.
Disagree.   Strongly disagree.   Other.
(Comment)

7. Roughly what percentage of the people in your electoral district (that is, those who can vote for you) are black?

8. Some people say it is important in the conduct of affairs in this city that blacks hold elective office. Do you:

Strongly agree. Agree. Disagree. Strongly disagree.
Other.

(Comment)

9. Have racial differences been responsible for serious civil disorder in your city at any time in the past five or six years?

   (If not, why? If so, why? When was the last incident? Is the potential for disorder different now? Why? etc.)

10. According to some, busing of children is a proper means to integrate schools. Do you:

    Strongly agree that it is. Agree. Disagree.

    Strongly disagree. Other.

    (Comment)

11. Some people say black elected officials see their responsibility mainly as representing the interests of the black community ahead of the entire city's. Do you:

    Strongly agree that they do. Agree. Disagree.

    Strongly disagree. Other.

    (Comment)

12. What are the major issues, in your judgment, that your city faces?

13. How long have you lived in this city?

14. What is your occupation (other than politician)?

15. What is your date of birth?

16. What is your religion?

17. Which of the following levels of formal schooling have you completed?

    Elementary. Some high school. Graduated high school. Some college. College degree. Some post-degree studies. Advanced college degree.

18. How long have you held public elective office, including elected positions before this one? What other offices have you held?

19. How long have you held this office?

20. Which political party are you a member of, or do you generally support?

21. Which of the following best describes relations here

between blacks and whites generally?
Excellent. Good. Fair. Poor. Other.
(Comment)

22. Do you think this city is getting its fair share of state and federal financial aid compared to other cities of this size?
(Comment)

23. How do you feel about this statement: The interests of blacks in this city are adequately represented at official levels of the city government? Do you:
Strongly agree. Agree. Disagree. Strongly disagree. Other.
(Comment)

24. What do the words "black power" mean to you?

25. What do the words "law and order" mean to you?

26. Based on trends of recent years, are you generally optimistic or pessimistic about the future of this city?
(Comment)

27. Which of the following terms best describes your political tendencies?
Radical. Liberal. Middle-of-the-road. Conservative. Reactionary. Other.
What does (self-described tendency) mean to you?

28. Do you care to comment further on any issues we've discussed, or any that we should have?
Name.
City.
Form of government.
Type of elections.
Office held.
Elected citywide or by district.
Sex.
Race.

(Though each questionnaire contained substantively identical questions, wording for some in the citizens survey was simplified. Officials were asked, for example, if they were optimistic or pessimistic about their city's future, citizens if their city's future looked good or bad.)

Questionnaire for Citizens Survey

Respondent's name   City   Date of call   Interviewer

1. How do you feel about the future of your city—does it generally look good or bad?
   (1. Optimistic. 2. Pessimistic. 3. Other ————.)

2. When an elected official feels differently about a particular issue than the people who elected him, should the official:
   1. Stick to his own belief. 2. Take the position of the people who elected him. (3. Other ————.)

3. Do you think your city is getting its fair share of state and federal financial aid compared to other cities of this size?
   (1. Yes. 2. No. 3. Other ————.)

4. Which of the following words best describes relations in your city between blacks and whites generally:
   1. Excellent. 2. Good. 3. Fair. 4. Poor.
   (5. Other ————.)

5. Some people say it is important in your city that blacks hold elective office. Do you:
   1. Strongly agree that it is. 2. Agree. 3. Disagree.
   4. Strongly disagree. (5. Other ————.)

6. According to some people, busing of children is a proper means to integrate schools. Do you:
   1. Strongly agree that it is. 2. Agree. 3. Disagree.
   4. Strongly disagree. (5. Other ————.)

7. How do you feel about this statement: Black elected officials tend to care more about the black community than they care about the entire city. Do you:
   1. Strongly agree. 2. Agree. 3. Disagree. 4. Strongly disagree. (5. Depends on the individual.
   6. Other ————.)

8. Do you think black elected officials should care more about the black community than the entire city? (1. Yes. 2. No. 3. Other ————.)

9. How do you feel about this statement: The *interests* of blacks are adequately represented in your city's government. Do you:
   1. Strongly agree. 2. Agree.   3. Disagree.
      4. Strongly Disagree. (5. Other ————.)

10. How many years have you lived in this city?
    (1. 1-5. 2. 6-10. 3. 11-15. 4. 16-20. 5. Over 20.)

11. What is your occupation?
    (1. Professional. 2. Bus. or ind. white collar. 3. Retail bus. owner/mgr. 4. Civil service. 5. Skilled worker. 6. Semi- or unskilled worker. 7. Housewife. 8. None.)

12. Are you employed now?
    (1. Yes. 2. No. 3. Other ————.)

13. What is your date of birth? ————.
    (1. 18-21. 2. 22-29. 3. 30-39. 4. 40-49. 5. 50-59. 6. 60-69. 7. 70 and over.)

14. What is your religion?
    (1. Cath. 2. Jew. 3. Presb. 4. Episc. 5. Meth. 6. Bapt. 7. 7th Day Advent. 8. Prot.: other or non-denomin. 9. None. 10. Other.)

15. What is your race? (1. White. 2. Black. 3. Other.)

16. What level of formal schooling have you completed?
    (1. Elem. 2. Some H.S. 3. Grad. H.S. 4. Some college. 5. College degree. 6. Some post-degree studies. 7. Advanced coll. degree.)

17. Which political party do you generally support?
    (1. Dem. 2. Rep. 3. Other party. 4. Independent.)

18. Off hand, what percentage of your city's population is black?
    (1. Accurate within 10%. 2. Under by 10-20%. 3. Under by 20% plus. 4. Over by 10-20%. 5. Over by 20% plus. 6. Other ————.)

19. Do you happen to know the name of the mayor of your city? (If yes, what is name according to respondent?)
(1. Yes. 2. No. 3. Approximately correct.)

20. Do you know the name of any one other councilman/commissioner/alderman? (If yes, what is name according to respondent?)
(1. Yes. 2. No. 3. Approximately correct.)

21. Do you know the name of either United States senator from New Jersey? (If yes, what is name according to respondent?)
(1. Yes. 2. No. 3. Approximately correct.)

22. Which of the following terms best describes your political tendencies? Are you:
1. Radical. 2. Liberal. 3. Middle-of-the-road. 4. Conservative. 5. Reactionary. (6. Other ———.)

23. At which of the following levels is your annual family income?
1. Under $5,000. 2. $5,000-$10,000. 3. $10,000-$15,000. 4. $15,000-$20,000. 5. Over $20,000. (6. Would not disclose.)

(The following questions should be marked
after interview)

24. Respondent's sex: 1. Male. 2. Female.

25. City ———.

Appendix III

Elected Officials Interviewed

Rita Avalo, *alderman, Paterson*
Frank H. Blatz, Jr., *mayor, Plainfield*
Peter J. Bonastia, *commissioner, Montclair*
Michael A. Bontempo, *councilman, Newark*
Michael P. Bottone, *councilman, Newark*
Joseph F. Bradway, Jr., *mayor, Atlantic City*
Alfred E. Brown, *councilman, East Orange*
Horace J. Bryant, Jr., *commissioner, Atlantic City*
Frank W. Burr, *mayor, Teaneck*
Harry J. Callaghan, *commissioner, Orange*
Carmen E. Capone, *commissioner, Orange*
Anthony P. Carabelli, *councilman, Trenton*
Matthew G. Carter, *mayor, Montclair*
Raymond Cassetta, *alderman, Paterson*
Daniel Ciechanowski, *councilman, Camden*
John R. Cipriano, *councilman, Trenton*
Charles H.L.D. Clark, *councilman, Plainfield*
Odis B. Cobb, *alderman, Paterson*
Thomas H. Cooke, Jr., *councilman, East Orange*
Aldrage B. Cooper, *councilman, New Brunswick*
Francis T. Craig, *councilman, East Orange*
Joseph Curtin, *alderman, Paterson*
Michael J. D'Arminio, *councilman, Hackensack*
John O. Davies, III, *councilman, Trenton*
Dominick DeMarco, *alderman, Paterson*
Michael J. DeMartino, *councilman, Elizabeth*

248

John P. Dougherty, *councilman, Teaneck*
Thomas G. Dunn, *mayor, Elizabeth*
Arthur C. Dwyer, *mayor, Paterson*
Judith W. Fernandez, *councilman, Englewood*
Mario Floriani, *commissioner, Atlantic City*
Walter H. Ganz, *councilman, Englewood*
Harry E. Gardiner, *alderman, Paterson*
Kenneth A. Gibson, *mayor, Newark*
Merton J. Gilliam, *councilman, Plainfield*
Anthony J. Giuliano, *councilman, Newark*
Gerald Goldman, *mayor, Passaic*
Thaddeus F. Gora, *councilman, Elizabeth*
Howard Gregory, *councilman, Hackensack*
Francis E. Hall, *councilman, Teaneck*
Earl Harris, *councilman, Newark*
William S. Hart, Sr., *mayor, East Orange*
Max A. Hasse, Jr., *councilman, Teaneck*
Elizabeth B. Hawk, *councilman, Camden*
George F. Hendricks, Jr., *councilman, New Brunswick*
Jerry J. Hersch, *councilman, Englewood*
William H. Hicks, *alderman, Paterson*
Martin J. Hillman, *councilman, Trenton*
Arthur J. Holland, *mayor, Trenton*
George B. Holman, *councilman, Hackensack*
William C. Holt, *councilman, East Orange*
Sharpe James, *councilman, Newark*
John Jaroski, *councilman, Jersey City*
Benjamin F. Jones, *commissioner, Orange*
Paul T. Jordan, *mayor, Jersey City*
Eugene E. Kalinowski, *councilman, Trenton*
L. Harold Karns, *councilman, East Orange*
John J. Kelaher, *councilman, Jersey City*
Eleanor M. Kieliszek, *councilman, Teaneck*
Kenneth M. King, *councilman, Englewood*
Fred Kuren, *councilman, Passaic*
John J. Lack, *councilman, Camden*
Karlos R. LaSane, *commissioner, Atlantic City*

Joseph Lazarow, *commissioner, Atlantic City*
W. Oliver Leggett, Jr., *councilman, Trenton*
William J. McCloud, *councilman, Elizabeth*
Joseph E. McGlynn, *councilman, Elizabeth*
Thomas F. McGovern, *councilman, Jersey City*
Theodore MacLachlan, *commissioner, Montclair*
Isaac G. McNatt, *councilman, Teaneck*
John R. Marini, *councilman, Camden*
William A. Massa, *councilman, Jersey City*
Frank G. Megaro, *councilman, Newark*
Bradford Menkes, *councilman, Teaneck*
Joseph E. Meyer, *councilman, Plainfield*
Robert M. Moran, *councilman, East Orange*
Edward Murphy, *alderman, Paterson*
Joseph M. Nardi, Jr., *mayor, Camden*
Joseph C. Nettleton, *councilman, Camden*
Maurice A. O'Keefe, *councilman, Elizabeth*
Paul J. O'Keeffe, *councilman, Plainfield*
Paul Ottavio, *alderman, Paterson*
Joseph Payne, *councilman, Passaic*
Aniello R. Pecoraro, *councilman, Jersey City*
Elijah Perry, *councilman, Camden*
Morris Pesin, *councilman, Jersey City*
John Petrone, *alderman, Paterson*
Richard G. Pettingill, *commissioner, Montclair*
Arthur W. Ponzio, *commissioner, Atlantic City*
Dominick J. Pugliese, *councilman, Jersey City*
Francis J. Quilty, *councilman, Jersey City*
Nat S. Raskin, *alderman, Paterson*
Victor D. Recine, *councilman, New Brunswick*
Patsy J. Riccio, *councilman, Elizabeth*
Samuel Rosenblatt, *commissioner, Montclair*
Abe Rosensweig, *councilman, Elizabeth*
David H. Rothberg, *councilman, Plainfield*
Richard L. Rountree, *councilman, Plainfield*
Joseph Russo, *councilman, Passaic*
Dan Ryan, *councilman, Passaic*

John L. Salek, *councilman, Passaic*
Nancy Jane Schron, *councilman, East Orange*
David J. Schroth, *councilman, Trenton*
Robert H. Schulte, *councilman, New Brunswick*
Joel L. Shain, *mayor, Orange*
Patricia Q. Sheehan, *mayor, New Brunswick*
John A. Smith, *councilman, New Brunswick*
Harold J. Smith, *councilman, East Orange*
Nicholas A. Soriano, *councilman, Elizabeth*
Herbert M. Sorkin, *councilman, Passaic*
Robert R. Stout, *councilman, Plainfield*
Junius C. Sturdifen, *alderman, Paterson*
Golden Sunkett, Sr., *councilman, Camden*
Nellie F. Suratt, *councilman, Plainfield*
Ben Sweetwood, *councilman, East Orange*
Walter S. Taylor, *mayor, Englewood*
William S. Thomas, *councilman, East Orange*
William J. Thornton, *councilman, Jersey City*
Vincente K. Tibbs, *councilman, Englewood*
John F. Trezza, *commissioner, Orange*
Louis M. Turco, *councilman, Newark*
Chester F. Turk, *councilman, Elizabeth*
Ralph A. Villani, *councilman, Newark*
Dennis A. Westbrooks, *councilman, Newark*
Earl Williams, *councilman, East Orange*
Kazmier Wysocki, *mayor, Hackensack*
Frank C. Zisa, *councilman, Hackensack*

Index

Aberbach, Joel D., 99n, 100
Abernathy, Ralph, 45n
accommodation, among elected
  officials, 232-33; as step toward
  integration, 229-30; on Newark
  city council, 163; political culture and, 96; political system
  and, 118, 153; in Teaneck,
  176-77
Adams, John, 107n
Addonizio, Hugh, 74-76, 140
affirmative action, 152, 157n; in
  East Orange, 181; in Newark,
  169
age, among interview sample, 241
aldermen, *see* councilmen
alienation, of blacks from the
  political process, 137
ambition and politics, 87
American Civil Liberties Union,
  207
Apgar, Wilbur E., 24n, 32n
Atlanta, 4, 57n, 136, 219
Atlantic City, 64, 172; black population and officials in, 13; civil
  disorder in, 138; divisions on
  board of commissioners of, 144-
  45; equitability of black representation, 58; proportion of
  interview sample, 240; socioeconomic level and black representation in, 66-68
at-large representation, effects on
  blacks, 62-63, 69
attitudes, affected by experience,
  214, 218; about future of cities,
  188; on busing for school in-

tegration, 200-207; racial, 135;
  relationship to behavior, 81-82;
  political representation a function of, 120; of whites toward
  black elected officials, 6
Auchincloss, Katharine L., 197n

Babcock, Richard F., 207n
Bailey, Harry A., Jr., 7n, 20n,
  22n, 228n
Baltimore, 4n
Banfield, Edward C., 57n, 61, 62n,
  227n
Banner, James M., Jr., 39n, 98n
Baptists, proportion among
  elected officials, 40-41, 54
Baraka, Imamu Amiri, 23, 75-76,
  167-71, 183
bargaining, as a step toward
  integration, 229
Barone, Michael, 12n
Beaton, W. Patrick, 154n
behavior, affected by philosophy
  and morality, 88. *See also* attitudes *and* perceptions
Bell, Michael D., 39n, 98n
Berry, Theodore M., 79
black and Puerto Rican political
  convention, 75, 161, 171, 224
black candidates, supported by
  black militants, 23
black citizens compared with
  white, on busing for school
  integration, 201-202; on identification of senators and mayors,
  108-10; ideologically scaled, 94,
  97; on importance of blacks

253

Library of Congress Cataloging in Publication Data

Cole, Leonard A   1933-
    Blacks in power.

    Includes index.
    1. Mayors—New Jersey.   2. Legislators—New Jersey.
3. Municipal officials and employees—New Jersey.
4. Negroes—New Jersey—Politics and suffrage.
I. Title.
JS451.N55C57   329'.009749   75-2985
ISBN 0-691-07573-5